This Day in Yankees History

This Day in Yankees History

RONALD L. MEINSTEREIFEL

McFarland & Company, Inc., Publishers
Jefferson, North Carolina, and London

Library of Congress Cataloguing-in-Publication Data

Meinstereifel, Ronald L., 1960–
    This day in Yankees history / Ronald L. Meinstereifel.
        p.   cm.
    Includes bibliographical references and index.
    ISBN 0-7864-1002-7 (softcover : 50# alkaline paper) ∞
        1. New York Yankees (Baseball team) — History — Chronology.
    2. New York Yankees (Baseball team) — Miscellanea. I. Title.
    GV875.N4 M45   2001
    796.357'64'097471 — dc21   2001030375

British Library Cataloguing data are available

Manufactured in the United States of America

On the cover: Yankee Stadium ©*1997 Wood River Gallery*

McFarland & Company, Inc., Publishers
  Box 611, Jefferson, North Carolina 28640
  www.mcfarlandpub.com

This book would not have been possible without the assistance of my wife LeAnn and son Henry, who have accepted my obsessive pursuit of date-related sports information and my monopolizing the computer.

CONTENTS

PREFACE

Some of my earliest childhood memories include falling asleep in my bed to the sounds of baseball on my father's radio in an adjacent room. Throughout childhood, adolescence and adulthood, sports have been a major source of gratification and positive distraction for me.

For two decades now, I have been a psychologist. I have worked in a variety of settings and currently have a private practice in rural northern Pennsylvania. Writing has always been part of my professional life, and over the past few years, my continued focus on sports information and statistics has gradually shifted from a hobby to an opportunity to write in my spare time as well.

For a number of years, I have written sports-related materials including chronologies, calendars and biographies. I refined my skills and eventually felt confident enough to submit some work to publishers for consideration. I was initially searching for feedback regarding my abilities as a writer, since my previous projects were self-published projects, sold over the Internet or through mail order. With each project, my writing abilities improved and the systems used to acquire and organize information became refined and specialized.

I remain fascinated by historical dates and facts. I have compiled various databases of information related to dates and chronologies. Throughout my education, I pursued the study of history and honed my skills in research techniques.

Last year, I produced a page-per-day desk calendar relating to Pittsburgh sports. To reach a larger market, I began researching New York City sports and began compiling information. I found too much data to include all New York sports and soon realized that choosing one specific team would be a more manageable and focused task. Because of their long-term success, recent championships, personalities and fan base, I chose the Yankees. As it turned out, this team provided a great wealth of research possibilities. Soon, I had compiled more than enough information for a daily calendar. I began to view this process as the outlet for something more inclusive. Several visits to libraries yielded books that had been written detailing team histories in a number of formats, some similar to the current project. I began to further refine my search by reviewing numerous books on baseball milestones, records and history. Each resource led to another until I had compiled a functional database of over 3000 Yankee entries. The book took approximately three years to complete, with many starts and stops.

Under each day of the calendar, events relating to the 1903–2000 Yankees are arranged in chronological order. The earliest events (births, for example) are from the mid–1800s, and coverage extends through the Subway Series of 2000.

Throughout my research, I encountered conflicting data. At times, a particular incident was reported as occurring on several dates or even years. When these discrepancies existed, a third resource was consulted and, at times, yet more resources. Usually, my rule of thumb, was "majority rules." Similarly, some misinformation inevitably was encountered in research. Therefore, I decided to exclude bits of information that appeared quite obscure and unlikely if I could not confirm them through another resource. To complete this process, a number of standard publications were used. Information from *The Baseball Encyclopedia* and *Total Baseball* were considered as the "industry standard" for purposes of verifying information included in this publication. Additionally, daily and weekly publications, online and printed, were accessed for fact checking and information compilation. Please refer to the bibliography for a complete list.

This project would not have been possible without the encouragement of my wife, son and family. The input and suggestions of friends and colleagues have been helpful and inspirational in completing the final product and keeping up with the demands of my work schedule and deadlines.

Ron Meinstereifel

JANUARY

1

William "Wee Willie" Keeler died in Brooklyn, NY, in 1923 at the age of 50. The Baseball Hall of Fame member played seven seasons with the Highlanders, batting .343 in 1904.

Clifford Torgeson, born in 1924 in Snohomish, WA, played 14 major league seasons, concluding his career as a part-time first baseman for the Yankees in 1961.

Pitcher Duane Maas was born in Utica, MI, in 1931. Maas was a Yankee 1958–61, going 14–8 in 1959.

2

The Brooklyn Dodgers traded outfielder, and New York icon, Casey Stengel and infielder George Cutshaw to the Pittsburgh Pirates for pitchers Burleigh Grimes and Al Mamau and infielder Chuck Ward in 1918.

David Cone was born in 1963 in Kansas City, MO. He pitched for the Mets 1987–92 and joined the Yankees in 1996, winning Game 3 of the World Series.

Adrian "El Duquecito" Hernandez defected from Cuba by sneaking aboard a flight to Costa Rica in 2000. He is the brother of major league pitchers Livan and "El Duque" Hernandez.

3

Stanley "Frenchy" Bordagaray was born in 1912 in Coalinga, CA. Frenchy was a reserve outfielder for the Yankees in 1941. He hit .315 as a regular with the 1936 Brooklyn Dodgers.

The Yankees traded catcher Al De-Vormer to the Boston Red Sox for pitcher George Pipgras and outfielder Harvey Hendrick in 1923.

Caracas, Venezuela, native Luis Sojo was born in 1966. Sojo played in five World Series games in 1996, going 3 for 5 with an RBI. He signed with the Pittsburgh Pirates in 2000, but returned to star in the World Series.

The Yankees held a press conference in 1973 to introduce shipbuilder George Steinbrenner III and Michael Burke as two "general partners" of a 12-man group who had purchased the Yankees from CBS for $10 million.

The Yankees signed Bill Virdon as manager in 1974. The former Pirate player and skipper managed in New York for two years and never won a game at Yankee Stadium because the team played home games at Shea Stadium during his tenure.

4

George "Twinkletoes" Selkirk played his entire nine-year career in the outfield for the Yankees (1934–42), batting .328 in 1937. He was born in Huntsville, Ontario, in 1899.

The Highlanders announced plans to play games on Sunday at Ridgewood Park on Long Island in 1904.

Pitcher Thomas Gorman was born in New York City in 1926. He pitched three seasons for the Yankees 1952–54 and compiled a 36–36 career record over eight major league seasons.

The Yankees purchased shortstop Lyn Lary and infielder Jimmy Reese from the Pacific Coast League in 1928.

Casey Stengel returned from the minor leagues to become a coach for the Brooklyn Dodgers in 1932.

Yankee pitcher Red Ruffing, nearly 37-years-old and missing four toes, was inducted into the Army in 1943 for service in World War II.

Former Yankee infielder Joe Dugan was injured in Boston in 1944 when he was struck by a car while crossing the street. Dugan was a regular third baseman on the 1927 Murderer's Row team.

New York City deputy mayor Randy Levine resigned in 2000 and accepted the position of president and chief executive in charge of business affairs with the Yankees the following day.

5

Middleport, OH, native Benjamin Kauff was born in 1891. Kauff started his career with the Highlanders in 1912 before finishing with the New York Giants 1916–20. He hit .308 playing regularly in 1917.

John Henry Kramer was born in New Orleans, LA, in 1918. He pitched 12 major league seasons, going 18–5 for the 1948 Boston Red Sox. He finished his career as a Yankee in 1951.

The Yankees officially announced in 1920 that they had purchased the contract of Babe Ruth from the Boston Red Sox for a total payment of $100,000.

Reggie Jackson was the only player elected to the Baseball Hall of Fame in 1993. "Mr. October" played 21 major league seasons, appeared on five championship teams, and hit 563 career home runs. He was the 29th player elected on the first ballot.

After receiving an apology from owner George Steinbrenner regarding his dismissal as Yankee manager in 1985 after only 16 games, Yogi

Berra stated that he would end his self-exile from Yankee Stadium and the organization in 1999.

The Yankees named Randy Levine president in 2000. He was a former New York City deputy mayor.

6

New York City native Thomas Ferrick was born in 1915. Ferrick pitched for the Yankees 1950–51. He posted a career 40–40 record over nine major league seasons.

Although he enjoyed his best seasons with the Brooklyn Dodgers, going 21–12 in 1947, Ralph "Hawk" Branca was 1–0 with the 1954 Yankees at the end of his career. He was born in 1926 in Mt. Vernon, NY.

Mickey Mantle signed a $75,000 contract with the Yankees in 1961 and became the highest paid player in the American League.

Johnny Keane died of a heart attack at the age of 55 in 1967. Keane managed St. Louis from 1961–64, then switched to the Yankees after the Cardinals 1964 World Series Championship, managing 1965 and part of 1966 in New York.

Thurman Munson signed a two-year contract extension in 1977 that paid $260,000 in 1980 and $275,000 in 1981.

The Yankees signed free-agent outfielder Danny Tartabull in 1992 after an all-star season with the Kansas City Royals in which he led the American League in slugging percentage. Tartabull played for New York 1991–95.

Phil Niekro became the 227th member of the Hall of Fame in 1997 when the Baseball Writers Association of America elected the Blaine, OH, native. The knuckleballer pitched for the Yankees 1984–85 and appeared in 24 major league seasons.

The Yankees acquired outfielder Terry Jones from the Los Angeles Dodgers for a player to be named later in 2000.

7

Hall of Fame member Johnny Mize was born in 1913 in Demorest, GA. Mize played his final four seasons with the Yankees. He hit .364 for the 1937 St. Louis Cardinals.

Yankee outfielder Joe DiMaggio had bone spurs removed from his heel at Beth David Hospital in New York in 1947.

Mickey Mantle was admitted to Room 202 of the Betty Ford Center in 1994 for treatment of alcoholism.

Jose Cardenal, who quit the New York Yankees coaching staff when denied a pay raise, joined the Tampa Bay Devil Rays coaching staff in 2000.

8

Frank Chance became the manager of the New York Yankees in 1913. New York was regarded as one of the weakest teams in history with controversial first baseman Hal Chase.

Brian Boehringer, born in 1969 in

St. Louis, MO, pitched for the Yankees 1995–97, mostly in long relief. Boehringer won Game 2 of the 1996 Divisional Playoffs over the Texas Rangers.

In 1998, the Yankees re-signed outfielder Darryl Strawberry to a one-year contract with a club option for 1999.

9

Frank Farrell and Bill Devery purchased the Baltimore franchise of the American League for a cost of $18,000 and subsequently moved the team to New York City to become the Highlanders in 1903.

Charles Stanceu, a Canton, OH, native born in 1916, pitched for the Yankees in 1941 and 1946 compiling a 3–3 record.

Ralph Terry, who pitched for the Yankees 1956–57 and 1959–64 and finished his career with the Mets, was born in 1936 in Big Cabin, OK. Terry led the American League in win with 23 in 1962.

Speedy outfielder Otis Nixon started his career with the Yankees in 1983. He batted .297 and stole 72 bases with the Atlanta Braves in 1991. He was born in Evergreen, NC, in 1959.

Spurgeon "Spud" Chandler died on this date in 1990. A native of Commerce, GA, the right-handed pitcher won the 1943 American League MVP, with a 20–4 record with the Yankees.

Darryl Strawberry signed a one-year contract with Yankees for $750,000 in 1998. In 1999, Darryl Strawberry had surgery to relieve pain caused by scar tissue from his October 1998 operation for colon cancer.

10

Derrill "Del" Pratt played second base for the 1918–20 Yankees. Born in Walhalla, SC, in 1888, he hit .314 in 1920.

The New York Supreme Court issued a preliminary injunction barring the Yankees from opening their season against the Detroit Tigers in Denver in 1983. The Yankees were uncertain if renovations to Yankee Stadium would be completed by opening day.

The Yankees re-signed first base coach Lee Mazzilli and major league catching instructor Bob Didier. They announced that coaches Willie Randolph, Chris Chambliss, Mel Stottlemyre and Don Zimmer would return for the 2000 season.

11

Colonel Jacob Ruppert and Colonel Tillinghast L'Hommedieu Huston purchased the Yankees in 1915 for $460,000 from Frank Farrell and Bill Devery.

In 1929, at the age of 31, Babe Ruth's first wife, Helen, died of suffocation in a fire. Adopted daughter Dorothy, who was eight at the time, was away at boarding school.

Following his dismissal by the Oakland A's, Billy Martin was signed by the Yankees to manage the team for the third time by George Steinbrenner in 1983.

Bob Lemon, Baseball Hall of Fame pitcher, who had a brilliant pitching career and managed the Yankees 1978–82 including a 1978 World Series Championship, died at the age of 79 in 2000.

12

The Chicago Cubs purchased the Yankees top farm team since 1932, the Newark Bears, in 1950 and planned to move the team to Springfield, MA.

Former Yankee utility player Andy Fox was born in Sacramento, CA, in 1971. He started his career with the Yankees in 1996 before being traded to the Arizona Diamondbacks.

13

No relation to the Yugoslavian leader, Michael Milosevich was born in Zeigler, IL, in 1915. He played for the Yankees 1944–45 as a utility infielder.

The Yankees acquired catcher John Grabowski and infielder Ray Morehart from the Chicago White Sox for infielder Aaron Ward in 1927.

Yankee owner for 24 years, Colonel Jacob Ruppert, died at the age of 71 in 1939. Six days after his death, Ed Barrow succeeded Ruppert as Yankee president.

Infielder Ray Morehart, member of the 1927 Yankee World Championship team, died in 1989 at the age of 89. That left Mark Koenig as the only living member of the Murderer's Row team (he passed away in 1993).

14

Joe DiMaggio married actress Marilyn Monroe at City Hall in San Francisco, CA, in 1954. Their marriage lasted less than a year.

Three-time all-star pitcher John J. "Johnny" Murphy died of a heart attack in New York City in 1970 at the age of 61. Murphy pitched for the Yankees 1932–46 compiling a 93–53 record. Murphy was a baseball executive with the New York Mets.

Yankee pitcher Jim "Catfish" Hunter and long-time Chicago Cub Billy Williams were elected to the Baseball Hall of Fame in 1987.

Pitcher Hideki Irabu married Kim Kyong in Chiba, Japan in 1997.

15

Raymond Chapman was born in McHenry, KY, in 1891. He was the only major league player killed in a game when he was struck on the head by Yankee pitcher Carl Mays in 1920.

Babe Ruth accepted a pay cut of $17,000 and signed a 1934 contract with the Yankees for $35,000.

The Yankees announced that they would televise 140 games during the

1958 season in a deal worth over one million dollars.

Power hitter Johnny Mize, a New York Giant, St. Louis Cardinal and New York Yankee who hit 359 career home runs, was elected by the Veteran's Committee to the Baseball Hall of Fame in 1981.

16

Former Yankee pitcher Jack McDowell was born in Van Nuys, CA, in 1966. "Black Jack" spent the 1995 season with New York. He twice won 20 games in a season and captured the 1993 American League Cy Young Award with the Chicago White Sox.

The Baseball Writers Association of America elected former Yankee teammates Mickey Mantle and Whitey Ford to the Hall of Fame in 1974. Mantle became only the seventh player in history to be elected on his first try.

17

Former Brooklyn Dodger and New York Met infielder, major league manager, and long-time Yankee coach Don Zimmer was born in 1931 in Cincinnati, Ohio.

Ed Barrow was elected president of the Yankees and succeeded Colonel Ruppert, who died earlier in 1939.

Charles T. "Chili" Davis, outfielder/designated hitter was born in 1960 in Kingston, Jamaica. Davis was

a Yankee 1998–99. He hit 19 home runs in 1999 and hit .286 as a designated hitter in the 1998 World Series sweep over the San Diego Padres.

The Yankees drafted Fred Lynn in the January 1970 phase of the free-agent draft. The Chicago native chose not to sign with New York and eventually started his career with the Boston Red Sox.

18

Infielder Nolen Richardson was born in 1903 in Chattanooga, TN. Richardson played six major league seasons, including 1935 with the Yankees as a part-time shortstop.

Grover Cleveland Alexander was elected to the Hall of Fame in 1938. His bases loaded strikeout of Tony Lazzeri in the 7th inning of Game 7 of the 1926 World Series clinched the series for the St. Louis Cardinals.

Inter-league action for Major League Baseball was unanimously approved by baseball owners in both leagues, leading to the first regular season showdown between the New York Mets and the Yankees in 1996.

19

The New York Yankees football team was purchased for $300,000 by the National Football League and transferred to Dallas, TX, in 1952.

The Baseball Writers Association of America elected Sandy Koufax, Yankee catcher Yogi Berra and Early Wynn to the Hall of Fame in 1972.

The Yankees announced that coaches Jose Cardenal, Chris Chambliss, Tony Cloninger, Willie Randolph, Mel Stottlemyre and Don Zimmer agreed to terms on one-year contracts for 1999.

In 1999, the Yankees agreed to terms with pitcher Andy Pettitte on a one-year contract, and avoided salary arbitration.

The Yankees agreed to a one-year contract with catcher Jorge Posada in 2000. Posada joined Bernie Williams as the only teammates to switch-hit home runs in the same game on April 23, 2000.

Darryl Strawberry tested positive for cocaine and was subsequently suspended for one year for violating his probation in 2000.

20

After his release by the Cleveland Indians, Joe Sewell signed with the Yankees in 1931. He went on to have three more successful seasons, hitting .302 in 1931 and batting .333 in the 1932 World Series sweep of the Chicago Cubs.

Jesse Gonder, who also caught for the New York Mets, was born in 1936 in Monticello, AR. Gonder started his career as a Yankee 1960–61, playing briefly. He hit .270 as a regular for the Mets in 1964.

George Steinbrenner's first trade as head of the Yankees sent pitcher Jack Aker to the Chicago Cubs for outfielder Johnny Callison in 1973.

The Yankees claimed pitcher Hector Ramirez off waivers from the Baltimore Orioles in 1998.

21

Following a great year in 1937, which included a World Series Championship, Joe DiMaggio met with owners for 30 minutes and rejected a $25,000 contract. DiMaggio held out until April 20, 1938.

Former catcher and major league manager Johnny Oates was born in 1946 in Sylva, NC. He concluded his 11-year career as a player with the Yankees 1980–81.

Pitcher Dizzy Dean and outfielder Al Simmons were elected to the Baseball Hall of Fame in 1953 by the Baseball Writers Association of America and Joe DiMaggio, controversially, was not.

Pitcher Andy Hawkins was born in 1960 in Waco, TX. Hawkins played for the Yankees 1989–91, going 15–15 in his first season in New York. He lost a 4–0 no-hitter to the Chicago White Sox in 1990.

22

The first baseball convention was held in New York in 1857. It was called by the Knickerbockers and attended by 16 baseball clubs, all located on Manhattan and Long Island.

Catcher Ira Thomas spent two seasons as a Highlander catcher, 1906–07, playing 124 games behind the plate. He was born in Ballston Spa, NY in 1881.

The New York Giants officially gave the Yankees permission to play at the Polo Grounds for the 1913 season after their Hilltop Park lease expired. They remained at the Polo Grounds until moving to Yankee Stadium in 1923.

The Yankees announced they would put numbers on their uniform backs in 1929, becoming the first baseball team to start continuous use of numbers. Initially, numbers were based on positions in the batting order thus, Ruth wore #3 and Gehrig #4.

Reggie Jackson officially ended his five-year stay with the Yankees, choosing to sign with the California Angels in 1982. His deal was worth close to $1 million per year for four years.

Don Mattingly announced the end of his 13-year baseball career with the Yankees. Owner George Steinbrenner immediately pronounced Mattingly's #23 retired.

23

Utility infielder Otto Hamlin "Jack" Saltzgaver played for the Yankees during five of his six major league seasons (1932–37). Saltzgaver was born in Croton, IA, in 1903.

Johnny Sturm played first base for the Yankees in his only major league season, 1941, when he batted .286 in the World Series victory over the Brooklyn Dodgers. Sturm was born in 1916 in St. Louis, MO.

Pitcher Randy Gumpert was born in Monocacy, PA, in 1918. He played ten major league seasons including 1946–48 with the Yankees. He was 11–3 in 1946.

Outfielder Charlie Spikes broke in with the Yankees in 1972 and went on to have consecutive 20 home run seasons with the Cleveland Indians 1973–74. Spikes was born in Bogalusa, LA in 1951.

Veracruz, Mexico, native Alfonso Pulido appeared in ten games for the 1986 Yankees. He was born in 1957.

24

Second baseman Earle Gardner was born in 1884 in Sparta, IL. Gardner played his entire five-year major league career with the Highlanders 1908–12.

The Baseball Writers Association of America elected George Sisler, Eddie Collins, and former Highlander Willie Keeler to the Baseball Hall of Fame in 1939. Keeler played for the Highlanders 1903–10, his final major league stop.

Pitcher Tim Stoddard played ten major league seasons with six teams, including 1986–88 with the Yankees. He recorded 26 saves with the 1980 Baltimore Orioles. He was born in 1953 in East Chicago, IN.

The Yankees gave Mickey Mantle a $10,000 raise for the 1956 season, signing him to a $30,000 contract. He was reported to be the highest paid 24-year-old in baseball history at the time. Mantle went on to win the triple crown and MVP that season.

Pitcher Neil Allen started his 11-year major league career in 1979 with the New York Mets. Allen pitched for the Yankees twice, in 1985 and 1987–88. He recorded 22 saves for the 1980 Mets. Allen was born in 1958 in Kansas City, KS.

Tom Zachary died in Burlington, NC in 1969. Zachary was famous as the pitcher who surrendered Babe Ruth's 60th home run in 1927 as a member of the Washington Senators. He pitched for the Yankees 1928–30. a.k.a. Zach Walton in 1918.

Yankees infield prospect D'Angelo Jimenez fractured a bone in his neck in a car accident in 2000.

25

Roy Sherid pitched for the Yankees his entire three-year career (1929–31), compiling a career 23–24 record. He was born in 1908 in Norristown, PA.

The Boston Braves bought pitcher Lefty Gomez from the Yankees in 1943. He was released before playing a game and later signed with the Washington Senators in May. Grove played all but the final game of his 14-year career with the Yankees.

The Ruppert estate sold the Yankees to Dan Topping, Del Webb and Larry MacPhail for $2.8 million in 1945.

Outfielder Paul O'Neill joined the Yankees in 1993 after eight seasons with the Cincinnati Reds. A member of three Yankee World Championship teams, he was born in 1963 in Columbus, OH.

WPIX, Channel 11 in New York City, had aired Yankee games for nearly 50 years until it was announced that the New York Mets would be on WPIX in 1999 and the Yankees would be on Channel 5, a Fox affiliate.

The Oakland A's signed free-agent Yankee outfielder Tim Raines for $600,00 in 1999. Raines played for the Yankees 1996–98, batting .321 on a part-time basis in 1997. Raines led the National League in stolen bases 1981–84 with the Montreal Expos.

The Yankees signed pitcher Andy Pettitte to a three-year contract with a club option for a fourth year in 2000.

26

Joe DiMaggio was elected to the Baseball Hall of Fame in 1955. DiMaggio played his entire career with the Yankees and was the American League Most Valuable Player three times, in 1939, 1941, and 1947. He finished second in 1937 and 1948.

Roger Maris and Mickey Mantle signed contracts with Columbia Pictures in 1962 to star in *Safe at Home!*, a baseball movie shot during spring training that featured Whitey Ford and Ralph Houk. Mantle appeared as himself in several movies.

Darryl Strawberry was arrested for alleged assault with a deadly weapon during an argument with his wife. He was released on $12,000 bail in 1990.

The Yankees signed outfielder Roberto Kelly to a minor-league contract and invited him to spring training. They also signed pitcher

Jason Grimsley to a one-year contract in 2000.

27

Al Wickland was born in 1888 in Chicago, IL. The outfielder finished his career with the Yankees in 1919. He led the Federal League in walks with 81 in 1914 as a member of the Chicago Chifeds.

Pitcher Milt Gaston was born in 1896 in Ridgefield Park, NJ. He pitched 11 major league seasons, losing 39 games for the Boston Red Sox over two seasons 1929–30. He started his career in 1924 with the Yankees.

Frederick "Lefty" Heimach was born in 1902 in Camden, NJ. He pitched for the Yankees 1928–29 and later pitched for the Brooklyn Dodgers. He was 14–12 with the 1924 Philadelphia A's.

The New York football Giants announced in 1956 that they were switching their National Football League home games to Yankee Stadium. This fueled speculation that the Major League Baseball Giants would also leave the Polo Grounds.

In 1999, the Yankees announced that Darryl Strawberry, Jason Grimsley, and Jeff Juden were asked to attend spring training as non-roster invitees.

28

Infielder Lynford "Broadway" Lary was born in Armona, CA, in 1906. He played for the Yankees 1929–34. He

hit .290 as the regular shortstop for the Cleveland Indians in 1937.

Bill White, former Yankee infielder, broadcaster, cardiologist, and first black president of the National League was born in 1934 in Lakewood, FL.

First baseman Dale Long died in 1991 at the age of 64 in Palm Coast, FL. Long set a record by hitting home runs in eight consecutive games as a member of the Pittsburgh Pirates, a record tied by Don Mattingly. Long played for the Yankees 1960, 1962–63.

The Yankees signed pitcher Ramiro Mendoza to a one-year contract in 2000. Mendoza was 10–2 with New York in 1998.

29

The Baseball Hall of Fame announced the election of the five charter members in 1936, Babe Ruth, Ty Cobb, Honus Wagner, Christy Mathewson and Walter Johnson.

Commissioner Happy Chandler fined the Yankees, Chicago Cubs, and Philadelphia Phillies $500 each in 1948 for signing high school players to contracts.

John Williams Cox bought Yankee Stadium in 1955. He sold the grounds to the Knights of Columbus, and left the structure to Rice University in 1962.

Infielder Steve Sax was born in 1960 in Sacramento, CA. A long-time Los Angeles Dodger, Sax played for the Yankees 1989–91. He was an American League all-star in 1989–90, batting .315 in 1989 for New York.

John Habyan, Yankee pitcher from

1990–93 was born in 1964 in Bay Shore, NY. He appeared in 66 games in 1991 out of the bullpen.

Former Yankee catcher and baseball executive Branch Rickey joined outfielder Lloyd Waner when they were elected by the Baseball Writers of America to the Baseball Hall of Fame in 1967.

Third baseman Graig Nettles was named the sixth captain in Yankee history in 1982, after over two years without a captain, succeeding Thurman Munson.

Darryl Strawberry's wife, Lisa, filed a petition for legal separation in Los Angeles Superior County Court in 1987.

Five-time all-star pitcher Jimmy Key retired from baseball in 1999 due to a shoulder injury at the age of 37. He appeared in the playoffs with all the teams he played with including the Toronto Blue Jays, Baltimore Orioles, and the Yankees.

30

The Yankees acquired Herb Pennock from the Boston Red Sox in 1923 for outfielders Norm McMillan and Camp Skinner, pitcher George Murray and $50,000. The future Hall of Fame pitcher blossomed as a Yankee, going 162–90 over 11 seasons in New York.

Herb Pennock, Yankee star of the 1930s and then general manager of the Philadelphia Phillies, collapsed in the lobby of a New York hotel in 1948 and later died at a local hospital. He was elected to the Baseball Hall of Fame in 1948.

Dallas Cowboys defensive back/kick returner Deion Sanders, who started his baseball career with the Yankees, decided to play baseball again and signed with the Cincinnati Reds in 1997.

31

Outfielder Timothy Hendryx was born in 1891 in LeRoy, IL. He played eight major league seasons including 1915–16 with the Yankees.

George "Tioga" Burns was born in 1893 in Niles, OH. Burns was a career .317 hitter in 16 years in the American League, spending parts of two seasons with the Yankees (1928–29).

Joe Sewell, the hardest man in history to strike out, played for the Yankees 1931–33. He was elected to the Baseball Hall of Fame on this date in 1977.

The Yankees signed pitcher Mike Grace to a minor league contract and invited him to spring training as a non-roster player in 2000.

FEBRUARY

1

Outfielder Ron Woods was born in 1943 in Hamilton, OH. Woods played for the Yankees 1969–71 before moving on to the Montreal Expos to finish his career.

Outfielder Paul Blair was born in 1944 in Cushing, OK. A long-time Baltimore Oriole, Blair played for the Yankees 1977–79, 1980. He was an all-star two times with the Orioles and led the American League with 12 triples in 1967.

Ford Frick was elected to the Baseball Hall of Fame in 1970. He is best remembered for suggesting that an asterisk be placed next to the name of anyone who broke Babe Ruth's home run record during a 162-game season.

The Yankees traded highly regarded third base prospect Mike Lowell to the Florida Marlins for minor league pitchers Eddie Yarnall, Todd Noel and Mark Johnson in 1999.

The Yankees signed outfielder Tim Raines to a minor league contract and invited him to spring training in 2000.

2

George Halas, born in 1895 in Chicago, IL, briefly tried professional baseball with the Yankees in 1919, batting .091. He went on to become a successful football executive.

Pitcher Wesley Farrell was born in 1908 in Greensboro, NC. Farrell pitched for the Yankees 1938–39. He won at least 20 games six different seasons with the Cleveland Indians and Boston Red Sox.

In 1950 Yankee shortstop Phil Rizzuto became the first mystery guest on the television game show, "What's My Line?"

Mickey Mantle was admitted to a Springfield, MO, hospital for removal of a fluid filled cyst from the back of his right knee, impairing his spring training in 1954.

The Hall of Fame Special Veterans

15

Committee elected Burleigh Grimes and Miller Huggins, among others, for induction in the biggest veteran class ever in 1964. Huggins had a .645 career winning percentage and won six pennants as Yankee manager.

The Special Veterans Committee selected three players, including former Yankee pitcher Lefty Gomez, to the Baseball Hall of Fame in 1972. Gomez pitched for the Yankees 1930–42, winning over 20 games four times, twice leading the American League in wins.

The Yankees named Billy Connors director of player personnel and Stump Merrill special assistant to the general manager for player development and scouting in 1999.

3

Houston, TX native Nathaniel "Mike" Garbark played his entire two-season major league career with the Yankees 1944–45. He caught 149 games with a career .244 batting average.

Thurman Munson became the highest paid Yankee catcher in history when he signed a 1974 contract for $75,000.

The special Veterans Committee elected Bucky Harris to the Hall of Fame in 1975. Harris spent 40 years in Major League Baseball as a player, manager and executive. He managed the 1947 World Champion Yankees.

Bill White, a six-time all-star with the Yankees and a popular New York

sportscaster, was elected the first black president of the National League in 1989. He began his term April 1, when Bart Giamatti became baseball commissioner.

Darryl Strawberry entered Smithers Center for alcohol rehabilitation in 1990.

The Yankees announced the resignation of general manager Bob Watson and named Brian Cashman general manager in 1998.

The Yankees signed shortstop Derek Jeter to a one-year contract in 2000 after reports of a long-term record breaking deal were not finalized.

4

Born in 1875 in Nashville, TN, Alphonzo "Lefty" Davis played four major league seasons. He was a regular in the Highlander outfield in 1903, batting .245. Coincidentally, he died on this date in 1919.

Germany Schaefer was born in 1877 in Chicago, IL. Schaefer played 15 major league seasons. He played for the Yankees in only one game in 1916, recording one at-bat near the end of his career.

Jackie Robinson was appointed director of communication for NBC's New York radio and television stations in 1952, becoming the first black to hold a post of that nature.

The Yankees obtained third baseman Toby Harrah and minor league player Rick Brown from the Cleveland Indians for Dan Boitano, Otis

Nixon and minor leaguer Guy Elston in 1984.

5

Wooster, OH, native Roger Peckinpaugh played for the Yankees 1913–21. Born in 1891, Peckinpaugh hit .305 in 1919.

Yankees announced the purchase of 10 acres of property in the west Bronx from the estate of William Waldorf Astor for $675,000 in 1921 for the construction of Yankee Stadium.

Los Angeles, CA, native Hank Workman was born in 1926. Workman played first base for the Yankees briefly in 1950.

Lee Thomas was born in 1936 in Peoria, IL. The outfielder/first baseman played eight major league seasons, starting with the Yankees in 1961 before moving to the Los Angeles Angels, where he hit 26 home runs and drove in 104 runs in 1962.

The Yankees traded Tommie Holmes (the eventual National League MVP in 1948) to the Milwaukee Braves for Gene Moore and Buddy Hassett in 1942.

Catcher/outfielder Mike Heath started his 14-year major league career with the Yankees in 1978. Heath was born in Tampa, FL, in 1955. He hit .281 for the 1983 Oakland A's.

6

Born in Baltimore, MD, in 1895, George Herman "Babe" Ruth hit 714 major league home runs and twice won over 20 games as a pitcher for the Boston Red Sox. He was a charter member of the Baseball Hall of Fame and a .342 lifetime hitter.

The St. Louis Browns acquired catcher Wally Schang from the Yankees for pitcher George Mogridge and cash in 1926.

Yankee pitcher 1992–96, Bob Wickman was born in 1969 in Green Bay, WI. He was 14–4 as a starter in 1993.

In 1986, the Yankees signed free-agent pitcher Al Holland, who saved five games for three different teams in 1985.

Darryl Strawberry was suspended from baseball for 60 days in 1995 due to his involvement with drugs.

The Yankees acquired second baseman Chuck Knoblauch from the Minnesota Twins for pitchers Eric Milton and Danny Mota, outfielder Brian Buchanan, shortstop Cristian Guzman and cash considerations in 1998.

7

First baseman Frank Leja played briefly in two seasons with the Yankees 1954–55.

Leja was born in Holyoke, MA, in 1936. Joe DiMaggio signed with the Yankees for $100,000 in 1949, the first six-figure contract in the major leagues.

Infielder Damaso Garcia played his first two major league seasons with the Yankees 1978–79. Garcia was born in 1955 in Moca, Dominican Republic. He was an all-star for the Toronto Blue Jays in 1984 and 1985.

8

"Sad Sam" Jones departed the Yankees for the St. Louis Cardinals, traded for pitcher Joe Giard and outfielder Cedric Durst in 1927.

Pitcher Fred "Fritz" Peterson was born in 1942 in Chicago, IL. Peterson pitched for the Yankees 1966–74, compiling a 20–11 record in 1970. He won 15 or more games in three other seasons for New York.

One day after taking a job as director of sports promotions for Claridge Hotel and Casino in Atlantic City in 1983, Mickey Mantle was ordered to sever his ties with Major League Baseball by commissioner Bowie Kuhn.

The Oakland A's "stole" pitcher Tim Belcher from the Yankees in 1984. The Yankees signed Belcher on February 2, but lost him because they had already submitted their list of protected players.

Former Yankee Dave Winfield announced his retirement in 1996. Winfield was a Yankee for ten years. He produced five consecutive 100+ RBI seasons with New York.

9

Julie Wera was born in Winona, MN, in 1902. He played only two major league seasons, 1927 and 1929, both

with the Yankees. He hit one career home run, with the Murderer's Row team in 1927.

Infielder Clete Boyer was born in 1937 in Cassville, MO. Boyer played 16 major league seasons, including 1959–65 with the Yankees. He hit the go-ahead home run in Game 1 of the 1962 World Series, won by the Yankees in seven games.

Robert Eenhoorn was born in Rotterdam, Holland in 1968. Eenhoorn played sparingly in his first three seasons for the Yankees 1994–96. He went on to play with the California/Anaheim Angels.

Yankee catcher Thurman Munson was posthumously inducted into the Kent State University (Ohio) Athletic Hall of Fame in 1980.

Darryl Strawberry made his debut as spokesman for the National Council on Alcoholism and Drug Dependence in 1999.

10

Bethany, OK, native Allie Reynolds was born in 1915. Reynolds pitched for the Yankees 1947–54, going 20–8 in 1952 and compiling a career 182–107 record with the Cleveland Indians and Yankees.

Newark of the Federal League sold Germany Schaefer to the Yankees in 1916. Schaefer appeared in one Yankee game in his career. Schaefer played in the 1907 and 1908 World Series with the Detroit Tigers.

Bill White was hired by WPIX-TV to broadcast Yankees games in 1971, becoming the first black play-by-play announcer in major league baseball.

11

Scott Pose was born in Davenport, IA, in 1967. He started his career with the Florida Marlins, moving to the Yankees in 1997. He appeared as a pinch runner in the 1997 American League Divisional Playoff Series against the Cleveland Indians.

The Chicago Cubs traded Bill Madlock and Rod Sperring to the San Francisco Giants for former Yankee Bobby Murcer, Steve Ontiveros and a minor leaguer in 1977.

The Yankees announced that former baseball star Tim McCarver would join their broadcast team after he was released as an announcer for the New York Mets in 1999.

12

Born in 1902 in Bridgeport, CT, George "Kiddo" Davis started his career with the 1926 Yankees. Kiddo played eight major league seasons, hitting .309 with the 1932 Philadelphia Phillies.

Walter "Monk" Dubiel was born in Hartford, CT, in 1918. Dubiel started his pitching career with the Yankees 1944-45 and played seven major league seasons.

The wife of Frank "Home Run" Baker, Ottalee, died at age 31. Baker missed the entire 1920 season to stay home and take care of his two young children, hitting .294 upon his 1921 return.

First baseman Don Bollweg was born in 1921 in Wheaton, IL. He played five major league seasons, including 1953 with the Yankees. He struck out in both World Series at-bats in 1953, his only appearance in post-season play.

Colonel Ruppert named George Weiss to head the Yankee farm system in 1932. Weiss had been VP and GM of the Baltimore Orioles of the International League.

Pat Dobson was born in 1942 in Depew, NY. Dobson was 20–8 with the 1971 Baltimore Orioles. He played for the Yankees 1973–75, recording a 19–15 record in 1974 with New York.

Lenny Randle was born in Long Beach, CA, in 1949. He played 12 major league seasons, including 1979 with the Yankees. He hit .304 and stole 33 bases for the 1977 New York Mets.

Dave Revering was a first baseman in five major league seasons, including 1981-82 with the Yankees. He was born in 1953 in Roseville, CA. He hit 19 home runs with the 1979 Oakland A's.

Juan Bonilla was born in Santurce, Puerto Rico, in 1955. Bonilla played six major league seasons including two with the Yankees, 1985 and 1987. He was the regular second baseman for the 1983 San Diego Padres.

13

Harold "Prince Hal" Chase, Highlander great from 1905 to 1913, was born in Los Gatos, CA, in 1883. Prince Hal was one of the first superstar Highlanders, hitting .323 in 1906.

Edward "Kid" Foster was born in 1888 in Chicago, IL. He started his career in 1910 with the Highlanders and went on to play 13 major league seasons, hitting .285 for the 1912 Washington Senators.

Catcher Ron Hassey, who had recently been acquired by the Chicago White Sox from the Yankees, was traded back to New York along with three minor-league players for Neil Allen, Scott Bradley and a minor leaguer.

14

First baseman Tim Jordan was born in New York City in 1879. Jordan played briefly for the 1903 Highlanders and went on to lead the National League with 12 home runs in 1906 and 1908 with the Brooklyn Dodgers.

Mel Allen, long-time Yankee broadcaster, known for his "going, going, gone!" home run call, was born in 1913 in Birmingham, AL.

Infielder Larry Milbourne played eleven major league seasons with six teams. He was a Yankee twice, in 1981-82 and 1983, batting .462 in the 1981 ALCS. Milbourne was born on Valentines Day 1951 in Port Norris, NJ.

15

The Yankees purchased the contract of Philadelphia A's third base-

man Frank "Home Run" Baker in 1916 for $37,500, after he had sat out the 1915 season. Baker hit 48 of his 93 lifetime home runs as a Yankee.

The Yankees renamed their spring training site in St Petersburg, FL, "Miller Huggins Field" in honor of their former manager in 1931.

With doctors unable to do any more for his throat cancer, Babe Ruth was released from the hospital in 1947.

A 1950 Associated Press poll selected Babe Ruth as the best athlete in baseball for the first half of the 20th century.

Owners refused to open the spring training camps in 1990 without a new agreement with the Players' Association. The lockout lasted 32 days and postponed the start of the regular season.

Darryl Strawberry angered owner George Steinbrenner by missing an autograph session in 1999.

Harvey Schiller was hired as the head of the Yankee Nets in 2000.

16

James "Alex" Ferguson was born in 1897 in Montclair, NJ. Ferguson started his career with the Yankees 1918 and 1921. He played ten major league seasons with only two winning records.

Yankee pitcher Bill Terry and National League outfielder Mel Ott received the most votes, but failed to be elected to the Baseball Hall of Fame in 1950.

Yankee pitcher Red Ruffing was

elected to the Baseball Hall of Fame in 1967. Ruffing compiled 273 major league wins.

17

First baseman Wally Pipp was born in Chicago, IL, in 1893. He played for the Yankees 1913–25 and was replaced by Lou Gehrig. Pipp hit .329 in 1922.

Babe Dahlgren, the player who eventually replaced Lou Gehrig, was bought by the Yankees from the Boston Red Sox in 1937.

Joe DiMaggio, earning $43,500 as a Yankee, enlisted in the military for a salary of $50 a month in 1943. By report, in his customary quiet style, he gave no notice to the team.

Yankee Don Mattingly won a $1.975 million arbitration case in 1987, breaking the record for the largest amount ever awarded to a player, set four days earlier by Detroit Tiger's pitcher Jack Morris.

Vernon Louis "Lefty" Gomez died on this date in 1989 in Larkspur, CA. The Hall of Fame member pitched four 20-win seasons for the New York Yankees between 1931 and 1937.

18

Infielder Joseph "Flash" Gordon played his first seven seasons with the Yankees 1938–43, 46. He hit .322 in 1942 and won the American League MVP award over Ted Williams. Flash was born in 1915 in Los Angeles, CA.

Pitcher Luis Arroyo was born in 1927 in Penuelas, Puerto Rico. Arroyo finished his eight-year career with the Yankees 1960–63. In 1961, he went 15–5 and led the league with 29 saves. He was named to the all-star team that year, but didn't play.

The Yankees signed outfielder Bernie Williams to a one-year contract, avoiding salary arbitration in 1998.

The Toronto Blue Jays traded pitcher Roger Clemens to the Yankees for pitchers David Wells and Graeme Lloyd and infielder Homer Bush in 1999.

19

Herbert Jefferis "Herb" Pennock was born in 1894 in Kennett Square, PA. He played for the Yankees 1923–33 and was elected to the Baseball Hall of Fame in 1948. He recorded a 23–11 record in 1926.

Lou Gehrig signed a $30,000 contract with the Yankees in 1935. Gehrig led the American League in RBIs for the final of five times in his career in 1934.

The Yankees announced that they would admit 5,000 uniformed servicemen free to each of their home games during the 1942 season.

Alvaro Espinoza played shortstop for the Yankees 1988–91, batting .282 in 146 games in 1989. He was born in 1962 in Valencia, Venezuela.

20

Carroll "Boardwalk" Brown was born in 1887 in Woodbury, NJ. He pitched for the Yankees 1914-15 with mediocre results. Brown was 18–11 with the 1913 Philadelphia A's. He once walked 15 batters in a game as a Yankee.

Catcher Herold "Muddy" Ruel played parts of four seasons with the Yankees (1917–20). He batted .316 in 1923 for the Washington Senators. He was born in 1896 in St. Louis, MO.

Massillon, OH, native Thomas Henrich was born in 1913. Henrich played his entire career with the Yankees 1937–42, 46–50. He hit .308 in 1948. He was named to the American League all-star team five of six seasons and led the league in triples 1947-48.

Outfielder/designated hitter Shane Spencer was born in Key West, FL, in 1972. Spencer hit home runs in Games 2 and 3 of the 1998 American League Division Series against the Texas Rangers to lead the three game sweep.

The era of "Billy Ball" began in Oakland in 1980 when Billy Martin was hired as manager of the A's for $125,000.

The Yankees and manager Joe Torre agreed on a $1.05 million, two-year contract extension in 1997.

21

Outfielder Tom Shopay was born in Bristol, CT, in 1945. Shopay played his first two major league seasons with the Yankees in 1967 and 1969 and his final five seasons with the Baltimore Orioles. Shopay hit two home runs in 27 at-bats in eight 1967 games.

Terry Ley pitched for the Yankees briefly in his only major league season in 1971. Ley was born in 1947 in Tonawanda, NY.

Catcher Joel Skinner was born in LaJolla, CA, in 1961. Skinner played for the Yankees 1986–89. He is the son of former Pittsburgh Pirate outfielder Bob Skinner, a two-time National League all-star.

22

Pitcher Rinold "Ryne" Duren was born in 1929 in Cazenovia, WI. Duren pitched for the Yankees 1958–60, leading the American League with 20 saves in 1958. Duren won Game 6 of the 1958 World Series in relief of Whitey Ford.

The Yankees added pitcher Dwight Gooden to their 40-man roster in 1996. Gooden went 11–7 with the team that year and was 9–5 in 1997 before leaving New York for the Cleveland Indians.

A 2000 Florida Department of Corrections report indicated that Darryl Strawberry tested positive for cocaine on a January 19 drug test.

23

Spavinaw, OK, native Roy Johnson was born in 1904. He played two seasons with the Yankees, 1936–37. Johnson hit .320 for the 1934 Boston Red Sox.

Catcher and Hall of Fame member Elston Howard was born in 1929 in St. Louis, MO. Howard was the 1963 American League MVP. He played for the Yankees 1955–67, finishing his career with the Boston Red Sox in 1968.

Brooklyn coach Casey Stengel replaced Max Carey and signed a two-year deal to manage the Dodgers in 1934.

The YankeeNets, the new company that controls the Yankees and the New Jersey Nets, announced it was offering $250 million in junk bonds to complete the acquisition of the baseball team in 2000.

Baseball ordered Darryl Strawberry off the field at spring training, suggesting he would be suspended for the 2000 baseball season because of a positive drug test.

24

The Yankees' star first baseman Lou Gehrig was given a screen test for the role of "Tarzan" in 1937, a part that eventually went to Johnny Weismuller. Gehrig did appear in a B-western, "Rawhide," in 1938.

The Yankees traded catcher Aaron Robinson and pitchers Bill Wright and Fred Bradley to the Chicago White Sox for pitcher Eddie Lopat in 1948.

New York icon Casey Stengel recorded his 3,000th victory as a manager in the New York Mets win over the San Francisco Giants, 7–6 in 1965.

The Yankees agreed on a two-year contract extension in 1999, worth an estimated $4 million, with manager Joe Torre.

25

Outfielder Cyril "Stormy" Weatherly played in parts of two seasons with the Yankees in the 1940s. He was born in Warren, TX in 1915.

The Veterans Committee elected Phil Rizzuto to the Baseball Hall of Fame in 1994. Rizzuto played his entire 13-year career in New York and won the 1950 American League MVP Award, having finished second the previous season.

The Yankees announced in 1998 that they would no longer allow the "Marlboro Man" to appear at Yankee Stadium, ending a long tradition of permitting cigarette advertisement.

The Yankees signed a letter of intent with the NBA's New Jersey Nets that would merge the teams into a new company entitled "YankeeNets" in 1999.

26

Yankee catcher of the 1950s and 1960s Johnny Blanchard was born in

Minneapolis, MN, in 1933. He batted .305 in 1961.

In the twilight of his career at age 40, the Yankees' Colonel Jacob Ruppert officially released Babe Ruth in 1935. He signed a contract with the Boston Braves for $20,000 and a profit-sharing plan and played one final season with six home runs.

Born in Long Beach, CA, in 1968, Jack "JT" Snow appeared in seven games for the Yankees in 1992 before establishing himself at first base for the Angels, hitting 24 home runs in 1995.

The Yankees announced that Tom Seaver would join their television broadcast team in 1989.

27

The Highlanders announced in 1912 that they would begin wearing pinstripes on their uniforms. It took until 1915 to become reality.

The Baseball Writers elected Yankee pitcher Herb Pennock and Pittsburgh Pirate infielder Pie Traynor to the Hall of Fame. Pennock played in 22 major league seasons, 11 with the Yankees.

In 1963, Mickey Mantle signed his first $100,000 contract with the Yankees.

An original Texas Ranger, infielder Toby Harrah was traded by the Yankees back to Texas for outfielder Billy Sample and a player to be named later in 1985.

Dale Berra's entered his first day as a New York Yankee in 1985 at spring training. His manager at the time was his father, Yogi.

28

The Yankees opened their first spring training in Ft. Lauderdale, FL. The Yankees had trained in St. Petersburg prior to the move to Florida's Atlantic coast in 1962.

Don Mattingly became only the 10th player to be named "Captain" of the Yankees in 1991. He retained the title until his retirement in 1997.

In 1997, The Yankees, one of the teams that voted against baseball's proposed contract with Nike, were reported negotiating with Adidas.

Yankee outfielder/designated hitter Darryl Strawberry was suspended for one year by commissioner Bud Selig in 2000 after testing positive for cocaine, his third drug-related suspension in five years.

29

Ernest Courtney, born in Des Moines, IA, in 1875, died on this date in 1920. Courtney played for the Highlanders in 1903.

If Darryl Strawberry wanted to play baseball during his one-year suspension, the Newark Bears announced in 2000 that he was welcome to join the independent New Jersey team, based near Strawberry's home in Fort Lee.

MARCH

1

The Yankees traded spring training sites with the New York Giants, opening their 1951 campaign in Phoenix, AZ, with rookie Mickey Mantle in camp.

Mickey Mantle announced his retirement to the press in Ft. Lauderdale, FL, in 1969. "I just can't play any more."

Reggie Jackson arrived at spring training in 1977, his first appearance as a member of the Yankees.

George Steinbrenner was reinstated as general partner in 1993, after his 30-month suspension due to his association with alleged gambler Howard Spira. Steinbrenner assumed control of the Yankees at the Ft. Lauderdale, FL, training site.

Darryl Strawberry checked himself into a drug rehabilitation clinic for the third time in ten years in 2000.

2

The Yankees purchased first baseman George Burns from the Detroit Tigers and traded him to the Philadelphia Athletics for outfielder Ping Bodie (real name Francesco Stephano Pezzolo) in 1918. Bodie was the first major league rookie to have over 100 RBIs.

Richard Starr, Born in 1921 in Kittanning, PA, pitched for the Yankees in 1947-48 with a 1–0 record.

Babe Ruth became the highest paid player in major league history in 1927 when the Yankees announced that he will earn $70,000 per season for the next three years.

At spring training 1951, Yankee Joe DiMaggio hinted that this would be his last season and he would retire at the end of the year.

The Yankees renewed the contract of catcher Jorge Posada in 1999.

3

John "Rowdy Jack" O'Connor played 21 professional seasons including 64 games at catcher for the 1903 Highlanders. He was born in St. Louis, MO in 1867.

William "Wee Willie" Keeler was born in 1872 in Brooklyn, NY. A 1939 Baseball Hall of Fame inductee, Keeler played for the Highlanders 1903–10. He hit .432 for Baltimore in 1897. He finished with a career .345 batting average.

In 1994, Darryl Strawberry was investigated by the IRS and U.S. Attorney's Office for allegedly failing to file tax returns on $300,000 of income derived from autograph and memorabilia shows.

The Yankees signed a controversial ten-year deal with sportswear giant Adidas in 1997, which led to a feud between George Steinbrenner and Major League Baseball over licensing rights.

4

Frank "Lefty" O'Doul was born in San Francisco, CA, in 1897. O'Doul began his career as a pitcher with the Yankees 1919–22 before playing outfield for the New York Giants and the Brooklyn Dodgers.

The Yankees become the first major league team to train outside the United States when they broke spring training in Bermuda in 1913. They played exhibition games on the island against the minor league New Jersey Skeeters.

Pitcher Melvin Queen was born in 1918 in Maxwell, PA. He pitched for the Yankees in his first four seasons, 1942, 1944–47 before finishing his eight-year major league career with the Pittsburgh Pirates.

Hall of Fame baseball announcer Red Barber began his career at WRUF in Florida in 1930. He broadcast games for the Cincinnati Reds, Brooklyn Dodgers and New York Yankees in his career.

Infielder Willie Randolph and pitcher Ron Guidry were named co-captains of the Yankees in 1986. The position had been vacant for approximately two years following the 3/30/84 trade of Graig Nettles to the San Diego Padres.

Replacement Yankees beat the New York Mets 2–1 in 1995 as a baseball players' strike forced teams to sign replacements to play in preparation for the regular season.

5

Catcher Walt Alexander concluded his playing career with the Yankees 1915–17, hitting his only major league home run in 1915. Alexander was born in Atlanta, GA, in 1891.

Catcher Chick Autry, one of two players with that name to play major league baseball, was born in Martindale, TX, in 1903. Autry began his six-year career with the Yankees in 1924.

Elmer Valo played major league baseball for 20 years, appearing with ten teams. He was a Yankee in 1960. He hit .364 for the Kansas City A's in

1955. Valo was born in 1921 in Rib-nik, Czechoslovakia.

Doug Bird was born in 1950 in Corona, CA. The right-handed pitcher saved 20 games as a rookie with the Kansas City Royals in 1973. Bird pitched for the Yankees 1980-81 compiling an 8–1 record.

In 1973, Yankee teammates Mike Kekich and Fritz Peterson announced they had traded wives, children and dogs.

6

Babe Ruth signed a three-year deal, for an estimated $52,000 annual salary, in 1922. Home Run Baker, with a $16,000 salary, was the second highest paid Yankee player at the time.

Yankee outfielder Bobby Murcer was inducted into the Army in 1967. He lost two years of his major league career to military service.

The Special Veterans Committee elected outfielder Enos "Country" Slaughter to the Baseball Hall of Fame in 1985. Slaughter played 19 major league seasons, six with the Yankees. He led the National League in RBIs in 1946.

7

Born in Columbus, OH, in 1901, Frank "Inch" Gleich was a Yankee outfielder his entire career 1919-20.

In 1914, at the Fayetteville, NC, Fair Grounds, George Ruth, a minor league pitcher from St. Mary's

School, smashed a long home run in an exhibition game that set the tone for his baseball career.

In 1955, baseball commissioner Ford Frick, former New York sports-writer and broadcaster, announced he favors legalizing the spitball.

The Yankees waived pitcher Jeff Juden in 2000. Juden played with eight major league teams in eight seasons. He was 11–5 with the Montreal Expos in 1997.

8

Davis, CA, native Myril Hoag played the first seven years of his career with the Yankees 1931–38. He hit .301 in 1936 and 1937.

New York City native Robert Grim was born in 1930. He started his career with a 20–6 season with the Yankees in 1954 and was named Rookie of the Year. He failed to win more than 12 games in a season the remainder of his seven-year major league career.

Babe Ruth signed a two-year contract in 1930 for $160,000, earning a larger salary than President Herbert Hoover. Ruth responded to questions regarding his worth with, "Why not? I had a better year."

Pitcher and author of "Ball Four," Jim Bouton, was born in 1939 in Newark, NJ. Bouton played his first seven seasons with the Yankees, 1962–68, going 21–7 as an all-star in 1963. Bouton was 2–0 in the 1964 World Series loss to the St. Louis Cardinals.

The Brooklyn Dodgers beat the

Yankees 1–0 in Havana's new del-Cerro Stadium in 1947. New York managed only one hit, Snuffy Stirnweiss's 10th inning single.

The Yankees traded infielder Andy Fox to the Arizona Diamondbacks for pitchers Marty Janzen and Todd Erdos in 1998.

Joe DiMaggio, the Yankee Clipper, died in Florida in 1999 at the age of 84 following a lengthy illness.

9

Born in 1895, Whitman, MA, native Francis "Sugar" Kane appeared once for the Yankees in 1919. He had previously appeared for the Brooklyn Dodgers in a short professional career.

Jack Jensen started his career with the Yankees 1950–52. He hit .315 for the 1956 Boston Red Sox. Jensen was born in 1927 in San Francisco, CA.

Babe Ruth turned down an offer by Cincinnati Reds General Manager Larry MacPhail to make a comeback as a player in 1936.

The Yankees announced in 1961 that the team would leave its spring training home in St. Petersburg, FL, and move to Fort Lauderdale, FL, by 1963.

In 1961, Yankee owners encouraged the new unnamed National League New York franchise (to become the Mets) to play home games at the Polo Grounds and not consider Yankee Stadium.

10

Second baseman Jim Curry was born in 1893 in Camden, NJ. He played briefly for the Highlanders in 1911.

FBI director J. Edgar Hoover revealed in 1951 that he turned down the baseball commissioner job that subsequently went to former New York sportswriter Ford Frick.

Troubled pitcher Steve Howe was born in 1958 in Pontiac, MI. He pitched for the Yankees from 1991 to 1996. He had eight drug and alcohol suspensions in his major league career.

Darryl Strawberry, still undergoing chemotherapy, went 1 for 4 in a 1999 exhibition game, his first appearance for the Yankees since colon cancer surgery in 1998.

11

Des Moines, IA, native Herm McFarland played outfield for the Highlanders in their first season, 1903. He was born in 1870.

Pitcher Doc Ellis was born in 1945 in Los Angeles, CA. Ellis was 17–8 for the 1976 Yankees. He pitched a no-hitter as a member of the Pittsburgh Pirates on 6/12/1970 against the San Diego Padres, apparently under the influence of drugs.

After a 10-day holdout in 1960, Mickey Mantle signed a contract for $65,000, a $7,000 cut from his 1959 salary.

12

New York Highlanders were approved as a member of the American League in 1903.

Born in Martinsburg, WV, in 1936, Ray "Buddy" Barker played infield for the Yankees 1965–67, to finish his career. He hit all ten of his major league home runs in a New York uniform.

Johnny Callison played 16 major league seasons, ending his career as a Yankee in 1972-73. Callison twice led the National League in triples and once in doubles as a Philadelphia Phillie. He was born in 1939 in Qualls, OK.

Joe DiMaggio signed a one-year contract for the 1942 season with the Yankees for $43,750. DiMaggio led the American League in 1941 with 125 RBIs.

Outfielder Ruppert Jones played twelve major league seasons and was an all-star once in each league. He hit over 20 home runs in three different seasons. He played for the Yankees in 1980. Jones was born in 1955 in Dallas, TX.

Born in Los Angeles, CA, in 1962, Darryl Strawberry was a member of four New York World Championship teams, the 1986 New York Mets and the 1996, 1998, and 1999 Yankees. Strawberry led the National League with 39 home runs in 1988.

13

Hall of Fame member Frank "Home Run" Baker was born in 1886 in Trappe, MD. He played the final six years of his career with the Yankees 1916–22. Baker hit .347 for the 1912 Philadelphia A's.

Lou Gehrig signed with the Yankees in 1937 for $38,000 and a $750 signing bonus.

During an exhibition game against the Yankees in 1954, Milwaukee's recently acquired Bobby Thomson broke his ankle and was replaced by a promising Brave prospect named Hank Aaron.

Infielder Mariano Duncan batted .340 for the 1996 Yankees, but was only 1–19 in the World Series. Duncan was born in San Pedro de Marcorís, Dominican Republic, in 1963.

14

Eugene Layden enjoyed a three-game career with the Yankees in 1915. The Pittsburgh, PA, native was born in 1894.

John Miller played briefly for the Yankees in 1966. He was born in Alhambra, CA, in 1944. He finished his career with the Los Angeles Dodgers in 1969.

Catcher Harold "Butch" Wynegar was an all-star in his first two seasons with the Minnesota Twins. He caught for the Yankees 1982–86, hitting .296 in 1983. Wynegar was born in York, PA, in 1956.

The New York Mets lured former Yankee general manager George Weiss out of retirement to become their first president in 1961.

15

Former Yankee Wilfred "Rosy" Ryan was born in 1898 in Worcester, MA. Ryan pitched for all three New York teams from 1919–1933, winning 17 for the 1922 Giants.

The Yankees sold pitcher Ray Fisher's contract to the Cincinnati Reds in 1919. He was 73–77 in eight Yankee seasons.

Outfielder Bobby Bonds was born in Riverside, CA in 1946. Bonds, whose son Barry has had great success in the National League, played for Yankees in 1975 and hit 32 home runs in his only season with New York.

The Yankees named Don Zimmer interim manager while Joe Torre received treatment for prostate cancer in 1999.

16

Babe Ruth signed a deal for $75,000 and a percentage of the exhibition gate in 1932. Legend has it that Ruth signed a blank contract and the amount was later filled in owner Jacob Ruppert.

The State of New York approved a bond issue for the construction of a 55,000-seat stadium on the site of the 1939-40 World's Fair in Queen's Flushing Meadow area, what was to be Shea Stadium.

Pitcher Andy Messersmith was injured covering first base in 1978. Messersmith was attempting a comeback from a 1977 injury and this es-

sentially ended his career (he was 0–3 that season).

17

Warren, PA native Edward "Big Ed" Klepfer was born in 1888. He started his career with the Yankees 1911–13. He was 14–4 with the 1917 Cleveland Indians.

Joe DiMaggio made his Yankee debut in 1936, recording four hits, including a triple, in an 8–7 exhibition loss to the St. Louis Cardinals.

In 1969, the St. Louis Cardinals traded Orlando Cepeda, who won the 1967 National League MVP, to the Atlanta Braves for Joe Torre, who would win the 1971 National League MVP. Torre went on to lead the Yankees as manager.

Baseball Commissioner Bowie Kuhn ordered an end to the 1976 spring training lockout.

In 2000, the Yankees announced they acquired pitcher Ted Lilly as the player to be named later in the trade that sent pitcher Hideki Irabu to the Montreal Expos.

18

John Cooney played the final 10 games of his 20-year major league career with the Yankees. He hit .319 for the 1941 Braves. In 1925, he was 14–14 as a pitcher. He was born in 1901 in Cranston, RI.

For the first time since the Baltimore Orioles moved to New York to become the Highlanders (Yankees) in

1903, a baseball team changed cities with the National League Braves moving to Milwaukee in 1953, after 77 years in Boston.

Baseball Commissioner Peter Ueberroth reinstated Hall of Fame members Mickey Mantle and Willie Mays in 1985. They had been banned from associating with Major League Baseball due to their employment arrangement with an Atlantic City casino.

Yankees first baseman Joe Pepitone was arrested after running a red light in New York in 1985. Police found a loaded handgun, $6,300 and a shoulder bag containing cocaine.

Yankee manager Joe Torre had prostate cancer surgery in 1999.

19

Utility player Clyde "Hack" Engle started his career with the Highlanders in 1909-10. He had a career high 71 RBI for the 1909 club. Engle was born in 1884 in Dayton, OH.

Wichita, KS native Fritz Brickell, born in 1935, played portions of two seasons for the Yankees 1958-59. He hit his only career home run for New York in 1958

The Yankees traded catcher Joel Skinner and a minor league player to the Cleveland Indians for outfielder Mel Hall in 1989.

20

Al Shealy was born in Chapin, SC, in 1900. Shealy played one season for the Yankees, compiling an 8–6 record in 1928.

Steve Blateric was born in 1944 in Denver, CO. Blateric pitched in three major league seasons, 1971-72 and 1975. He appeared with the 1972 Yankees in relief.

Paul Mirabella was born in Belleville, NJ in 1954. Mirabella played 13 seasons in the American League, including 1979 with the Yankees. He made 52 appearances for the 1984 Seattle Mariners.

The Yankees sold outfielder-first baseman Joe Collins' contract to the Philadelphia Phillies in 1958. The deal was voided when Collins decided to retire. He had played his entire career with the Yankees.

The Yankees announced in 1961 that they would oppose any plan for the new National League expansion franchise to use Yankee Stadium, leaving the Polo Grounds as the only viable option for the new team until their new stadium was completed.

21

William Stumpf, born in 1892 in Baltimore, MD, played his entire 52-game career as a shortstop for the Highlanders/Yankees 1912-13.

William "Good Time Bill" Lamar was born in 1897 in Rockville, MD. Lamar played for the Yankees 1917–19. He hit .356 for the 1925 Philadelphia Athletics as a regular outfielder.

Joe DiMaggio increased his average to 12 for 20 in an 11–2 Yankee victory over the Boston Bees in 1936. The prize rookie was left unattended with his foot in a diathermy machine. The resulting burn ended his spring training and delayed his debut until May 1936.

garding Dave Winfield, after a contract dispute.

The Yankees announced the retirement of outfielder Tim Raines in 2000.

22

New York Highlanders tickets went on sale for the first time in 1903 after the franchise was purchased and moved from Baltimore to New York.

Born in Spokane, WA, in 1916, Norman "Red" Branch compiled a 5–2 major league record in two seasons with the Yankees 1941-42.

The Yankees traded outfielder Danny Cater to the Boston Red Sox for pitcher Sparky Lyle in 1972.

The Yankees announced in 1986 that pitcher Britt Burns, an 18-game winner with the Chicago White Sox in 1985, would miss the entire season due to a degenerative hip condition.

Joseph A. Molloy was elected general partner of the Yankees in 1992.

23

The Yankees agreed to stay in New York in 1972 after the city agreed to renovate Yankee Stadium.

The Yankees purchased the contract of Texas Ranger outfielder Elliott Maddox. He hit .303 for the Yankees that year, 1974.

Howard Spira was arrested in 1990 for extorting money from George Steinbrenner. The Yankee owner allegedly paid Spira $40,000 in January 1990 for damaging information re-

24

Pitcher Ernie Shore won 19 games for the 1915 Boston Red Sox and was 2–0 with a1.53 ERA in the 1916 World Series. Shore was born in East Bend, NC in 1891. He was a Yankee 1919-20.

Babe Ruth accepted a $23,000 pay cut in 1933, the depths of the depression era.

Catcher Bob Tillman was born in Nashville, TN, in 1937. He played for the Yankees in 1967. He enjoyed his most successful season in 1964, batting .278 with 17 home runs for the Boston Red Sox.

Thurman Munson became the sixth Yankee to earn $100,000 in a season when he signed a four-year progressive salary contract in 1976.

25

Woodie Held was born in 1932 in Sacramento, CA. He played 14 major league seasons, all in the American League. The utility player started his career with the Yankees in 1954, reappeared in 1957, and played for six other teams before retiring in 1969.

The Yankees purchased pitcher Pat Malone from the Cubs in 1935. Malone led the National League in wins in 1929 and 1930.

26

The New York Highlanders played their first exhibition game, a 9–0 triumph at Piedmont Park in Atlanta in 1903. Ernie Courtney was the first batter, who walked and scored the first run.

Joe DiMaggio, on the advice of Ty Cobb, switched from a 40-oz. bat to a 36 or 37 oz. bat to avoid getting tired at the end of the season. He hit .346 during 1937 with 46 home runs—the most he ever hit in a season.

Yankee manager Casey Stengel was arrested and released on $50 bail after he allegedly cursed and kicked a newspaper photographer during a 1957 St. Petersburg, FL, exhibition game.

The Yankees gave infielder Rafael Bournigal his unconditional release in 2000.

27

Pitcher Stephen "Smokey" Sundra compiled a 21–11 record in four seasons with the Yankees from 1936–40. He was born in Luxor, PA, in 1910 and appeared in the 1939 World Series.

William "Suds" Sudakis was a catcher/infielder for eight major league seasons, mostly with the Los Angeles Dodgers. Sudakis spent the 1974 season with the Yankees, hitting seven home runs. He was born in 1946 in Joliet, IL.

Born in 1950, Monroe, LA, native

Lynn McGlothen was an all-star with the St. Louis Cardinals in 1974. He finished his 11-year major league career with the Yankees in 1982.

George Steinbrenner named Al Rosen president of the Yankees, succeeding Gabe Paul in 1978.

The New York Mets traded catcher Ed Hearn, pitcher Rick A. Anderson and pitching prospect Mauro Gozzo to the Kansas City Royals for future Yankee David Cone and minor leaguer Chris Jelic in 1987.

28

Pitcher Vic Raschi was born in 1919 in W. Springfield, MA. Raschi pitched for the Yankees 1946–53, posting three consecutive 21-win seasons from 1949–51. He was a member of five consecutive World Series winners.

The Boston Red Sox traded designated hitter Mike Easler to the Yankees for designated hitter Don Baylor in 1986.

The Yankees waived knuckleball pitcher, and future Baseball Hall of Fame member Phil Niekro four days shy of his 47th birthday in 1986.

29

San Francisco, CA, native Herbert McQuaid was born in 1899. McQuaid was 1–0 for the 1926 Yankees.

The Yankees and the Boston Red Sox tied 2–2 in 17 innings in a 1948 spring training game.

The Yankees gave Mel Stottlemyre, suffering from a torn rotator cuff, his unconditional release in 1975. He compiled a 164–139 record with a 2.97 ERA and 40 shutouts. He later became a Yankee pitching coach.

The Yankees released veteran major league catcher Tom Pagnozzi in 2000. Pagnozzi played 12 seasons with the St. Louis Cardinals and was a National League all-star in 1992.

30

The San Diego Padres obtained third baseman Graig Nettles from the Yankees for pitcher Dennis Rasmussen and prospect Darin Cloniger in 1984. The trade ended Nettles' tenure as New York captain.

The Yankees met the Baltimore Orioles in the first exhibition baseball game played at Miami's Joe Robbie Stadium in 1991.

Izzy Molina and Ben Ford were traded from the Arizona Diamondbacks to the Yankees in exchange for Darren Holmes in 1999.

The Yankees helped the Astros inaugurate Houston's new Enron Field with an exhibition game in 2000. New York played the first exhibition game in the Houston Astrodome in 1965.

31

Infielder Frank Truesdale played four major league seasons, including 1914 with the Yankees. He was born in 1884 in St. Louis, MO.

Grand Ridge, IL, native Tom Sheehan was born in 1894. He pitched six major league seasons including 1921 with the Yankees.

The Yankees made a 1981 spring training trade with the San Diego Padres, sending outfielders Ruppert Jones and Joe Lefebvre and pitchers Chris Welsh and Tim Lollar to the Padres for outfielder Jerry Mumphrey and pitcher John Pacella.

In the first baseball game at Coors Stadium, replacement Colorado Rockies defeated the Yankees 4–1 before a near capacity crowd of 47,563 in Denver in 1995.

APRIL

1

Babe Ruth hit his first home run as a Yankee, in a spring training game in 1920 in Florida.

The Baseball Hall of Fame officially opened in Cooperstown, New York in 1938.

"Snuffy" Stirnweiss, who starred for the Yankees 1943–50 and finished third in the 1945 American League MVP vote, was traded to the Cleveland Indians by the St. Louis Browns in 1951, his last major league stop.

The Yankees made an April Fool's trade that was vetoed by Commissioner Bowie Kuhn. The Yankees acquired slugger Jason Thompson from Pittsburgh, but the amount of money exchanged doomed the 1981 deal.

In the first Yankees game against the New York Mets since 1983, the Yankees defeated their cross-town rivals 4–3 in 1989.

2

Chattanooga Lookouts pitcher Jackie Mitchell, a seventeen-year-old girl, struck out Babe Ruth and Lou Gehrig on six straight pitches in a 1931 exhibition game.

Pitcher Mike Kekich, who played nine major league seasons, was born in 1945 in San Diego, CA. Kekich pitched for the Yankees 1969–73, winning ten games in 1971 and 1972.

Bill Sample played nine major league seasons for three teams, including the 1985 Yankees. Sample was born in Roanoke, VA in 1955. He hit .274 as a regular outfielder for the 1983 Texas Rangers.

Pete Incaviglia was born in Pebble Beach, CA, in 1964. He played for the 1997 Yankees in the twilight of his career. Incaviglia hit over 20 home runs in his first five major league seasons with the Texas Rangers, hitting 30 in 1986, his rookie year.

3

Pomona, CA, native Harry Kingman played his entire, yet brief, major league career with the Yankees in 1914. He was born in 1892.

Pitcher Arthur Ditmar pitched for the Yankees 1959–61, going 15–9 in 1960. Ditmar was born in 1929 in Revere, MA. He played in nine American League seasons.

Darryl Strawberry failed to show up for the Los Angeles Dodgers' final exhibition game against California at Anaheim Stadium in 1994. He was not located until that night.

In 2000, the Yankees purchased the contract of outfielder Roberto Kelly. Kelly started his career in New York 1987–92, making the American League all-star team in 1992 and the National League team in 1993 as a member of the Cincinnati Reds.

4

Outfielder "Silent John" Mummel was born in 1883 in Bloomsburg, PA. He played the final 22 games of his career with the Highlanders. Mummel hit .282 for the 1912 Brooklyn Dodgers.

Hank Aaron tied Babe Ruth on the all-time list with his 714th home run against Jack Billingham in Cincinnati in against the Reds in 1974.

On Opening Day 1989, Yankee Tommy John tied a record by playing in his 26th major league season. John beat the Minnesota Twins, 4–2, for his 287th victory, reaching 19th place in career wins at the time.

The 1994 Opening Day crowd of 56,706 was the largest in Yankees history and the largest regular-season crowd at the new Yankee Stadium.

The Los Angeles Dodgers announced that Darryl Strawberry had a substance abuse problem and placed him on the disabled list in 1994.

5

The Brooklyn Dodgers played their first game at Ebbets Field, a 1913 exhibition game against the Yankees in front of 25,000 spectators. Brooklyn defeated New York, 3–2. Casey Stengel hit the park's first home run, inside-the-park.

Babe Ruth collapsed in an Asheville, North Carolina railroad station in 1925 and was subsequently hospitalized in New York City. He later had ulcer surgery and was bedridden until May.

In 1934, Babe Ruth agreed to do weekly NBC radio broadcasts, sponsored by Quaker Oats. His thirteen-week salary of $4000 was more than his baseball contract.

Infielder Ron Hansen was born in 1938 in Oxford, NE. Hanson played 15 major league seasons including 1970-71 with the Yankees. He was an all-star with the 1960 Baltimore Orioles, when he hit a career high 22 home runs.

6

For the first time in major league history, the season failed to open due to a player strike. The strike erased 86 games from the 1972 schedule.

Ron Blomberg of the Yankees became the first designated hitter in the 1st inning of the opener against the Red Sox in 1973. Blomberg walked with the bases loaded to drive in a run, but Boston won 15–5.

The Yankees began a two-year stint at Shea Stadium while Yankee Stadium was remodeled, defeating the Cleveland Indians, 6–1.

A rare April blizzard produced a foot of snow and postponed 1982 Opening Day between the Yankees and the Texas Rangers at the Stadium.

7

Mel Stottlemyre won his third straight season opener for the Yankees, 8–4 over the Senators, with President Nixon in attendance at Washington in 1969. Bobby Murcer hit a home run to spoil Ted Williams' managerial debut.

Reggie Jackson made his Yankee debut with two hits and Catfish Hunter hurled a three-hitter for a 3–0 Opening Day win at the Stadium in 1977 against the Milwaukee Brewers.

Yankee first baseman and captain Don Mattingly collected his 1000th career RBI on a 4th inning fielder's choice against the Texas Rangers in 1987.

In 1989, Darryl Strawberry was named in a lawsuit in Missouri charging that he fathered a son with Lisa Clayton.

Bernie Williams hit a home run into the centerfield bleachers in 1994 at Yankee Stadium as they defeated the Texas Rangers 18–6.

Cuban defector Adrian "El Duque-cito" Hernandez agreed to a four-year contract with the Yankees in 2000.

8

First baseman Hal Chase contracted smallpox at spring training for the Highlanders in 1909. The entire team was vaccinated and quarantined.

James Augustus "Catfish" Hunter was born in 1946 in Hertford, North Carolina. Hunter was one of the first big free-agent acquisitions by the Yankees. He died of ALS in 1999.

Brave "Hammering" Hank Aaron passed Babe Ruth on the all-time home run list with his 715th off Los Angeles Dodger pitcher Al Downing at Fulton County Stadium in Atlanta in 1974.

Making his debut as the first black manager in the major leagues in 1975, Frank Robinson put himself in the lineup as designated hitter. He hit a home run to help the Cleveland Indians win, 5–3, over the Yankees.

The Yankees opened the 1978 season with a 2–1 loss in Texas against the Rangers as Richie Zisk hit a home run off Goose Gossage in the debut of each player with their new team.

Ford Frick, New York sportswriter and broadcaster who served as National League President and Baseball Commissioner, died in 1978 at age 83.

Baritone Robert Merrill of New York's Metropolitan Opera became the first person to sing the anthem and throw out the first pitch at the 1986 Home Opener at Yankee Stadium.

Indian infielder Carlos Baerga became the first player in major league history to hit a home run from both sides of the plate in the same inning in a 15–5 Cleveland rout of the Yankees in 1993.

Darryl Strawberry entered the Betty Ford Center in Rancho Mirage, CA for treatment of a substance abuse problem in 1994.

posed to throw out the first pitch, but arrived late.

The Houston Astrodome (the proclaimed Eighth Wonder of the World), was officially opened for baseball in front of 47,876 fans in a 2–1 Astros exhibition win over the Yankees.

Graeme Lloyd, Yankee reliever who won Game 4 of the 1996 World Series, was born in Geelong, Australia in 1967.

Mickey Mantle and Whitey Ford appeared as guests on *The Dick Cavett Show* in 1970.

On Opening Day 1981, Bobby Murcer hit a pinch-hit grand slam home run to lead the Yankees over the Texas Rangers 10–3 at Yankee Stadium. Bucky Dent hit a three-run home run and Tommy John got the win on the mound.

9

James "Hippo" Vaughn was born in 1888 in Weatherford, TX. He pitched for the Highlanders from 1908–1912 and won 178 games over 13 major league seasons.

Baseball Commissioner Happy Chandler suspended Yankee coach Charley Dressen for 30 days in 1947 following a feud over the signing of Brooklyn Dodger coaches by the Yankees.

Mickey Mantle and the Yankees initiated the Houston Astrodome. Mickey Mantle hit the first indoor home run in an exhibition game in 1965 with Mel Stottlemyre pitching. President Lyndon Johnson was sup-

10

President Woodrow Wilson threw out the first ball in the Washington Senators home opener as the Yankees lost, 2–1, to Walter Johnson in 1913. It was their first official game as the Yankees (previously known as the Highlanders or Hilltoppers).

Yankee general manager Bob "The Bull" Watson was born in 1946 in Los Angeles, CA. The first baseman/designated hitter played for the Yankees 1980–82. Watson hit .318, hit two home runs, and led the Yankees with 7 RBIs in the 1981 World Series.

Ken Griffey Sr., father of Ken Griffey Jr., was born in 1950 in Donora,

PA. Griffey played most of his career with the Cincinnati Reds, but played for the Yankees 1982–86, batting .306 in 1983. He played 19 major league seasons.

Yankee slugger Roger Maris was interviewed in a 1962 "Look" magazine article entitled, "I Couldn't Go Through That Again," revealing the stress he experienced as he broke Babe Ruth's home run record.

Demolition began on the Polo Grounds in 1964, the former home of the Yankees, to clear the way for a housing project.

Due to crowd noise at Milwaukee's County Stadium, reliever Dave Pagan did not hear time-out called at first base and pitched. Brewer Don Money hit a grand slam, which was nullified, then hit a sacrifice fly. The Yankees won 9–7 despite protest in 1976.

The Yankees acquired shortstop Roy Smalley from the Minnesota Twins for pitcher Ron Davis, two other players and cash. This supplanted star shortstop Bucky Dent, traded later in 1982 to the Texas Rangers.

Toronto Blue Jay pitcher Dave Stieb tossed his third one-hitter in four starts in an 8–0 victory over the Yankees in 1989.

The Yankees drew the largest regular-season crowd ever at the new Yankee Stadium, 56,717, in 1998's home opener. The Yankees crushed the Oakland A's 17–13.

11

Babe Ruth beat the Yankees on a three-hitter for a 10–3 Boston Red Sox win in the season opener. Ruth had his best year as a pitcher in 1917 with a 24–13 record, leading the league with 35 complete games.

Jackie Robinson became the first black player in major league baseball when he appeared in an exhibition game for the Brooklyn Dodgers against the Yankees in 1947.

The St. Louis Cardinals traded Enos Slaughter to the Yankees for outfielder Bill Virdon, pitcher Mel Wright and outfielder Emil Tellinger in 1954. Virdon became the 1955 National League Rookie of the Year.

Born in Shreveport, LA, in 1964, Wally Whitehurst started his career with the Mets (1989–1992). He joined the Yankees in 1996, going 1–1 in two starts.

The Yankees scored 12 runs in the 7th inning against the 1987 Kansas City Royals. Designated hitter Chili Davis was named American League player of the week in 1999.

12

Joe McCarthy made his Yankee debut as manager in 1931. By the time he resigned in 1946, McCarthy had won eight American League Championships. He went on to manage the Boston Red Sox 1948–50.

Mel Stottlemyre lost his no-hit bid on a brilliant one-hitter over the Detroit Tigers in 1968. Jim Northrup recorded the only hit. Twelve days later, he had the only hit against Cleveland Indian Steve Hargan (4/24), and twelve days after that he had the only hit against Baltimore Oriole pitcher Dave Leonhard (5/6).

The Yankees hit ten doubles in a game against the Toronto Blue Jays in 1988.

The New York Yankees raised the World Series banner for the 25th time at their home opener against the Texas Rangers in 2000.

13

Pomeroy, OH, native Norman "Kid" Elberfeld was born in 1875. Elberfeld played shortstop for the Highlanders 1903–09. He served as player-manager for 98 games in 1908. He hit .309 playing regularly for the Detroit Tigers in 1901.

Pitcher George Shears was born in 1890 in Marshall, MO. He appeared for the Highlanders in 1912, his only major league season.

Outfielder Charlie "Goggy" Meara played briefly for the 1914 Yankees, hitting one major league home run. He was born in New York City in 1891.

Born in 1915 in Minerva, OH, Oscar Grimes played nine major league seasons, including 1943–46 with the Yankees. He was named to the 1945 all-star team, but was replaced due to injury.

On Reggie Candy Bar Day at Yankee Stadium, Reggie Jackson was showered with chocolate following his home run that defeated the

Chicago White Sox, 4–3, on Opening Day 1978.

At Yankee Stadium, a 500-pound steel and concrete structural joint fell from the upper deck and crushed section 22, seat 7 in 1998, forcing the Yankees to abandon the stadium for Shea for two games.

14

When fire severely damaged the Polo Grounds in 1911, the Highlanders graciously offered the New York Giants the use of Hilltop Park until they returned to their home field in June.

Elston Howard became the first black player to wear a Yankees uniform in 1955 with a single in his first at-bat against the Boston Red Sox in an 8–4 Yankee win.

Red Sox pitcher Billy Rohr was one out from a no-hitter in his major league debut in 1967 when Yankee Elston Howard singled to ruin it. His mother, Jackie Kennedy, consoled six-year-old fan John-John Kennedy, sitting near the Boston dugout.

In 1974, Graig Nettles became the 10th American League player, and the third Yankee, to hit four home runs in a doubleheader.

Darryl Strawberry was charged with possession of cocaine and soliciting a prostitute in 1999 in Florida. He was released on $6,000 bond.

15

The American League season opened with Babe Ruth pitching a four-hit,

7–1 victory over the Philadelphia A's. Red Sox manager Ed Barrow started Ruth's conversion to slugger by playing him 72 games in the outfield and first base in 1918.

The Yankees dedicated a plaque to long-time baseball executive Edward Barrow in 1954.

The remodeled Stadium opened with the Yankees defeating the Minnesota Twins, 11–4, in 1976 despite the fact that the new $3 million scoreboard didn't work. Winner of the 1923 Yankee Stadium opener, Bob Shawkey, threw out the first pitch.

Yankee and Cleveland Indian second baseman Joe "Flash" Gordon died in Sacramento, CA, in 1978. Gordon, the 1942 American League Most Valuable Player, was a Yankee 1938–46. Gordon hit .500 in the 1941 World Series and hit the first home run in Game 1.

The Yankees and New York Mets teamed for a unique doubleheader at Shea Stadium in 1998. The Yankees beat the Anaheim Angels, 3–2, in the afternoon and the Mets beat the Chicago Cubs, 2–1, at night. Yankee Stadium was closed due to structural problems.

Mickey Mantle Field in Commerce, OK, was dedicated on this date in 2000.

16

Hall of Fame member Paul "Big Poison" Waner played sparingly in the final two years of his spectacular career with the Yankees in 1944-45. The

lifetime .333 hitter was born in 1903 in Harrah, OK.

The Yankees became the first team to permanently add numbers to the backs of their uniforms in 1929.

In his first National League game, in 1935, Babe Ruth hit a home run for the Boston Braves against New York Giant pitcher, and future Hall of Fame member, Carl Hubbell. It was his last professional appearance in Fenway Park.

The Yankees unveiled their first message scoreboard in 1959 at Yankee Stadium.

The Yankees defeated the Boston Red Sox, 7–6 in 18 innings, in 1967.

17

Babe Ruth, after collapsing earlier in April 1925 in North Carolina, had ulcer surgery in New York City, remaining lost to the Yankees until May 26.

Actress Claire Hodgson wed Babe Ruth at 5 AM, to avoid Opening Day crowds in New York City in 1929. The opener against the Boston Red Sox was subsequently rained out.

Yankee public address announcer Bob Sheppard's first game was in 1951. Sheppard has announced over 4000 regular season games and began his sixth decade at Yankee Stadium in 2000.

Mickey Mantle hit what was probably his longest home run, a 565-foot shot out of Washington's Griffith Stadium, off Senator pitcher Chuck Stobbs in 1953.

After nearly 25 years without a

captain, catcher Thurman Munson was named the third captain in Yankee history in 1976, succeeding Lou Gehrig.

18

Icon John McGraw made his debut as manager of the Baltimore Orioles (later the Highlanders/Hilltoppers) in 1899. The Orioles won, 5–3, over the New York Giants, whom McGraw would manage for more than 30 years.

Yankee Stadium opened at 161st Street and River Avenue in the Bronx. 74,200 attended the opening game in 1923, won by the Yankees 4–1 over the Boston Red Sox behind a Babe Ruth home run. It cost $2.5 million and took 185 working days to complete.

In his first at-bat since his marriage the previous day, Babe Ruth hit a home run and tipped his cap to his bride, Claire Hodgson, as he rounded second base in 1929.

Trailing 9–0 in the 6th inning to the Red Sox in 1950, the Yankees staged a miraculous comeback to defeat Boston 15–10.

Mickey Mantle went 1 for 4 in his first major league game in 1951. The Yankees defeated the Boston Red Sox, 6–1.

Ed Rommel became the first umpire to wear glasses in a game between the New York Yankees and Washington Senators in 1956.

19

The Yankees fell out of first place for the first time since May 1926 after losing to the Boston Red Sox in a morning Patriots Day game in Boston in 1928.

The Yankees switched their dugout from the third base side to the first base side of Yankee Stadium in 1946.

A granite monument honoring Babe Ruth was dedicated and plaques honoring Lou Gehrig and Miller Huggins were unveiled in centerfield during 1949 Opening Day at Yankee Stadium.

Pitcher Scott Kamieniecki was born in Mt. Clemens, MI, in 1964. He started his career with the Yankees in 1991.

George Steinbrenner replaced Mike Burke with Gabe Paul as Yankee president in 1973.

Baltimore Oriole Al Bumbry hit an inside-the-park home run against the Yankees in 1974.

In the wake of a 6–3 loss to the Baltimore Orioles, Yankee reliever Goose Gossage and catcher Cliff Johnson were involved in a clubhouse brawl in 1979. Gossage sustained a sprained ligament in his thumb and was sidelined until July.

20

Following two days of rain, the first game was finally played at Boston's Fenway Park in 1912 with the Red Sox staging an 11th inning win over the

New York Highlanders, 7–6, before an estimated crowd of over 27,000.

Babe Ruth scored five runs in a game for the second and final time of his career in 1926.

Yankee pitcher Red Ruffing struck out Ted Williams of the Boston Red Sox in his first major league at-bat in 1939.

Yankee Bill Skowron became third player to hit a baseball out of Boston's Fenway Park in 1957.

First baseman Don Mattingly was born in 1961 in Evansville, IN. Mattingly totaled over 2000 hits as a Yankee and won the 1984 American League batting title. He also won the Golden Glove at first base 1985-89 and 1990–94.

Outfielder Claudell Washington hit the 10,000th home run in New York Yankee history, the first team to reach the milestone, in a 1988 win over the Minnesota Twins, 7–6.

21

Joe McCarthy, Baseball Hall of Famer and Yankee manager from 1931–46, was born in 1887 in Philadelphia, PA. McCarthy managed the Yankees to seven World Series Championships.

The Highlanders and the New York Giants played a benefit game in 1912, won by the Giants, for the survivors of the Titanic.

Lou Gehrig was named the second captain in the history of the Yankees in 1935. Babe Ruth had been captain for five days in 1922, before he was stripped of the title due to his behavior.

Billy Martin pulled a Yankee lineup out of a hat and it was enough to defeat the Toronto Blue Jays, 8–6 in 1977.

22

In the New York Highlanders first game in 1903 in Washington, the Nationals chose to bat first to have more chances to hit the new ball. They defeated the Highlanders 3–1.

Hilltop Park was jammed with 30,000 fans when the Highlanders offered free admission in 1905 after failing to issue rain checks for the previous day's storm that caused cancellation.

Babe Ruth, in his first professional baseball game, shutout Buffalo 6–0 on six hits to give Baltimore the win in the International League game in 1914.

The Yankees took the field wearing pinstriped uniforms for the first time in 1915. The idea, the brainchild of owner Jake Ruppert, obviously caught on.

Babe Ruth played centerfield in his first regular season game as a Yankee in 1920, making an error to cost them the season opener, 6–5 in Philadelphia against the A's.

Yankee Don Larsen, who pitched a perfect Game 5 of the 1956 World Series, hit a grand slam home run in 1956 off Boston Red Sox pitcher Frank Sullivan. He was the third Yankee pitcher to hit a grand slam.

Yankee pitcher Whitey Ford struck out 14 Washington Senators en route to a 1–0, complete game win, in 14 innings in 1959.

Jimmy Key, born in Huntsville, AL, in 1961, won the deciding Game 6 of the 1996 World Series for the Yankees over the Atlanta Braves.

The Washington Senators defeated the Yankees in 18 innings in 1970, 2–1.

Yankee star shortstop Mark A. Koenig died in 1993 at the age of 88 in Willows, CA. He was the last surviving member of the 1927 World Championship team. Koenig hit .319 for the 1928 Yankees.

The Yankees traded Ruben Rivera and Rafael Medina to the San Diego Padres for the rights to Hideki Irabu, Homer Bush, Gordon Amerson and a player to be later in 1997.

23

Handsome Harry Howell was the winning pitcher in the Highlander's first American League win, 7–2 vs. the Senators in Washington in 1903.

Lou Gehrig's consecutive game streak was threatened in 1933 after Washington Senator pitcher Earl Whitehill knocked him unconscious. He recovered to finish the game.

The Yankees dedicated a plaque to long-time owner Jacob Ruppert in 1940.

Roy White hit home runs from both sides of the plate for the third time in his career in 1975.

Bernie Williams and Jorge Posada became the first switch-hitting team mates to hit home runs from both

sides of the plate in the same game in the Yankees 10–7 win over the Toronto Blue Jays at SkyDome in 2000.

24

Born in Hackensack, NJ, in 1895, Harry Harper pitched ten major league seasons. He was 4–3 with the 1921 Yankees and appeared in the World Series that season. He was 14–10 with the 1916 Washington Nationals.

The White Sox won the first official American League game, 8–7 over the Cleveland "Bronchos" (subsequently the "Naps" and "Indians") in Chicago in 1901.

The most lopsided shutout win in Highlander-era history was a 17–0 victory over the 1909 Washington Nationals.

George Mogridge became the first Yankee to win a no-hitter, 2–1 over Boston at Fenway Park in 1917. He allowed three walks and three Red Sox batters reached on errors.

Pitcher Joe Verbanic was born in Washington, PA in 1943. Verbanic played his final three major league seasons with the Yankees, 1967-68, 1970, appearing in 40 games in 1968.

Eleven former players, including Highlander star pitcher Jack Chesbro, were named to the Baseball Hall of Fame in 1946.

The Yankees scored eight runs before making an out in 1960 against the Orioles, tying an American League record. Baltimore rallied, but the Yankees won 15–9.

Mike Blowers was born in 1965 in Wurzburg, West Germany. He played with the Yankees his first three seasons, 1989–91. Blowers hit 23 home runs as a regular infielder for the 1995 Seattle Mariners.

Yankee Graig Nettles recorded an RBI in his 10th consecutive game. Nettles drove in 18 of his 75 RBIs in 1974 in the ten game span.

Darryl Strawberry was ordered to repay $350,000 in back taxes and sentenced to six months of home confinement in 1995. The order permitted him to leave home for practice and games, and allowed him to travel to road games with a baseball team.

Darryl Strawberry was placed on administrative leave in 1999 by Major League Baseball, pending a review of his arrest on drug charges.

25

Russ Ford was born in 1883 in Brandon, Manitoba, Canada. Ford set a record with 26 wins as a Highlander rookie in 1910. His 8 shutouts that season established a major league record. Ford pitched in New York 1910–1913.

Pitcher Jack Chesbro of the Highlanders recorded the first of his 41 victories of the 1904 season, an American League record and franchise mark that still stands. No other Yankee pitcher has ever won over 30 games in a season.

Russ Van Atta made a spectacular debut for the Yankees, winning 16–0 and getting four hits against the Washington in 1933. After a wild free-for-all, Ben Chapman, Buddy

Myer, and Earl Whitehill were suspended for five days and fined $100.

Joe DiMaggio, believing he was worth $40,000, signed a $25,000 contract with the Yankees for one season in 1938.

Yankee manager Bob Lemon was replaced by Gene Michael after a 3–1 win in the Yankees 14th game of the 1982 season. Michael would not finish the season as manager either, replaced in August by Clyde King.

26

Yankee Fritz Maisel set a record by being caught stealing three times in one game in 1915. He was caught only 12 times that season in 63 attempts.

Sal Maglie, born in 1917 in Niagara Falls, NY, pitched for the Yankees 1957-58, in the twilight of his career. Maglie was 23–6 for the 1951 New York Giants.

Virgil "Fire" Trucks was born in 1917 in Birmingham, AL. He spent 18 years in the American League, compiling a 177–135 career record. He was 2–1 in his final season, 1958 with the Yankees.

Lou Gehrig hit a home run but was called out when he passed the runner, which cost him the 1931 American League home run championship. He tied with Babe Ruth at 46.

Mickey Mantle hit home runs from both sides of plate for the eighth time in his career in 1961. Roger Maris began his assault on the single season home run record with the first of 61 home runs in 1961. Number one came in the 5th inning against Detroit pitcher Paul Foytack at Tiger Stadium in a 13–0 Yankee victory.

The Yankees traded pitchers Fred Beene, Tom Buskey, Steve Kline and Fritz Peterson to the Cleveland Indians for first baseman Chris Chambliss and pitchers Dick Tidrow and Cecil Upshaw in 1974.

27

Catcher Bob Williams was born in 1884 in Monday, OH, on a Sunday. He played his entire three-year career with the Highlanders 1911–13.

Enos "Country" Slaughter played 22 major league seasons including parts of six seasons with the Yankees. The career .300 hitter was born in 1916 in Roxboro, NC.

"Babe Ruth Day" in every baseball park in the United States and Japan in 1947. Although too frail to wear his uniform at the time, Babe made an appearance at Yankee Stadium. New York lost to Sid Hudson of the Washington Senators, 1–0.

Hank Bauer and Andy Carey became the first Yankees to hit back-to-back home runs to lead off a game, in 1955 off Virgil Trucks of the Chicago White Sox.

28

Former Yankee pitcher Tom Sturdivant, who won 16 games in 1956 and 1957, was born in 1930 in Gordon, KS.

A fight erupted on the field and bottles flew from the stands after St. Louis Brown "Scrap Iron" Courtney spiked Phil Rizzuto in the 10th inning. The Yankees won in the 11th when Gil McDougald scored, 7–6, in St. Louis in 1953.

Much traveled catcher Barry Foote hit a home run in his first Yankee at-bat against the Detroit Tigers after going 0 for 22 to start the season with the Chicago Cubs in 1981.

In 1985, Billy Martin was named manager of the Yankees for the fourth time after the firing of Yogi Berra.

In 1989, Yankee Rickey Henderson set a major league record when he led off a game with a home run for the 36th time in his career, breaking the previous mark set by former Yankee Bobby Bonds.

29

Marvin "Baby Face" Breuer pitched for the Yankees 1939–43 with a career 25–26 record. The Rolla, MO, native was born in 1914.

The Yankees signed Lou Gehrig to a major league contract for $3,500 in 1923. He debuted in June against the St. Louis Browns.

The Little-Bigger League officially changed their name to the Babe Ruth League in 1953.

Pitcher Sterling Hitchcock broke in with the Yankees in 1992 and appeared in two Divisional Playoff games in 1995. He was born in 1971 in Fayetteville, NC.

As a member of the Boston Red

Sox, pitcher Roger Clemens set a major league record for a nine-inning game by striking out 20 Seattle Mariners in 1986. "The Rocket" was named American League MVP and Cy Young Award winner in 1986.

30

The New York Highlanders won their home opener at Hilltop Park (a.k.a. Highlander/American League Park) in 1903 before an estimated 16,000 fans, 6–2 against the Washington Nationals. Jack Chesbro recorded the win.

Lou Gehrig, the Iron Horse, played in his 2,130th and final game in a streak that began on June 1, 1925. Gehrig went hitless in a 3–2 loss to the Washington Senators at Yankee Stadium in 1939.

Cleveland Indian pitcher Bob Feller threw his second career no-hitter. A 9th inning solo home run by Frank Hayes edged the Yankees, 1–0, in 1946.

The Yankees shutout the 1960 Baltimore Orioles 16–0. Three Baltimore Oriole pitchers walked 14 Yankees in a nine-inning game in 1968.

With RBIs #28 and #29 in 1988, Yankee Dave Winfield tied the major league record for runs batted in for the month of April.

The Yankees and the Baltimore Orioles played the longest nine-inning game in major league history, four hours and 21 minutes, with the Yankees overcoming a five-run deficit to win, 13–10, in 1996.

MAY

1

Boston Red Sox shortstop Freddy Parent recorded the only hit against Highlander pitcher Bill Hogg in a 1906 New York win.

At the Polo Grounds in 1920, Babe Ruth hit his first home run as a Yankee, and the 50th of his career, in a 6–0 win over the Boston Red Sox.

Minnie Minoso became the first black player for the Chicago White Sox, hitting a home run against Yankee Vic Raschi in his first plate appearance in 1951.

Chicago White Sox pitcher Randy Gumpert gave up Mickey Mantle's first major league home run in an 8–3 Yankee victory in 1951.

Free-agent pitcher Ron Guidry re-signed with the Yankees in 1987.

Rickey Henderson, American League MVP with the Oakland A's in 1990, broke Lou Brock's record for career steals in 1991 with his 939th in a 7–4 Yankee loss to the Oakland A's.

Former Yankee Rickey Henderson became the first man to steal 1,000 bases in the major leagues in 1992.

In 1996, Gerald Williams became the first Yankee since 1934 to record six base hits in a game.

2

William "Wild Bill" Percy was born in 1896 in El Monte, CA. He played two seasons with the Yankees, 1917 and 1921, compiling a 5–5 pitching record.

Walter "Big Train" Johnson became the first and only pitcher to record 100 career major league shutouts in a 1923 victory over the Yankees, 3–0.

Yankee Hall of Fame member, former catcher and manager Lawrence "Yogi" Berra was born in St. Louis, MO, in 1925.

Lou Gehrig benched himself in 1939, ending his consecutive game streak at 2,130. The Yankees won 22–2 over the Detroit Tigers with his replacement, Babe Dahlgren, hitting a home run and a double.

Jim McDonald of the Yankees

walked twice in the 5th inning of a 1954 game.

The Yankees threatened to broadcast games nationwide in 1958 in response to a National League plan to broadcast Los Angeles Dodger and San Francisco Giant games to New York City.

Don Mattingly's 7th inning hit ended Chicago pitcher Lamarr Hoyt's perfect game bid. The opposite field single was followed by a double play. The White Sox hurler faced the minimum 27 batters defeating the Yankees, 3–0, in 1984.

3

Charles "Red" Ruffing, born in 1904 in Granville, IL, pitched 15 of 22 American League seasons with the Yankees, posting four consecutive 20-win seasons from 1936–39.

Born in Chicago, IL, in 1916, Kenneth "Hatch" Silvestri caught 33 games over three seasons with the Yankees in the 1940s.

New York mayor Hylan closed streets in the Bronx to aid in the construction of Yankee Stadium in 1922.

Joe DiMaggio made his major league debut against the St. Louis Browns in 1936, hitting two singles and a triple and scoring three runs in a 14–5 Yankee win.

Yankee pitcher Vic Raschi balked four times in one game due to his failure to comply with the new rule requiring a one second stop with men on base. New York beat the Chicago White Sox 4–3 despite his difficulty in 1950.

In a 17–3 rout over the St. Louis Browns at Sportsman's Park in 1951, Gil McDougald tied a major league record with six RBIs in one inning (9th). The Yankee rookie hit his first career home run, a grand slam, and added a two-run triple.

Detroit Tigers Charlie Maxwell hit four consecutive home runs in a doubleheader sweep of the Yankees, 4–2 and 8–2, at Briggs Stadium in 1959.

In the third Mayor's Trophy Game, the New York Mets defeated the Yankees 2–1 in 10 innings in 1965.

Don Mattingly became the sixth player in major-league history to hit three sacrifice flies in a game in a Yankee win over the Texas Rangers in 1986, 9–4.

Following a major league suspension, Darryl Strawberry signed with the St. Paul Saints, a Northern League AA independent team, in 1996.

4

In 1929, Lou Gehrig hit three home runs in the same game for the second time in his career as a Yankee. Babe Ruth, Gehrig, and Bob Meusel hit back-to-back-to-back home runs in the 7th inning, the second time in team history.

Due to injury, Babe Ruth played first base and Lou Gehrig moved to right field. Gehrig committed an error to help the Boston Red Sox defeat the Yankees in 1931.

Joe Borowski was born in 1971 in Bayonne, NJ. Borowski came to the Yankees in 1997 from the Atlanta

Braves. He was 1–0 in 1998 with New York before moving to the Milwaukee Brewers.

Yankee Reggie Jackson recorded an RBI in his 10th consecutive game. It was the longest RBI streak of his career, with 20 of his 97 RBIs in 1978 coming in the ten-game stretch.

In 1981, Yankee Ron Davis struck out eight consecutive California Angels to end the game. He set a record for consecutive strike outs by a reliever, eclipsing Denny McLain's previous mark of seven straight strikeouts.

Bernie Williams hit home runs from both sides of the plate for the fourth time in his career on this date in 1999.

5

The White Construction Company of New York began building the first triple-decked stadium (Yankee Stadium) in the country in 1922 in the Bronx.

Yankee shortstop Everett Scott's record-setting consecutive game streak ended at 1,307 in 1925 when manager Miller Huggins replaced him with Pee Wee Wanninger (Lou Gehrig, ironically, pinch-hit for Wanninger to begin his streak on 6/1/25).

The baseball musical "Damn Yankees" premiered on Broadway in 1955.

Japanese sensation Hideki Irabu was born in 1969 . Irabu refused to play with the San Diego Padres and his rights were eventually traded to the Yankees. He fell out of favor in

New York and was traded to the Montreal Expos.

6

Boston Red Sox pitcher/outfielder Babe Ruth hit his first major league home run off pitcher Jack Warhop in his 18th major league at-bat in a 5–3 loss to the Yankees in 1915. Ruth had two other hits but lost the game in 13 innings.

The Yankees signed a deal with United Airlines in 1946 to transport the team to and from road games making them the first professional sports franchise to travel primarily by air in a season.

Mickey Mantle hit home runs from both sides of plate for the ninth time in his career in 1962. Mantle hit three home runs this day off Dave Stenhouse, Pete Burnside, and Jim Hannan of the Washington Senators.

The Yankees lost at the Kingdome in Seattle, 7–3, in 1982. The "Ancient Mariner," Gaylord Perry, became the 15th player in major league history to win 300 games.

Darryl Strawberry finished his 28-day stay at the Betty Ford Clinic in 1994.

7

The Highlanders played the Boston Pilgrims (later the Red Sox) for the first time in team history in 1903, recording a 6–2 win and initiating a heated rivalry.

American League umpire Tim

Hurst punched Highlander manager Clark Griffith and was suspended for five days in 1906.

Boston Red Sox ace left-hander Babe Ruth allowed only two hits and out-dueled Walter "Big Train" Johnson. Ruth drove in the winning run with a sacrifice fly in a 1917 shutout victory over the Washington Senators, 1–0.

In 1921, Outfielder Bob Meusel became the second Yankee to hit for the cycle in team history. Babe Ruth hit a long home run in a game against the Washington Senators.

Lou Gehrig hit a 9th inning grand slam home run off Chicago White Sox pitcher Ted Lyons in an 8–0 Yankee win in 1927.

Cleveland Indian pitcher Herb Score suffered a season-ending injury when he was struck in the face with a Gil McDougald drive in during a 1957 Yankee game.

Roy White hit home runs from both sides of the plate for the first time in his career on this date in 1970.

On Helmet Day at the Stadium, Chris Chambliss hit a 12th inning home run to send the Yankees home with a 3–2 victory in 1978. Goose Gossage got the win in relief.

Medical tests revealed that pitcher David Cone had an aneurysm in his right arm and required career-threatening surgery in 1996.

played for the Yankees 1911–13. He lived to the age of 107, making him the oldest living Yankee at the time of his 1998 death, and likely the oldest Yankee in history.

Roger Peckinpaugh of the 1915 Yankees hit a 9th inning home run and Guy Clarke, a chauffeur, tried to get away with the ball at the Polo Grounds. Police stated that between 25 and 30 balls were lost at the park each week. Clarke was fined $3.

Gene Woodling scored five runs in a game in 1949. Woodling played for the Yankees 1949–54. He hit 15 home runs and batted .309 in the outfield for New York in 1951.

In front of only 6,298 Oakland A's fans, Jim Catfish Hunter hurled the first American League perfect game in 46 years, defeating the Twins, 4–0, in 1968.

Danny Tartabull hit a long home run into the centerfield bleachers at Yankee Stadium in 1994. Tartabull played for the Yankees for over three seasons (1992–95), hitting 31 home runs in 1993 in New York.

Yankee Doc Gooden recorded his first American League win with a 10–3 victory over the Detroit Tigers. Gooden allowed three runs on two hits, striking out eight over 8 innings in 1996. It was his first win in almost two years.

8

Chester "Red" Hoff was born in 1891 in Ossining, NY. The former pitcher

9

Babe Ruth collected four extra-base hits for the first time in his career as a member of the Boston Red Sox. Ruth hit three doubles and a triple in this 1918 game.

Joe McCarthy returned as Yankee manager after missing most of spring training and the beginning of the 1944 season due to illness.

In 1966, after only four victories in the first twenty games, Yankee manager Johnny Keane was fired and replaced by general manager, Ralph Houk.

The Yankees won 3–2 in the 9th inning against the Minnesota Twins on Joe Pepitone's home run that hit the right field foul pole in 1966.

St. Louis Cardinal outfielder # 9 Roger Maris hit his first National League home run on the 9th day of the month in seat 9 in section 9 in 1967.

10

Edward G. Barrow was born near Springfield, IL on this date in 1868. He was regarded as baseball's first real general manager and was the man behind the New York Yankee dynasties of the 1920s and 1930s.

The Highlanders committed eight errors but still defeated the Detroit Tigers, 10–9 in 10 innings in 1909.

Ben Chapman, who led the protest against Jackie Robinson in 1947, shouted a racial slur at a Jewish fan in 1934.

Lou Gehrig played five innings, then removed himself from the game because of illness. Gehrig accounted for two home runs, two doubles, and seven RBIs in 1934 against the Chicago White Sox.

Joe DiMaggio hit his first big league home run in 1936 at Yankee Stadium off Philadelphia A's pitcher George Turbeville, from Turbeville, SC, in a 7–2 New York win.

The Boston Red Sox won their 15th straight game, defeating the Yankees 5–4 despite Joe DiMaggio's grand slam home run in 1946.

In the ninth Mayor's Trophy Game, the New York Mets defeated the Yankees 8–4 in 1973.

11

First baseman John Ganzel hit the first home run in Highlander history in an 8–2 win over the Tigers in Detroit in 1903. Wid Conroy hit a home run later in the game for New York.

Washington Senator pitcher Walter Johnson retired 28 straight batters in a 0–0 pitching contest. The game was called due to darkness after 12 innings in 1919. The future owner of the Chicago Bears, Yankee leadoff hitter George Halas, was 0–5.

The Kansas City A's traded pitcher John "Sonny" Dixon and cash to the Yankees in exchange for outfielder Enos Slaughter and pitcher Johnny Sain in 1955.

Yankee catcher Yogi Berra ended his errorless string at 148 games in a 7–6 loss to the Cleveland Indians at Yankee Stadium in 1959.

Due to a no-trade clause in his contract, Yankee outfielder Dave Winfield refused to report to the California Angels after being traded for Mike Witt. Winfield eventually accepted the trade five days later ending his tenure with New York in 1990.

12

Joseph "Jumping Joe" Dugan was born in 1897 in Mahanoy City, PA. He was the third baseman for the Yankees 1922–28. He hit .322 for the 1920 Philadelphia A's.

Bloomfield, NJ native Henry Borowy pitched his first four years with the Yankees, posting a 17–12 record in 1944. He was born in 1916.

In 1919 the Yankees and the Washington Senators played a second straight extra-inning tie, 4–4 in 15 innings.

Catcher Lawrence "Yogi" Berra was born in St. Louis, MO, in 1925. A member of the Hall of Fame, Yogi played on 14 championship teams in New York was the American League MVP three times. He managed the Yankees in 1964 and 1985.

Jim Bouton made his first start of the 1963 season and pitched a 2–0, two-hitter for the Yankees over the Orioles in Baltimore.

Yankee catcher Fran Healy announced his retirement in 1978. The following day, Healy began a broadcasting career.

13

Ed Barrow Day was celebrated at Yankee Stadium in 1950. Barrow was the successful general manager behind the New York Yankee dynasties of the 1920s and 1930s.

Mickey Mantle hit a home run from each side of the plate for the first time in his career in 1955. Mantle also hit three home runs for the first time in his career against Detroit Tiger pitchers Steve Gromek (2) and Bob Miller.

Former Yankee Reggie Jackson, as a member of the California Angels in 1983, became the first major league player to record 2000 career strike outs.

After trailing 8–0, the Yankees rallied to defeat the Minnesota Twins 9–8 on Don Mattingly's 9th inning, two-out, three-run home run in 1985.

Yankee Stadium fans serenaded Oakland A's outfielder Jose Canseco, singing "Like a Virgin" in 1991.

Yankee owner George Steinbrenner was suspended from baseball's executive council in 1997 after his team filed a lawsuit against Major League Baseball in a dispute over a reported 10-year, $95 million contract with the sportswear company Adidas.

14

Hall of Fame outfielder Earle "Colonel" Combs was born in 1899 in Pebworth, KY. Combs played his entire career with the Yankees 1924–35. He hit .356 in 1927.

The New York Giants notified the Yankees in 1920 that the lease allowing them to play in the Polo Grounds would not be renewed for the 1921 season.

Dick Howser was born in 1936 in Miami, FL. Howser managed the Yankees twice and played his final two major league seasons as an infielder for New York 1967-68. He was an all-star during his first major league season, with the Kansas City A's in 1961.

Charlie Keller, Joe DiMaggio, and Johnny Lindell hit back-to-back-to-back home runs for the fourth time in Yankee history in the 6th inning of a 1947 game.

Pitcher Dick "Dirt" Tidrow was born in 1947 in San Francisco, CA. Acquired from the Cleveland Indians, Tidrow played for the Yankees 1974–79, appearing in three straight World Series 1977–79.

Mickey Mantle's 500th career home run, off Baltimore's Stu Miller in 1967, helped the Yankees defeat the Orioles, 6–5, making Mantle the sixth player to reach the plateau.

Bucky Dent hit an inside-the-park home run to power the Yankees over the Kansas City Royals in 1980. Dent hit only five home runs that season and 40 in his career. He is remembered for one playoff home run that defeated the Boston Red Sox in 1978.

Dwight Gooden pitched a 2–0 no-hitter for the Yankees in 1996. Gooden struck out five and walked six Seattle Mariners.

15

Ty Cobb went into the Hilltop Park stands to fight a heckler, precipitating a brawl and near riot in 1912. This caused heightened security at major league ballparks.

Lou Gehrig stole home for the 15th and final time of his career in 1935 in a 4–0 Yankee victory over the Detroit Tigers.

Joe DiMaggio singled, going 1 for 4 against the Chicago White Sox in 1941, the first of 56 consecutive games with a hit.

In the 11th Mayor's Trophy Game in 1975, the Yankees defeated the New York Mets, 9–4.

16

Pitcher Frank "Stubby" Overmire was born in 1919 in Moline, MI. Stubby played for the Yankees in 1951. Stubby started and lost Game 3 of the 1945 World Series as a member of the Detroit Tigers.

Outfielder Bob Meusel stole second, third, and home in the 2nd inning of the Yankees 1927 win over the Detroit Tigers, 6–2. He led the American League with 33 home runs and 138 RBIs in 1925.

The Yankees completed their fourth consecutive shutout to tie an American League record. Johnny Allen, George Pipgras, Red Ruffing, and Lefty Grove got the wins in 1932. This was Allen's rookie season, he compiled a 17–4 record.

After winning 11 consecutive games over two years, Yankee pitcher Hank Borowy finally lost, 10–4, to the Chicago White Sox in 1944.

Rick Reuschel pitched in 19 major league seasons with four teams, including part of 1981 with the Yankees. He was born in 1949 in Quincy, IL.

Yankees Hank Bauer, Mickey Mantle, Whitey Ford, Yogi Berra, Johnny Kucks and Billy Martin celebrated

Martin's 29th birthday at the Co-pacabana Club. After an alleged fight, the Yankees fined all six players in 1957.

Jim Mecir pitched for the Yankees in 51 games in 1996–97. He was born in 1970 in Bayside, NY, and went on to play with the Tampa Bay Devil Rays.

Thurman Munson hit a home run and had two other hits in a 1973, 11–4, victory over the Milwaukee Brewers. Munson also picked a runner off third base.

New York Met Rookie Darryl Strawberry hit his first major league home run in an 11–4 win over the San Diego Padres in 1983.

17

Due to Sunday restrictions in Cleveland, OH, a major league game was played in Columbus, OH, as the "hometown" Blues (Indians) defeated the Highlanders, 9–2, pitcher/manager Clark Griffith took the loss for New York.

Yankee Frank "Home Run" Baker had a good day on the bases in 1917. Home Run stole four bases in a game for the only time in his career. He stole 40 bases for the 1912 Philadelphia A's.

Grants Pass, OR, native James "Hot Rod" McDonald was born in 1927. Hot Rod pitched for the Yankees 1952–54, going 9–7 in 1953.

In the first televised baseball game, Princeton beat Columbia 2 1 at Co lumbia's Baker Field in 1939. The contest was aired on an experimental station in New York City, W2XBS.

The Yankees and St. Louis Browns set a major league record by using 41 players in a game in 1953.

Roger Maris hit his first home run of the year at Yankee Stadium, and his fourth of the season, off Washington Senator pitcher Pete Burnside, on his way to a record of 61 home runs in 1961.

Mickey Mantle generated the winning run in the top of the 9th inning at Fenway Park against the Boston Red Sox. Mantle walked, stole second, went to third on a bad throw, and scored on a sacrifice in 1962.

18

Modum, Norway native Arndt "Art" Jorgens was a part-time Yankee catcher, born in 1905. 1929–39 Jorgens caught 306 games with a career .238 average.

Dan Topping was born in 1912. He was the owner of the Yankees 1945–66.

In 1942, night games were banned in New York City over fears that the lights would create a danger to the city during World War II.

Reggie Jackson was born in 1946 in Wyncotte, Pa. A Hall of Famer, Jackson led the American League in home runs four times. He is the all-time major league strikeout leader with 2,597.

Mickey Mantle hit home runs from both sides of plate for the third time in his career, off Billy Pierce and Dixie Howell, in a win over the

Chicago White Sox, 8–7 in ten innings, in 1956.

The Yankees obtained Carlos May from the Chicago White Sox in 1976.

Darryl Strawberry's wife filed a divorce petition in Los Angeles in 1989.

Joe Torre returned to manage the Yankees in 1999, exactly two months after prostate cancer surgery.

19

Infielder Gil McDougald was born in 1928 in San Francisco, CA. He played his entire career with the Yankees 1951–1960 and was named American League Rookie of the Year in 1951. He led the league in triples in 1957 and appeared in eight World Series.

Tragedy struck in 1929 at Yankee Stadium when two people were killed and 62 injured when the crowd stampeded the right field exits to escape a cloudburst.

Rick Cerone, a catcher with 18 years of major league experience, was born in 1954 in Newark, NJ. He played for the Yankees 1980–84 and 1990 and went on to manage in the Yankees farm system. Cerone hit a home run in Game 3 of the 1981 World Series.

Pitcher Ed Whitson played for the Yankees after signing as a high priced free-agent in 1984. He was subsequently traded back to his former club, the San Diego Padres in 1986. Whitson was born in 1955 in Johnson City, TN.

Steve Sax, who had played all of his previous two seasons at second base, became the Yankee third base-man in 1991. He played only five career games at third for New York.

20

Babe Ruth and Bob Meusel, both suspended the previous October by Judge Kennesaw Mountain Landis, returned to the Yankees lineup and went hitless in 1922. Ruth began his brief stint as Yankee team captain.

The Cleveland Indians scored six runs in the bottom of the 9th inning to defeat the Yankees, 10–9, in 1925. Tris Speaker scored the winning run from first base on a single.

One-armed outfielder Pete Gray starred in the St. Louis Browns sweep of the Yankees, 10–1 and 5–2. Gray had two RBI and three hits in the opener. He scored the winning run and made three spectacular catches in game two of the 1945 doubleheader.

Bobby Murcer, successor to Mickey Mantle in centerfield for the Yankees, was born in 1946 in Oklahoma City, OK.

In front of only 5,001 fans in Chicago, Yankee Joe DiMaggio hit for the cycle and drove in six runs in a 13–2 rout of the White Sox in 1948. It was the second and final time he hit for the cycle and the fourth time he had four extra-base hits in a game.

In 1959, the Yankees dropped into last place for the first time since 1940.

David Wells, Yankee pitcher who hurled a perfect game in 1998, was born in 1963 in Torrance, CA. He was traded back to the Blue Jays, for

Roger Clemens, before the 1999 season.

After a 12-inning loss to the Yankees, the California Angels team bus crashed on the way to Baltimore with manager Buck Rodgers suffering a broken rib, elbow and knee in 1992.

21

Pitcher Henry Johnson was born in 1906 in Bradenton, FL. He pitched the first seven years of his career for the Yankees 1925–32, going 14–9 in 1928.

Colonel Ruppert bought out Colonel Huston's interest in the Yankees for $1,500,000 in 1922.

In 1930, at age 35, Babe Ruth had his first three home run game in the regular season. The Yankees lost to the Philadelphia A's 15–7 at Shibe Park. Ruth attempted to bat right-handed in the 9th inning, got two strikes, then struck out left-handed.

Joe DiMaggio and five other players were fined $100 for failing to fulfil contractual requirements for promotional duties to the Yankees in 1947.

Yankee Whitey Ford made his final appearance, a start against the Tigers in Detroit in 1967. The Chairman of the Board lasted only one inning and later retired.

The Yankees defeated the Boston Red Sox in 12 innings, 6–5, in 1976. After a two-out error, Graig Nettles and Kerry Dineen singled for the win.

Roger Clemens earned his 200th career victory, allowing only four hits

and striking out 12 over eight innings as the Toronto Blue Jays defeated the Yankees, 4–1, in 1997.

22

For the second consecutive game, a Yankee batter hit three home runs in a game when Lou Gehrig hit three against the Philadelphia A's in 1930. Babe Ruth hit three the previous day. Gehrig had 8 RBIs in the game.

Lou Gehrig collected an RBI in his 10th consecutive game. Gehrig had two previous ten game RBI streaks, one in 1930 and one in 1931. He drove in 22 of his 165 RBIs in 1934 in these ten games.

The Yankees turned a triple play on their way to a 5–3 victory over the Detroit Tigers in 1946.

The Yankees defeated the Washington Senators 12–4 in 1953. Yankee Irv Noren hit into a triple play.

Roger Maris set a record receiving four intentional walks. He also tied a record with five walks in the nine-inning game in 1962.

Mickey Mantle barely missed hitting the first ball out of Yankee Stadium, striking the top of the right-field façade on a home run off pitcher Bill Fischer in an 8–7 win over the Kansas City, A's in 1963.

Yankee Mel Stottlemyre set a major league record for the most walks in winning a shutout in 1970. Stottlemyre walked eleven, but won 2–0 in 1970.

After a stint on the disabled list and a rainout in 1999, Yankee pitcher Roger Clemens finally broke the

American League record for consecutive victories with 19.

23

Joe DiMaggio, Nick Etten, and Joe Gordon became the third Yankee trio to hit back-to-back-to-back home runs in the 5th inning of a 1946 game. Meusel-Ruth-Gehrig (1925) and Ruth-Gehrig-Meusel (1929) had previously achieved it.

Joe DiMaggio hit three consecutive home runs, the first two off Bob Feller, as the Yankees defeated the Cleveland Indians in 1948, 6–5.

William "Buck" Showalter was born in 1956 in DeFuniak Springs, FL. Showalter managed the Yankees 1992–95 before being replaced by Joe Torre.

Yankee first baseman Joe Pepitone hit two home runs in the 8th inning to pace New York over the Kansas City A's in 1962, 13–7.

The Yankees traded pitcher Dick Tidrow to the Chicago Cubs for pitcher Ray Burris in 1979.

Dave Winfield hit his first home run as a Yankee at the Stadium off Cleveland Indian pitcher Rick Waits in 1981. Dave Righetti won his first major league game for New York.

The Yankees hit six home runs to beat the Minnesota Twins in 1990, 12–0.

The Yankees played in their fourth straight extra inning game in 1992.

24

The Yankees played the longest game, in innings, in Polo Grounds history in 1918. They lost to the Cleveland Indians 3–2 in 19 innings on a home run by Smokey Joe Wood. Frank "Home Run" Baker tied an American League record with 11 assists at third base.

A record 13 future Baseball Hall of Fame players appeared in the New York Yankees' 9–7 victory over the Philadelphia Athletics in 1928. Both managers, Miller Huggins and Connie Mack, were also elected to the Hall of Fame.

Babe Ruth hit a home run in both games of a doubleheader, giving him nine in one week in 1930.

Tony Lazzeri hit two grand slam home runs and accumulated 11 RBIs in a 25–2 Yankee win over the Philadelphia A's in 1936. Ben Chapman set a major-league record by reaching base seven times, five by walks.

Joe McCarthy resigned as Yankees manager in 1946. Hall of Fame catcher Bill Dickey replaced him. McCarthy managed two more years, 1948–50, with the Boston Red Sox.

Mickey Mantle went 5 for 5 with an intentional walk in an 11–5 victory over the Detroit Tigers in 1956. Mantle hit his 17th home run of the season off Duke Maas.

Yankees reliever Lee Guetterman gave up five runs in the 9th inning of an 11–4 loss to the California Angels. This ended his consecutive scoreless streak at 30⅔ innings in 1989.

Despite trailing 7–1, the Yankees tied the Milwaukee Brewers and scored the winning run in the 9th to avoid their fifth straight extra inning game in 1992.

Ken Griffey Jr. hit three home runs against the Yankees en route to a 10–4 Seattle Mariners victory in 1996. It was the first three home run game in the "Kid's" career.

25

Babe Ruth was suspended for one game and fined $200 for throwing dirt on an umpire and going after a fan, costing him his position as the first Yankee team captain (which lasted only five days) in 1922.

At Forbes Field in Pittsburgh, Babe Ruth hit his final three major league home runs to bring his career total to 714. Ruth played briefly in the National League in his final season, 1935 with the Boston Braves.

Future Hall of Fame catcher Mickey Cochrane had his skull fractured after Yankee pitcher Bump Hadley hit him in the head in 1937. Cochran had hit a home run earlier in the game. He retired later that season at age 34.

The longest nine-inning major league baseball game ever played lasted three hours and 52 minutes as the Boston Red Sox defeated the Yankees, 14–10 in 1953.

The Yankees completed a doubleheader sweep over the Indians in Cleveland in 1958 to raise their record to 25–6. They led the league by nine games.

The Yankees scored nine runs before their first out in the 8th inning

in a 1992 victory over the Milwaukee Brewers, 13–7.

Ramiro Mendoza made his major league debut with the Yankees in 1996, earning the 5–4 victory. He pitched six innings and struck out six.

Todd Stottlemyre recorded his 100th career victory in 1997 to join Mel Stottlemyre as the first father and son combination to each win 100 major league games.

26

Chicago White Sox pitcher Ed Walsh threw a no-hitter against the Highlanders in a five-inning game in 1907, 8–1.

Manager Joe McCarthy was named to manage the 1937 American League all-star team. He led the Yankees to World Series Championships 1936–39.

In the largest single-game crowd to date, 74,747, witnessed the Yankees 5th straight win, defeating the Boston Red Sox 9–3 at Yankee Stadium in 1947.

Rob Murphy was born in 1960 in Miami, FL. Murphy pitched 11 seasons in the major leagues, never starting a game. He was a Yankee in 1994. Murphy led the National League appearing in 76 games in 1988 with the Cincinnati Reds.

Yankee outfielder Darryl Strawberry received 18 months probation in 1999 after pleading no contest to a charge of solicitation and drug possession in Florida.

27

Babe Ruth was ejected from his first game as a Yankee after trying to stretch a single into a double. Afterwards, Ruth entered the stands and battled a heckler. Ruth received a one-game suspension and a fine in 1922.

The 1932 Yankees scored 12 runs in the 8th inning against the Chicago White Sox.

In the top of the 3rd inning, the Chicago White Sox had runners thrown out at the plate on consecutive singles to Yankee leftfielder Lou Piniella in 1974.

28

Joe DiMaggio started a 61-game hitting streak in the second game of a double-header against Portland while playing for the 1933 San Francisco Seals of the Pacific Coast League.

George Selkirk became the first Yankee, and 10th American Leaguer, to pinch-hit a grand slam home run, off Washington Senator pitcher Sid Hudson in 1941

The Yankees won the first night game in the history of Griffith Stadium in Washington D.C., 6–5 over the Senators in 1941.

The first night game was played at Yankee Stadium in 1946 before 49,917. The Yankees lost to the Washington Senators 2–1 with General Electric president Charles E. Wilson throwing out the first pitch.

Pittsburgh Pirate Dale Long hit a home run in his eighth consecutive game in 1956, a major league record later tied by Yankee first baseman Don Mattingly. Long played for the Yankees in 1960 and 1962-63, hitting eight home runs for New York in 1962.

American League batters hit 27 home runs in seven games on one day in 1961, setting a record. Yankee Roger Maris contributed to the total with his ninth of the season in a 5–3 victory over the Chicago White Sox in game two of a doubleheader.

In 1995, Mickey Mantle was admitted to the hospital for evaluation of stomach pain.

The Yankees claimed pitcher Greg McCarthy off waivers from the Seattle Mariners and added him to the 40-man roster in 1999.

29

Frank "Home Run" Baker hit his first career home run in 1909. He later became one of the first stars of the Yankees.

Third baseman on the 1996 World Championship team, Charlie Hayes was born in Hattiesburg, MS, in 1965. He played two stints with the Yankees in 1992 and 1996-97.

Oakland A's outfielder Rickey Henderson stole the 893rd base of his major league career, breaking Ty Cobb's American League record in 1990.

The Yankees signed Hideki Irabu to a four-year, $12.8 million deal in 1997.

30

The Yankees recorded a shutout win in 15 innings over the Philadelphia A's, 2–0, in 1917. Yankee Nick Cullop pitched a 6–0 shutout in game one of the doubleheader sweep. Slim Love pitched the victory in the second game.

The first of the outfield monuments at Yankee Stadium was dedicated to manager Miller Huggins in 1932.

A record Yankee Stadium crowd of over 81,00 saw the Yankees sweep a doubleheader 10–0, 5–4 from the Boston Red Sox in 1938. Yankee outfielder Jake Powell was involved in a famous fight with Red Sox player/manager Joe Cronin in the nightcap.

Yankee Eddie Robinson set a franchise record when he grounded into three double plays in a game in 1955. Robinson was 2 for 3 in the 1955 World Series with an RBI for New York.

Mickey Mantle missed by a reported 18 inches of becoming the first player to hit a home run out of Yankee Stadium. By report, the shot was still climbing as it hit the facade in the upper deck in 1956 off Washington Senator pitcher Pedro Ramos.

Mickey Mantle, Roger Maris and Bill Skowron each hit two home runs and Yogi Berra added a one to lead the Yankees to a 12–3 victory over the Boston Red Sox in 1961.

Pitcher Whitey Ford, suffering from circulatory problems, retired in 1967. The "Chairman of the Board" played his entire career with the Yankees 1950–67, compiling a 236–106 lifetime record and an ERA of 2.75.

In the 10th Mayor's Trophy Game, The Yankees defeated the New York Mets in 1974, 9–4.

Roy Smalley hit home runs from both sides of the plate for the second and final time in his career in 1986.

Scott Sanderson became the ninth pitcher to defeat all 26 major league teams in the Yankees 8–1 victory over the Milwaukee Brewers in 1992.

31

After a conflict with manager Frank Chance, Yankee star first baseman "Prince Hal" Chase was traded to the Chicago White Sox for infielder Rollie Zeider and first baseman Babe Borton in 1913.

The Yankees set an attendance record at the Polo Grounds in 1920, playing before 38,688 fans in the second game of a doubleheader. New York defeated the Washington Senators 10–7.

Babe Ruth hit his 12th home run of the month. The Yankees collected 24 hits in an 18–5 win over the Philadelphia Athletics in 1927. Babe Ruth hit home runs number 15 (off Jack Quinn) and 16 (off Howard Ehmke). Lou Gehrig hit his 12th against Quinn.

Babe Ruth played his last major league game going 0 for 1 against the Philadelphia Phillies in 1935.

Lou Gehrig appeared in the 2,000th consecutive game of his career in 1938.

Ranger Cesar Tovar recorded the only hit in Yankee Catfish Hunter's one-hit victory over Texas in 1975. It was the fifth time in Tovar's career that he recorded the only hit in a game.

Joe Torre was named manager of the New York Mets in 1977, replacing Joe Frazier.

American League President Lee MacPhail suspended Yankees owner George Steinbrenner for one week for his public criticism of umpires. George was banned from his Yankee Stadium and from attending games during the 1983 suspension.

JUNE

1

Third baseman Frank "Home Run" Baker turned Chicago White Sox Chick Gandil's bases-loaded, 9th inning line drive into a triple play to preserve a 5–4 Yankee win in 1918.

With the Yankee pitching staff limited by injury, Babe Ruth pitched his first game as a Yankee. He faced 17 batters, allowed three hits and picked up the win in a 1920 contest against the Washington Senators.

Lou Gehrig pinch hit for Pee Wee Wanninger in the 8th inning and replaced Wally Pipp at first base in 1925, playing in the first of 2,130 consecutive baseball games over 14 years.

Actress Marilyn Monroe was born in 1926 in Los Angeles, CA. She married Yankee Clipper Joe DiMaggio in 1954, a union that lasted less than a year. It was his second marriage.

The Yankees set a record in 1935 by hitting six solo home runs to defeat the Boston Red Sox, 7–2. Bill Dickey hit two and Frank Crosetti, Ben Chapman, George Selkirk, and Red Rolfe each hit one.

Mickey Mantle broke up Baltimore Oriole Hal Brown's no-hitter with a home run in 1960.

Baseball Commissioner Bowie Kuhn reprimanded pitcher Jim Bouton in 1970 for writing *Ball Four*, an inside look at the New York Yankees. The publicity put the baseball book on the bestseller list.

2

Roger Peckinpaugh drew five bases-on-balls in the same game in 1919, the second Yankee to achieve the distinction.

Babe Ruth announced his retirement from baseball in 1935 at the age of 40. He hit just .181 with six home runs for the Boston Braves in 28 games.

Gene Michael, Yankee infielder of the 1960s and 1970s, and manager, was born in 1938 in Kent, OH.

Yankee second baseman of the

1960s and 1970s Horace Clarke was born in 1940 in Frederiksted, Virgin Islands.

Yankee Lou Gehrig died of amyotrophic lateral sclerosis at the age of 37 in 1941. Gehrig was the American League MVP in 1927 and 1936. Gehrig was the second Yankee captain and set a consecutive game streak that stood for over 50 years.

Yankee pitcher Whitey Ford stuck out six consecutive Chicago White Sox batters, the second and final time he achieved the feat, in 1958. Ford led the American League with 7 shutouts that season.

Left-handed reliever Mike Stanton was born in 1967 in Houston, TX. Stanton appeared in 81 games with the Boston Red Sox and Texas Rangers in 1996 and was signed that winter as a free-agent by the Yankees.

triple-play in team history in a 1968 loss to the Minnesota Twins, 4–3.

The Yankees scored eight times in the 13th inning to defeat the Chicago White Sox in 1972, 18–10. Bobby Murcer tied a franchise record by scoring five runs.

Oakland A's first baseman Mike Hegan ended his record errorless streak at 178 games against the Boston Red Sox in 1973. Hegan was traded back to the Yankees later that season after spending his first three seasons in New York.

Orlando Hernandez made his major league debut defeating the Tampa Bay Devil Rays, 7–1. "El Duque," who escaped from Cuba by boat six months earlier, allowed just one run on five hits over seven innings in 1998.

The Baltimore Orioles claimed catcher Mike Figga off waivers from the Yankees in 1999.

3

In Philadelphia, Lou Gehrig became the first player in the 20th century to hit four home runs in one game and barely missed a fifth as the Yankees set a major league record for total bases with 50 against the Philadelphia A's in a 20–13 win in 1932. Gehrig collected 16 total bases and Tony Lazzeri hit for the cycle in the victory.

The Yankees scored ten 5th inning runs to overcome 11 scored in the 2nd by the Philadelphia A's in 1933 to record a 17–11 win.

The Yankees recorded the 21st

4

Pitcher Ray Caldwell was ejected as Ty Cobb completed his 5th career steal of home against the Yankees in 1915. New York lost to the Detroit Tigers 2–0. Caldwell enjoyed a 19–16 record in 1915.

Del Pratt hit a grand slam home run, becoming the second Yankee in two days to hit one in 1920, Ping Bodie hit a grand slam the previous day.

Shortstop Phil Linz was born in 1939 in Baltimore, MD. He played for the Yankees 1962–65. Linz hit two home runs in the 1964 World Series. He sparked the Yankees in the pennant race with his harmonica playing conflict with manager Yogi Berra.

The Yankees lost a heartbreaking shutout, 2–0 to the Chicago White Sox in 15 innings in 1965.

Yankee infielder Horace Clarke broke up a no-hitter in the 9th inning for the first of three times in less than a month in 1970 with a hit against Kansas City Royal pitcher Jim Rooker.

The longest baseball game in the history of Baltimore's Memorial Stadium lasted five hours and 46 minutes in 1970. The Yankees defeated the Orioles 7–6 in 14 innings.

Reggie Jackson hit two doubles in the same inning in 1977.

The Yankees completed a 1981 three-game series sweep of the Baltimore Orioles behind strong pitching by Gene Nelson, 12–3. Bobby Murcer collected his 1000th career RBI.

Rickey Henderson stole two bases in 1988, making him the all-time Yankee stolen base leader with 249.

The Yankees acquired pitcher Scott Brow and minor league pitcher Joe Lisio from the Arizona Diamondbacks for pitcher Willie Banks in 1998.

5

Hall of Fame pitcher John "Happy Jack" Chesbro was born in N. Adams, MA, in 1874. Chesbro pitched for the Highlanders 1903–09, going 41–13 in 1904.

Mickey Mantle hit a home run off Chicago White Sox pitcher Billy Pierce that was estimated to travel 550 feet, clearing the left field upper deck at old Comiskey Park in 1955.

Mickey Mantle broke a bone in his foot and damaged his left knee in a collision with a fence in Baltimore in 1963.

The Yankees defeated the Washington Senators behind Thad Tillotson's six-hitter, 4–2 in 1967. Mickey Mantle hit a home run off pitcher Darold Knowles in the 8th inning at the Stadium to break a 2–2 tie.

6

Hall of Fame catcher Bill Dickey was born in 1907 in Bastrop, LA. Dickey played his entire career with the Yankees 1928–43 and 1946 with a career .313 batting average. Dickey managed the 1946 Yankees to a 105–57 record.

The Yankees were beaten 2–1 at the Polo Grounds by the Cleveland Indians in 1913, their 13th consecutive loss, and the longest losing streak in team history.

The Yankees scored 14 runs in one inning on their way to a 17–0 win over the Washington Senators in 1920. The 14 runs in one inning set an American League record until the Boston Red Sox scored 17 in one frame in 1953.

Myril Hoag hit a major league record six singles, going 6 for 6, as the Yankees defeated the Boston Red Sox in 1934, 15–3. New York recorded 25 hits.

In Game 2 of a doubleheader, Tom

Tresh hit home runs from both sides of plate for the third and final time of his career in 1965. It was the only three-home run (consecutive) game of his career in a 12–0 shutout over the Chicago White Sox.

Yankee hurler Tommy John won his 200th major league game in 1980 with a 3–0 two-hitter over the Mariners in Seattle.

The New York Yankees played their 13,000th game in 1987.

Stump Merrill replaced Bucky Dent as Yankee manager in 1990. Bernie Williams hit home runs from both sides of the plate for the first time in his career against the Texas Rangers in 1994.

7

The Yankees defeated the Cleveland Indians, 5–4 in 16 innings in 1936. Yankee pitchers recorded zero strike outs, while pitcher Red Ruffing hit two home runs in a game for the second and final time in his career. He hit five home runs that season.

Hall of Fame member Thurman Munson, Yankee catcher 1969–79, was born in 1947 in Akron, OH. Munson had three consecutive seasons with at least 100 RBIs, 1975–77. Munson led the Yankees with a .529 average (9 for 17) in the 1976 World Series.

Yankee catcher Yogi Berra hit the first of his two career pinch-hit grand slam home runs, off St. Louis Browns pitcher Satchel Paige, in 1953. Paige allowed 12 home runs

that season, at age 47, his last regular season in the major leagues.

The last-place Yankees used the first pick in the 1967 free-agent draft to select Ron Blomberg, who would appear as the first designated hitter in major league regular season history.

The Yankees acquired pitchers Sudden Sam McDowell from the Cleveland Indians and Pat Dobson from the Atlanta Braves in separate transactions in 1973.

8

Yankee Hugh "Bunny" High became the first American League player to walk twice in the first inning, in 1917. He walked a total of 48 times in 103 games that year. Bunny played in the Yankees outfield in his final four major league seasons, 1915–1918.

Babe Ruth was arrested and fined $100 for speeding in New York City in 1921. Held until 4:00 PM in jail, Ruth changed into his uniform and received a police escort to the game, arriving late and sparking the Yankees to a 4–3, comeback win.

Babe Ruth hit a home run out of Detroit's Navin Field that landed two blocks from the stadium, an estimated 626 feet, in 1926.

Infielder Tony Lazzeri hit three home runs to lead the Yankees over the Chicago White Sox in 1927, 12–11, in 11 innings.

Jimmie Foxx hit home runs in his first three at-bats to give him four consecutive home runs in 1933. The Philadelphia A's defeated the Yankees 14–10.

Lou Gehrig collided at first base with Carl Reynolds, leaving the game with arm and shoulder injuries. A rainout the following day and a scheduled off day helped maintain his consecutive game streak in 1935.

Yankee Bill Dickey became the first catcher in franchise history to record an unassisted double play behind the plate in 1941.

Yankee pitcher Tommy Byrne walked 13 Detroit Tigers in a nine-inning game in 1949. Byrne walked 179 batters that season, compiling a 15–7 record. He started Game 3 of the World Series against the Brooklyn Dodgers.

Yankee pitcher Bob Turley walked 11 Washington Senators in a nine-inning game in 1955. He struck out 210, walked 177, finished with a 17–13 record and was named to the 1955 American League all-star team.

In 1969, 60,096 fans at Yankee Stadium watched as Mickey Mantle's #7 was retired. He exchanged plaques with Joe DiMaggio and New York swept the Chicago White Sox, 3–1 and 11–2, to celebrate.

In the longest game nine-inning game in American League history, the Baltimore Orioles beat the Yankees 18–9 in four hours and sixteen minutes in 1986.

Troubled Yankee pitcher Steve Howe was banned from baseball for the seventh time in his career in 1992.

Mickey Mantle received a liver transplant in 1995.

9

Babe Ruth hit a triple and stole home in the Yankees 8–3 win over the Chicago White Sox in 1927.

Bill Virdon, 12-year major league outfielder who later managed four teams including the Yankees, was born in 1931 in Hazel Park, MI.

66,545 fans helped Yankees break the one million mark in attendance on the earliest date in history in 1946.

Outfielder Chad Curtis was traded by the Cleveland Indians to the Yankees for pitcher David Weathers in 1997.

10

Babe Ruth became modern baseball's career home run leader, hitting his 120th career shot off Cleveland Indian Jim Bagby in the 3rd inning of an 8–6 New York loss in 1921.

The Yankees recorded their second most lopsided shutout in franchise history with an 18–0 win over the 1936 Cleveland Indians.

In Baltimore, Rocky Colavito became the sixth player to hit four home runs in one game, helping the Indians defeat the Orioles, 11–8. He joined Lou Gehrig as the only person to accomplish the feat with four consecutive home runs in 1959.

In Shea Stadium while Yankee Stadium was renovated, the Yankees marked Army Day with a pre-game ceremony. The 21-gun salute destroyed part of the outfield fence and set another portion on fire in 1975.

The Yankees swapped pitchers

with the Chicago Cubs, sending Ken Holtzman to the National League for Ron Davis in 1978. Davis became a successful reliever for New York.

11

Birdie Cree hit the first official grand slam home run in "Yankees" history in 1913, the first year the name changed from the Highlanders. It was the final home run in his major league career. He totaled 11 in eight years with New York.

In 1915, Yankee pitcher Ray Caldwell became the first major league pitcher to hit a pinch-hit home run in two consecutive games. As a starting pitcher the following day, Caldwell also hit a home run.

Yankee Red Rolfe hit three doubles and a triple in a 1936 game, the only time in his career he recorded four extra-base hits in one game.

Mickey Mantle returned to the lineup after a two week absence to hit two home runs off Boston Red Sox Bill Monbouquette in an 8–4 Yankee win at Fenway Park in 1964.

Mel Stottlemyre set an American League record with his 272nd consecutive start in a 1974 no-decision to the California Angels at Shea Stadium. Bill Sudakis hit a grand slam home run for the Yankees, who lost 5–4.

The Yankees acquired Mike Easler from Philadelphia for two minor league players in 1987. New York had traded Easler to the Phillies the previous December.

In 1988, Yankee Rick Rhoden became the first pitcher to start a game as designated hitter in New York's 8–6 win over the Baltimore Orioles in 1988. Rhoden recorded an RBI on a sacrifice fly.

As a member of the Cleveland Indians, former Yankee Dwight Gooden hit the only home run by an American League pitcher in the 1999 season in an 8–6 inter-league game win over the Cincinnati Reds.

The Yankees signed pitcher Dwight Gooden to a minor league contract in 2000.

12

The Highlanders committed eleven errors and lost to the Detroit Tigers in 1907, 14–6.

Hub Pruett struck out Babe Ruth three consecutive times in the St. Louis Browns 7–1 victory over the Yankees in 1922.

Yankee Lou Gehrig collected fourteen total bases to lead the Yankees to a 15–7 win over the Chicago White Sox in 1928. He hit two triples and two home runs for four extra-base hits and scored five times.

Centerfielder Harry Rice set a Yankee record with 11 putouts in a game against the Detroit Tigers in 1930. Rice led National League outfielders in fielding percentage in 1933 as a member of the Cincinnati Reds.

In 1939, ordained as the game's centennial, the Baseball Hall of Fame was dedicated in Cooperstown, NY, with the induction of Babe Ruth, Ty Cobb, Christy Mathewson, Honus Wagner, and Walter Johnson.

Mickey Mantle hit **home** runs from both sides of plate for the fifth time in his career in 1957 against Chicago White Sox pitchers Jack Harshman and Bob Keegan.

Bobby Richardson collected his 1000th major league hit in 1964.

The Yankees were in first place in 1981 when the Players Association went on strike. The Yankees made a pre-strike deal, obtaining Rick Reuschel from the Chicago Cubs for Doug Bird.

In 1990, Yankee reliever Dave Righetti became the ninth pitcher to record 200 career saves.

The Yankees traded pitcher Rich Monteleone to the Anaheim Angels for outfielder Mike Aldrete in 1996. Aldrete hit three home runs for the Yankees in 1996 and pitched one inning, allowing only one hit. He appeared in two 1996 World Series games.

The Yankees signed their 1998 first-round draft pick, outfielder Andrew Brown.

13

George Herman Ruth took his seven-year-old son to St. Mary's Industrial School for Boys and signed over custody of the boy to the Xaverian Brothers, a Catholic Order of Jesuit Missionaries, in 1902.

Babe Ruth pitched the first five innings and hit two home runs, the fourth consecutive game to hit a home run, to help the Yankees defeat the Detroit Tigers, 11–8, in 1921.

Yankee Bob Meusel threw his bat at Detroit Tiger pitcher Bert Cole after being hit by a pitch. The Yankees won by forfeit, 10–6, after fans charged the field and umpires were unable to restore calm in 1924.

Catcher Pat Collins hit the second grand slam home run of the 1927 season for the Yankees in the 6th inning of a 14–6 win over the Cleveland Indians. Ben Paschal collected a double, triple, and two home runs and scored five times.

Yankee Joe DiMaggio hit three consecutive home runs in a game for the first time in his major league career in 1937.

With the crowd of 49,641 singing "Auld Lang Syne" to the Babe, the Yankees celebrated the silver anniversary of Yankee Stadium by holding "Babe Ruth Day" in 1948. His uniform number 3 was retired and sent to Cooperstown.

Roy White hit a home run from each side of the plate, the fifth and final time in his career, as the Yankees beat the 1978 Oakland A's, 5–3.

In 1994, Don Mattingly played in his 1,469th game to move into second place in career games played at first base. He topped Wally Pipp, but fell short of Lou Gehrig's team record of 2,137.

14

Babe Ruth hit a home run in his fifth consecutive game, with two in this game, giving him seven in five games as the Yankees began a nine-game winning streak in 1921.

Joe McCarthy and Lou Gehrig

were both thrown out of the game. The Yankee manager was suspended for three games but the first baseman wasn1t and his consecutive game streak remained intact at 1249 games in 1933.

Before 74,708 fans, the Yankees swept the Cleveland Indians (6–2 and 3–0) to extend their winning streak to 18 consecutive games in 1953.

In the 12th Mayor's Trophy Game, the Yankees defeated the New York Mets, 8–4.

Yankee Paul Blair hit a game winning three-run home run with two outs in the 10th inning to erase a 9–7 deficit in 1978.

The Yankees traded pitcher Rawly Eastwick to the Philadelphia Phillies for outfielder/first baseman Jay Johnstone and a minor league outfielder in 1978.

Yankee outfielder Bobby Murcer hit a two-out, two-run home run in the 9th inning to lead the Yankees to a 2–1 victory in Oakland against the A's in 1980.

15

The Yankees set a team record for runs allowed in one inning when they gave up 13 in the 6th to the Cleveland Indians in 1925.

Yankee Yogi Berra became the second catcher in franchise history to record an unassisted double play behind the plate in 1947. Berra did it again in 1962.

Duane Pillette of St. Louis ended an 18-game Yankee winning streak in 1953. His 3–1 victory at Yankee Stadium erased a record 14-game losing streak for the Browns.

Johnny Mize became the 93rd player in baseball history to record 2,000 career hits when he singled in the lone run in the 5th inning of a 3–1 Yankee loss to the St. Louis Browns in 1953.

The Yankees traded infielders Billy Martin and Woodie Held, outfielder Bob Martyn and pitcher Ralph Terry to the Kansas City A's for pitcher Ryne Duran, infielder Milt Graff, and outfielder Harry Simpson (traded back one year later) in 1957.

A member of the 1996 World Champion Yankees, infielder Wade Boggs batted .273 in the Series. He won the American League batting title five times. He was born in Omaha, NE, in 1958.

The Yankees acquired pitchers Virgil Trucks and Duke Maas from the Philadelphia A's in exchange for 1954 Rookie of the Year Bob Grim and outfielder Harry "Suitcase" Simpson in 1958.

Yankee infielder-outfielder Tom Tresh was traded to the Detroit Tigers for outfielder Ron Woods in 1969.

Pitcher Ramiro Mendoza was born in 1972 in Los Santos, Panama. Mendoza won Game 3 of the 1998 World Series against the San Diego Padres in relief of David Cone.

Pitcher Andy Pettitte was born in 1972 in Baton Rouge, LA. Pettitte started with the Yankees in 1995 and led the American League with 21 wins in 1996. He shutout the San Diego Padres 3–0 in Game 4 of the 1998 World Series to finish the sweep.

The Yankees concluded a 10-player deal with Baltimore in 1976, acquiring pitchers Ken Holtzman, Doyle Alexander, and Grant Jackson, and catcher Elrod Hendricks. The Orioles acquired outfielder Carlos May, catcher Rick Dempsey, and pitchers Dennis Martinez, Scott McGregor, and Dave Pagan from New York.

Oakland A's owner Charlie Finley sold Vida Blue to the Yankees for $1.5 million in 1976.

The Yankees defeated the Oakland A's, 8–2 in 1980. Willie Randolph ended a string of 16 consecutive times on base and Reggie Jackson hit two home runs.

The Baltimore Orioles recorded their ninth triple play in a 1989 contest against the Yankees.

Pitcher "Steady" Eddie Lopat died in 1992 at the age of 73 in Darien, CT. He pitched for the Yankees 1948–55, winning 21 games in 1951. He was a member of five consecutive World Champions 1949–53 and pitched two complete game wins in the 1951 Series.

16

The Highlanders' first manager, Clark Griffith, doubled as a pitcher. "The Old Fox" hurled the first shutout in team history in 1903, 1–0 over the Chicago White Sox.

John Ganzel hit the first grand slam home run in franchise history for the Highlanders in 1904. Ganzel was the regular first baseman for New York 1903–04. He hit a career-high six home runs in 1904 and hit the first home run in franchise history.

Lefty Gomez struck out six consecutive Cleveland Indians in a game in 1937. Gomez led the league with 21 wins, 6 shutouts, and 194 strike outs that season. He pitched two complete game wins in the World Series against the New York Giants.

Boston Red Sox pitcher Boo Ferriss lost his first major league game after starting his career with eight victories, four of them shutouts, 3–2 to the Yankees in 1945.

Acquired from the New York Giants the previous year, four time home run champion (1939-40 and 1947-48) Johnny Mize began a comeback after being recalled by the Yankees in 1950. Mize went on to hit 25 home runs in 90 games for New York.

Yankee Johnny Mize recorded his 2000th career hit in his final major league season, 1953.

After a month on the disabled list, Mickey Mantle hobbled to the plate and pinch-hit a three-run home run in the top of the 9th inning against Cleveland's Gary Bell in 1962. The Indians won in the bottom of the 9th, 10–9.

Ron Guidry's first complete game was a 7–0 Yankee win over the Kansas City Royals in 1977.

Sammy Sosa became the youngest Dominican to play in the major leagues at the age of twenty years, seven months. The Texas Ranger rookie went 2 for 4 with a double against the Yankees in 1989.

New York Yankee announcer from 1939-64, and Baseball Hall of Fame member, Mel Allen died in 1996 at the age of 83.

17

Lou Gehrig recorded an RBI in his 10th straight game. Gehrig collected 27 of his American League leading 174 RBIs in 1930 in those ten games.

Joe DiMaggio was credited with a hit in his 30th consecutive game when Luke Appling had an easy grounder bounce off his shoulder. The Chicago White Sox defeated the Yankees, 8–7, in 1941.

With two out and two on in the 9th inning, Mickey Mantle hit a home run off pitcher Paul Foytack into the upper deck. Elston Howard followed with a home run but Detroit hung on for a 12–10 win in 1961.

Ron Guidry struck out 18 batters in a four-hit, 4–0 shutout of the California Angels, setting an American League record for lefthanders and breaking Bob Shawkey's team record. The victory raised his 1978 record to 11–0.

Former Yankee manager Dick Howser died of a brain tumor in 1987. Howser played eight major league seasons, finishing as an infielder with the Yankees 1967-68. He managed one game in 1978 and the entire 1980 season in New York.

18

The Yankees scored in every inning except the 8th in a 1916 victory over the Cleveland Indians, 19–3.

After signing with Brooklyn as a coach, Babe Ruth wore a Dodger uniform for the first time and took batting practice with the team in 1938.

Commissioner Bowie Kuhn ordered the Yankees to return Vida Blue to the Oakland A's in 1976, voiding the cash deal made three days earlier.

Yankee Reggie Jackson sauntered after a fly ball in a 10–4 loss to the Boston Red Sox. Manager Billy Martin replaced Jackson in a double switch. Jackson and Martin nearly came to blows on national TV in the dugout in 1977.

Bob Lemon was fired and replaced by Billy Martin as Yankees manager in 1979. It began Martin's second managerial stint with New York.

Yankee pitchers picked-off three Toronto Blue Jays base runners in a 1991 game.

Baseball Commissioner Bud Selig announced that Darryl Strawberry could return to baseball after a 120-day suspension in 1999.

19

In the earliest recorded baseball game under a set of adopted rules. The New York Baseball Club defeated the Knickerbocker Club 23–1 in one inning under Cartwright Rules in Hoboken, NJ, in 1846.

Lou Gehrig was born in 1903 in New York City. The Yankee first baseman played his entire career with the team and set a major league record with 2130 consecutive games played, which was broken in 1995 by Baltimore Oriole Cal Ripken.

The Washington Nationals defeated the Highlanders 7–4 in 1907 behind unusually wild pitching from Walter Johnson, who allowed just three hits and struck out ten, but threw four wild pitches and walked seven.

Babe Ruth received his fourth suspension of the year after coming in from the outfield to argue a call at second base. The Yankees lost their eighth game in a row in 1922.

On the way to 56 straight games with a hit, Joe DiMaggio hit in his 32nd consecutive game, going 3 for 3 with a home run against the Chicago White Sox in 1941.

Mickey Mantle hit his 100th career home run in 1955 off Chicago White Sox pitcher Sandy Consuegra.

Roger Maris' 25th home run of the 1961 season, a 9th inning shot off Kansas City A's pitcher Jim Archer, put him seven games ahead of Babe Ruth's record pace.

Yankee infielder Horace Clarke spoiled Boston Red Sox pitcher Sonny Siebert's s no-hitter in the 9th inning. It was the second time in less than a month that Clarke broke up a no-hitter in 1970.

Jim Bouton's controversial book *Ball Four* was published in 1970.

36,211 fans at Yankee Stadium witnessed the return of Billy Martin in a loss to the Toronto Blue Jays in 1979, 5–4.

Despite the fact he was under a 60-day suspension for drug abuse, Darryl Strawberry signed a one-year contract with the Yankees in 1995.

20

Three of the first four Yankee batters were hit by a pitch on the way to a record six hit batsman in this 1913 contest. Yankee Bert Daniels set an American League record by being hit by a pitch three times in a double-header.

As a Boston Red Sox shortstop, Everett Scott began a string of 1,307 consecutive games played in 1916. Scott's streak would end with the Yankees in 1925 and Lou Gehrig eventually broke the record.

In 1920, the Yankees won a protest of a 1–0 Chicago White Sox win, and the game was replayed.

The Yankees recorded 26 hits in a 1932 game against the Philadelphia Athletics.

At Detroit's Briggs Stadium, Mickey Mantle hit two Billy Hoeft pitches into the right-center field bleachers, a first, in the Yankees 7–4 win over the Tigers in 1956.

In the first Mayor's Trophy Game, the New York Mets beat the Yankees, 6–2.

The Yankees pounded the Boston Red Sox in 1978, 10–4. Fred Stanley hit a grand slam home run and Reggie Jackson added a three-run home run in the victory at Fenway Park.

Outfielder Bobby Murcer retired as an active player in 1983. Murcer played 17 major league seasons including 1965–74 and 1979–83 with the Yankees. He was an all-star five consecutive seasons, 1971–75.

The Yankees traded catcher Jim Leyritz to the Los Angeles Dodgers for infielder Jose Vizcaino in 2000.

21

The *Boston Herald*'s 1904 report of a Red Sox trade with the Highlanders, "Dougherty as a Yankee," was the first known reference to the New York club as the Yankees (which they officially became in 1913).

Russell "Sheriff" Van Atta, born in Augusta, NJ, in 1906, compiled a 15–9 record for the Yankees from 1933–35.

Red Sox Pitcher George "Rube" Foster tossed a 2–0 no-hitter against the Yankees at Fenway Park in Boston in 1916. Foster struck out three and walked three. Bob Shawkey took the loss for New York.

Pitcher Eddie Lopat was born in 1918 in New York City. He played for the Yankees for eight of his twelve major league seasons. He started seven World Series games for the Yankees, compiling a 4–1 post-season record between 1949–53.

Babe Ruth hit three home runs but the Yankees blew a 6–0 lead and lost, 15–7 in 1930.

Yankees announced Lou Gehrig's retirement as a player in 1939, based on the report that he had amyotrophic lateral sclerosis. The 36-year-old remained team captain.

The Yankees scored 13 runs in the 5th inning against the 1945 Boston Red Sox. The Yankees led the American League in runs scored in 1945 with 676.

Joe DiMaggio recorded his 2,000th career hit, a 7th inning single off Cleveland Indian pitcher Chick Pieretti, in an 8–2 Yankee win in 1950.

The Yankees took a 5–3 lead in the 11th inning of the first game, but lost 6–5. In the second game the Boston Red Sox led 3–2 in the 9th, but the Yankees came back for a 6–3 win in a 1967 doubleheader.

The Yankees traded outfielder Rickey Henderson back to the Oakland A's for pitchers Eric Plunk and Greg Cadaret and outfielder Luis Polonia in 1989.

At a 1990 Yankee Stadium rally, Nelson Mandela wore a Yankee baseball cap and stated "I am a Yankee!" during Nelson Mandela Day in the United States.

22

Catcher Jack Zalusky was born in Minneapolis, MN, in 1879. He played one season in the American League, with the 1903 Highlanders.

Outfielder Mike Fitzgerald was born in 1890 in San Mateo, CA. Fitzgerald played for the 1911 Highlanders and the 1918 Philadelphia Phillies.

Yankee pitcher Hank Johnson shut out the Philadelphia A's, 4–0. That team included stars Ty Cobb, Mickey Cochrane, Al Simmons, Jimmie Foxx, Eddie Collins, Tris Speaker, and Lefty Grove in 1928.

Pitcher Jim Bronstad was born in Fort Worth, TX, in 1936. Bronstad started his career with the Yankees in 1959 and reappeared in 1963-64 with the Washington Senators, winning only one major league game.

The Yankees defeated the Detroit Tigers 15–0 in 1958.

Yankee Ray Barker tied an American League record with his second consecutive pinch-hit home run in a 6–2 loss to the Kansas City A's. He hit seven home runs in 1965. Mickey Mantle added career home run #465 off John O'Donoghue.

The Detroit Tigers, and manager Billy Martin, got caught in traffic in 1973. Fearing they would be late, they got on the wrong subway. The Yankees won the game, 5–4, and Martin was ejected from the game.

The Yankees released veteran reliever Steve Howe in 1996.

23

The Yankees were helped by a record 16 walks and three wild pitches by Bruno Haas in their 15–0 win over the Philadelphia A's in 1915.

Catcher Aaron Robinson played his first four seasons with the Yankees 1943, 1944–47, batting .297 in 1946. He was born in 1916 in Lancaster, SC.

In 1917, the Yankees purchased the contract of Aaron Ward of Louisville of the Southern League. The infielder played 10 years with the Yankees, helping them win their first pennant in 1921 with a .306 batting average.

Red Sox reliever Ernie Shore replaced Babe Ruth, who had walked one Washington Senator before being ejected. Shore retired the next 26 consecutive batters after Boston threw the baserunner out trying to steal second in a 4–0 win in 1917.

Lou Gehrig hit three home runs in a 1927, 11–4, Yankee victory over the Boston Red Sox at Fenway Park. He hit his 19th off Del Lundgren and his 20th and 21st off Danny MacFayden.

The Yankees recorded a 15–0 shutout over the St. Louis Browns in 1930.

In 1932, Lou Gehrig played in his 1,103rd successive game as a Yankee equaling Joe Sewell's record of consecutive games with one team with the Cleveland Indians.

Hoot Evers' game-winning 9th inning home run gave the Detroit Tigers a 10–9 victory over the Yankees in 1950. The teams combined for a major league record 11 home runs with the Yankees hitting six and the Tigers five.

Yogi Berra hit a pinch-hit grand slam home run off Detroit Tiger pitcher Phil Regan in 1962. It was the second and final time Berra pinch-hit a grand slam.

In the 13th Mayor's Trophy Game, in 1977, the New York Mets beat the Yankees 6–4.

George Steinbrenner fired manager Billy Martin for the fifth and final time, replacing him with Lou Piniella in 1988.

Former Yankee "Marvelous" Marv Throneberry, best known for his antics as a New York Met, died from cancer at the age 60 in 1995.

In 1996, Yankees completed a game sweep of the Indians in Cleveland for the first time since 1964.

24

The Highlanders made their first managerial change, replacing Clark Griffith with Kid Elberfeld, an infielder on the team, in 1908. Griffith was the initial manager of the Highlanders, which debuted in New York in 1903.

Yankee George Selkirk walked twice in the 5th inning of a 1935 game. Selkirk achieved the feat of walking twice in the same inning on four different occasions in his career.

Yankee rookie Joe DiMaggio hit two home runs in the 5th inning of an 18–11 rout of the 1936 St. Louis Browns. DiMaggio hit two doubles for twelve total bases and four extra-base hits in the game.

In 1962, Jack Reed's 22nd inning home run, his only major league homer, won the longest game in Yankee history, 9–7 over the Detroit Tigers. Bobby Richardson batted 11 times in the game.

Bobby Murcer hit a home run in the 9th inning of game one of a 1970 doubleheader against the Cleveland Indians. He added three straight to start the nightcap in a 5–4 Yankee win, tying a major league record with home runs in four consecutive at-bats.

Baseball Commissioner Fay Vincent permanently banned pitcher Steve Howe from baseball in 1992 after Howe pleaded no contest to cocaine charges. The ban was overturned and Howe pitched four more seasons.

The Yankees and the Cleveland Indians played the first game suspended by curfew at Jacobs Field after three hours, ten minutes of rain delays in 1994. Concluded the following day, the 11–6 Yankee win ended Cleveland's 18-game home winning streak.

Seattle Mariner pitcher Randy Johnson broke Ron Guidry's American League record for strikeouts by a left-hander with 19 in a loss against the Oakland A's in 1997.

25

The Highlanders and the Chicago White Sox ended an 18-inning baseball game in a 6–6 tie in 1903.

In 1922 Yankee Everett Scott completed his 900th consecutive career game, a record that would be broken by Lou Gehrig.

In an 11–2 victory over the Chicago White Sox in 1934, Lou Gehrig hit for the cycle for the first of two times in his career and Yankee pitcher Johnny Broaca tied a major league record by striking out five consecutive times at the plate.

Catcher Bob Stanley played for the Yankees 1992–1995, batting .305 in 130 games in 1993. He was born in 1963 in Fort Lauderdale, FL.

After a batboy was hit by a line drive foul ball by Butch Wynegar in 1985, team officials enacted a rule mandating that Yankee batboys wear protective helmets during all games.

Darryl Strawberry underwent arthroscopic surgery on his left knee in 1997.

26

The Highlanders sold the contract of pitcher Hippo Vaughn to the Washington Senators on waivers in 1912, one of their worst personnel moves.

Vaughn went on to win more than 20 games four times with the Chicago Cubs.

Lou Gehrig received his first national recognition as a high school junior when he hit a grand slam in a high school championship game at Chicago's Wrigley Field in 1920.

Spud Chandler became the second Yankee pitcher to hit two home runs in a game. Chandler also became the second pitcher in team history to hit a grand slam home run, off Chicago pitcher Pete Appleton, in a win over the White Sox in 1940.

St. Louis Brown Glenn McQuillen hit a home run to spoil a no-hit bid by Yankee Marius Russo in 1941. Russo pitched a complete game win in Game 3 of the 1941 World Series against the Brooklyn Dodgers.

Outfielder Bill Robinson was born in McKeesport, PA in 1943. Robinson played for the Yankees 1967–69 before enjoying success in the National League 1972–83. Robinson hit 26 home runs and batted .304 for the 1977 Pittsburgh Pirates.

Before 50,000 fans at the Polo Grounds, the three New York teams played against each other in a six-inning three-team game to raise money for war bonds in 1944. Final score Dodgers 5, Yankees 1, and Giants 0.

Shortstop Derek Jeter was born in 1974 in Pequannock, NJ. He joined the Yankees in 1995 and starred in World Series Championship teams in 1996, 1998, 1999 and 2000. He shares his birth date with Pittsburgh Pirate all-star catcher Jason Kendall.

The Yankees, after falling behind 9–0 to the Boston Red Sox, scored 11 runs in the 3rd inning on their way to a 12–11, ten-inning victory in 1987.

27

The Yankees defeated the New York Mets 5–2 in the fourth Mayor's Trophy Game in 1966.

Mickey Lolich was staked to 4–0 lead when Detroit Tigers Aurelio Rodriguez, Al Kaline, and Willie Horton hit three consecutive 1st inning home runs against Yankee Wade Blasingame, making his American League pitching debut in 1972.

Milwaukee Brewer designated hitter Dave Parker got his 2,500th career hit in a 5–4, 1990 win over the Yankees.

Yankee first baseman Tino Martinez was named American League player of the week in 1999.

28

Branch Rickey, an early catcher for the Highlanders, allowed 13 Washington Senators stolen bases in a 16–5 New York loss in 1907.

Frank Gilhooley stole four bases in one game in 1916 for the Yankees. Gilhooley only stole 16 that season, his career high, and 37 total in nine major league seasons.

Lou Gehrig scored five runs in a game for the third and final time in his Yankee career in 1936. Gehrig led the American League in runs scored four times, including 1936 when he scored a career-best 167 runs.

The Yankees pounded eight home

runs in the first game of a double-header against the Philadelphia A's in 1939. They added five more in the second game of a 23–2, 10–0 sweep to set a record for home runs and total bases (53) in a doubleheader.

Pitcher Al Downing was born in 1941 in Trenton, NJ. Downing is most famous for surrendering Hank Aaron's 715th career home run, which broke Babe Ruth's record. Downing played for the Yankees 1961–69 and was 20–9 with the 1971 Los Angeles Dodgers.

Joe DiMaggio returned to the line-up after missing the first 69 games of the season due to a heel injury. Di-Maggio hit four home runs in a three-game sweep of the Boston Red Sox in 1949.

Outfielder Don Baylor was born in 1949 in Austin, TX. Baylor played for the Yankees three seasons in the 1980s, hitting 71 home runs for New York.

Frank "Home Run" Baker died in 1963 in Trappe, MD, at the age of 77. A Hall of Famer and Yankee (1916–22), "Home Run" never hit more than twelve in any one season. He led the American League in home runs 1911–14 (11, 10, 12, 9) with the Philadelphia A's.

Detroit Tiger rookie sensation Mark "the Bird" Fidrych amused a national television audience talking to the baseball and one-hitting the Yankees in 1976, 5–1.

In 1994 as a New York Met, pitcher Dwight Gooden was suspended from Major League Baseball for 60 days due to drug charges.

Mickey Mantle was released from the hospital following a liver transplant in 1995.

29

Yankee outfielder Lee Magee tied a major league record by getting caught stealing three times in the same game in 1916. Magee played for New York 1916-17. He recorded 29 steals and was caught 25 times in 1916.

Joe DiMaggio singled against Washington Senator knuckleballer Dutch Leonard in the 6th inning of the first game of a doubleheader to tie George Sisler's American League consecutive game hit record of 41 in 1941. DiMaggio broke the record in the game two.

The Yankees defeated the Washington Senators 3–1, the first win in a string of 19 victories in 1947.

The Yankees called up pitcher Whitey Ford from Kansas City (AA) in 1950.

Yankee pitcher Tom Morgan tied a major league record by hitting three batters in one inning in 1964.

Yankee infielder Bobby Brown played his last game in 1964, retiring to become a doctor.

Yankees Bobby Richardson, Mickey Mantle, and Joe Pepitone hit consecutive homeruns in the 3rd inning at Fenway Park in New York's 6–5 win over the Red Sox in 1966. It was the fifth set of back-to-back-to-back home runs in Yankee history.

The Yankees blew an 11–4 lead in 1987. Trailing 14–11, Dave Winfield hit an 8th inning grand slam home run to help defeat the Toronto Blue

Jays 15–14. Don Mattingly also hit a grand slam to pace the win.

The Yankees acquired outfielder Dave Justice from the Cleveland Indians for outfielder Ricky Ledee and two players to be named later in 2000.

30

Cy Young became the oldest man to toss a no-hitter at the age of 41 years, three months at Hilltop Park over the Highlanders, 8–0 in 1908. Young contributed three hits to the victory. Nolan Ryan would later become the oldest man to throw a no-hitter.

Babe Ruth, as a member of the Boston Red Sox, hit his first career grand slam home run in 1919. Ruth hit another one 18 days later.

Lou Gehrig hit three triples in 4½ innings. The game did not count when rain in Washington prevented the Senators from completing their half of the 5th inning in 1934.

Philadelphia A's outfielder Bob Johnson spoiled Yankee Lefty Gomez's no-hit bid with a home run in 1937. Gomez led the American League with six shutouts that season.

Outfielder Ron Swoboda was born in 1944 in Baltimore, MD. Swoboda finished his nine-year major league career with the Yankees 1971–73, but is remembered for his diving catch in Game 4, and his .400 average, in the 1969 World Series as a New York Met.

Joe DiMaggio completed his first series of the year, after an operation to remove a bone spur, with a sweep over the Boston Red Sox in 1949 at Fenway Park by batting .455. with four home runs and nine RBIs.

In 1950, Joe and Dom DiMaggio became the fourth set of major league brothers to hit home runs in the same game. Dom connected in the 6th off Yankee Joe Ostrowski while Joe hit an 8th inning home run off Boston Red Sox Walt Masterson.

Yankee designated hitter Cliff Johnson hit three consecutive home runs, including two in the 8th inning, in Toronto against the Blue Jays in 1977.

JULY

1

Yankee Waite Hoyt allowed 11 hits, but managed to shutout the Philadelphia A's, 7–0, in 1924.

Mickey Mantle hit a home run from each side of the plate for the fourth time in his career, off Dean Stone and Bud Byerly, as the Yankees swept a doubleheader from the Washington Senators in 1956.

The Yankees pulled out a dramatic victory over the Washington Senators at the Stadium. Mickey Mantle hit two home runs of pitcher Carl Mathias, the latter won the game in the bottom of the 9th inning, 7–6 in 1961.

Yankees defeated the Milwaukee Brewers 4–1, but the score was changed to 5–1 after the game when umpires ruled that Yankee Roberto Kelly scored before the conclusion of a double-play in 1989.

Comiskey Park celebrated its 80th birthday in 1990 as Yankee pitcher Andy Hawkins threw a no-hitter, but lost the game to the Chicago White Sox, 4–0.

2

The Highlanders won a game by forfeit in 1906, the first time in team history, 5–1 over the Philadelphia A's.

Yankee Whitey Witt became the third player in franchise history to receive five walks in a game in 1924.

Pitcher Harold "Porky" Reniff was born in Warren, OH, in 1938. Reniff played for the Yankees 1961–67, recording 18 saves in 1963. He pitched 3⅓ combined scoreless World Series innings in 1963 and 1964, allowing only two hits.

Joe DiMaggio extended his hitting streak to 45 consecutive games with a home run off Boston Red Sox pitcher Dick Newsome in 1941. This broke the 19th century record of 44 games set by Wee Willie Keeler with Baltimore in 1897.

The Cleveland Indians scored all of their runs in the 4th inning of a 12–0 shutout over the Yankees in 1943.

Detroit Tiger Joe Niekro had his no-hit bid broken up by Yankee Horace Clarke's 9th inning single in a

5–0 Tiger win in 1970. It was the third time in less than a month that Clarke broke up a no-hitter in the 9th inning.

Ron Guidry pitched a 3–2 win over the Detroit Tigers to raise his record to 13–0, the best start in team history, in 1978.

The Yankees claimed infielder Jeff Manto off waivers from the Cleveland Indians in 1999.

3

Catcher William "Curt" Walker, born in 1896 in Beeville, TX, started his career with the Yankees in 1919. He compiled a .304 career batting average .

Catcher Warren "Buddy" Rosar played for the Yankees 1939–42, playing 13 American League seasons with a career .261 average. He was born in Buffalo, NY, in 1914.

Bob Meusel hit for the cycle for the second of three times in his career, a Yankee record, in 1922.

Yankee pitcher Bullet Joe Bush pitched a 15-inning complete game victory. Bush hit a home run to tie the game and force extra innings in 1923. Babe Ruth's home run won it 2–1 in the 15th inning.

The Yankees defeated the Boston Red Sox 13–2 in 1932 in the first Sunday game at Fenway Park. Earle Combs and Lyn Lary became the first teammates to each hit two doubles in one inning in the same game.

Manager Casey Stengel experimented by putting outfielder Joe

DiMaggio at first base in 1950. The Yankees lost the game 7–2 but DiMaggio was perfect in the field, effectively handling 13 chances.

Yogi Berra drove in eight runs in a game in 1957, a personal best. However, after four straight years with 100+ RBIs, Berra dropped to 82 in 1957.

4

John "Chief" Warhop, Highlander/ Yankee pitcher 1908–15, was born in 1884 in Hinton, WV. He finished his eight-year career with a 69–92 record. He is the only pitcher in franchise history to steal home twice in his career.

Two great left-handers, Yankee Herb Pennock and Lefty Grove of the Philadelphia Athletics locked in a pitcher's duel in 1925, won by the Yankees 1–0 in 15 innings. Pennock gave up four hits and walked none in the complete game victory.

The Yankees completed a doubleheader sweep of the 1927 Washington Senators, 12–1 and 21–1. Lou Gehrig hit a home run in each game, a grand slam in game two. The Yankees scored nine runs in the 6th inning of the second game.

Yankee owner George Steinbrenner was born in 1930.

Lou Gehrig Appreciation Day at Yankee Stadium. "Today, I consider myself the luckiest man on the face of the earth." 61,808 fans turned out for Gehrig's 1939 farewell speech.

Shortstop Tony Kubek recorded eight hits, seven singles and a double, in 1959 to set a Yankee record for hits in a doubleheader.

Mickey Mantle's three-run 1st inning home run off Hal Woodeshick made him the 18th player with 300 career home runs. The Yankees lost, 9–8, to the Washington Senators in 1960.

Mickey Mantle hit two home runs in his final two at-bats against A's Dan Pfister and John Wyatt in Kansas City on his way to a string of four consecutive home runs in 1962. Mantle hit 30 in 1962.

At Yankee Stadium, Dave Righetti pitched a 4–0 no-hitter over the 1983 Boston Red Sox, the eighth in team history, and the first since Don Larsen's World Series perfect game in 1956.

Yankee knuckleballer Phil Niekro struck out Texas Ranger catcher Larry Parrish in 1984 to become the ninth major league pitcher to record 3,000 career strikeouts.

The Yankees purchased Darryl Strawberry's contract from St. Paul of the Northern League and assigned him to the Columbus Clippers of the International League in 1996.

5

John Picus Quinn (born John Quinn Picus) was born in 1883 in Janesville, PA. Quinn pitched in the majors 1909–1933, compiling a career 247–213 record. He pitched for the Yankees 1909–12, 1919–21.

Herbert "Lefty" Thormahlen, a Jersey City, NJ, native born in 1896, pitched for the Yankees from 1917–20, compiling a 29–19 record.

In 1919, Boston Red Sox pitcher/outfielder Babe Ruth hit two home runs in a game for the first of 72 times in his career.

In a 1934 win over the Washington Senators, 8–3, Lou Gehrig hit an inside-the-park home run to pass Babe Ruth with his 17th career grand slam home run. Gehrig totaled 23 at the end of his career.

Joe DiMaggio hit his first career major league grand slam home run against the Boston Red Sox in a 15–0 shutout win in 1937.

Richard "Goose" Gossage was born in 1951 in Colorado Springs, CO. Gossage was a star reliever who led the American League in saves three times. A Yankee 1978–83, Gossage pitched 14⅓ scoreless innings in the 1981 post-season.

Danny Tartabull hit a home run for the second time in the 1994 season into the centerfield bleachers at Yankee Stadium.

Yankee reliever John Wetteland tied Lee Smith's major league record of 19 consecutive saves in 1996.

By defeating the Baltimore Orioles 1–0 in 1998, the Yankees improved their record to 61–20, equaling the best 81-game start in history. The mark matched the record of the 1902 Pittsburgh Pirates and the 1907 Chicago Cubs.

6

The Highlanders recorded their first doubleheader shutout with a 4–0 win by Jack Chesbro in the first game and an 8–0 win by Doc Newton in the second game against the Boston Pilgrims in 1906.

The Yankees scored 14 runs in the 5th inning of a 17–0 victory over the 1920 Washington Senators to set a franchise record for runs in one inning. It was the third most lopsided shutout in Yankee history.

Babe Ruth hit his first grand slam home run as a member of the New York Yankees in 1922. Ruth hit four previous grand slams as a member of the Boston Red Sox.

The first all-star game, at Chicago's Comiskey Park in 1933 was part of the Century of Progress Exhibition. Babe Ruth hit a two-run home run, the first in all-star history, in the 3rd inning, to lead the American League victory.

At Crosley Field in Cincinnati, American League starting pitcher Yankee Lefty Gomez was defeated for the first time in four all-star starts as the National League won The 1938 all-star Game, 4–1.

Mickey Mantle hit two home runs in his first two at-bats against Camilo Pascual in Minnesota against the Twins to go with two home runs in his previous two at-bats to tie a major league record with four straight home runs in 1962.

Outfielder Lance Johnson was born in Lincoln Heights, OH, in 1963. Johnson has played 14 major league seasons, through 2000. He led the American League in hits with 186 in 1995 and led the National League the following year with 227 as a New York Met.

Andy Pettitte recorded his first career shutout in 1997.

7

After heavy losses to Federal League competition, Baltimore Orioles owner Jack Dunn offered Babe Ruth and two others to Connie Mack for $10,000 in 1914. Mack refused the deal. Cincinnati chose two other players, George Twombley and Claud Derrick.

The Yankees purchased the contract of pitcher Bob Shawkey from the Philadelphia Athletics in 1915 for $18,000. Shawkey went on to become the first Yankee pitcher to record four 20-win seasons.

Lou Gehrig led the American League all-stars over the National League, 8–3, with a home run, a double, and 4 RBIs in Washington in 1937. Dizzy Dean's toe was fractured during the game.

Joe DiMaggio tore cartilage in his left knee and sprained his ankle sliding into second base at Philadelphia's Shibe Park in 1946.

Second baseman Chuck Knoblauch was born in 1968 in Houston, TX. Knoblauch's argument while play continued in Game 2 of the 1998 American League Championship Series cost the Yankees in extra innings against the Cleveland Indians.

Milwaukee Brewer pitcher Mike Caldwell beat the Yankees and Ron Guidry 6–0 for Guidry's first loss of the 1978 season (13–1).

Okay numerology fans, the Yankees, on 7/7, trailed by 7, but scored 7 in the 7th (and five in the 8th) to defeat the Minnesota Twins 12–7 in 1987.

Darryl Strawberry was promoted

to the Yankees from the Columbus Clippers in 1996 and went hitless in a 4–1 Yankee loss to the Milwaukee Brewers.

Yankee first baseman Tino Martinez won the 1997 All-Star Home Run Derby at Jacobs Field in Cleveland.

8

Highlander Doc Newton walked 11 St. Louis Browns batters in a nine-inning game in 1905. Newton walked 24 and struck out 15 for New York that season.

Babe Ruth's apparent home run over the fence at Fenway Park scored Amos Strunk in the Boston Red Sox 1–0 over the Cleveland Indians in 1918. Rules at the time credited Ruth with a triple, the amount of bases required for the winning run to score.

Infielder/outfielder Hector Lopez was born in 1932 in Colon, Panama. Lopez played for the Yankees 1959–66. Lopez hit a home run in the final game of the 1961 World Series to help the Yankees defeat the Cincinnati Reds in five games.

The feud between Joe DiMaggio and Casey Stengel caused the manager to replace DiMaggio in center field in 1950 with reserve outfielder Jackie Jenson after he had taken his position, due to a misplay by DiMaggio in the 1st inning.

Yankee manager Casey Stengel and outfielder Mickey Mantle testified before a special House of Representatives subcommittee on Capitol Hill in Washington, D.C., in 1958, regarding baseball's antitrust exemption.

Yankee shortstop Jim Mason tied a major league record with four doubles in a nine-inning game in 1974.

Billy Martin recorded his 1,000th career win as a manager. Ironically, Martin managed the Oakland A's to a 6–3 win over the Yankees in 1982 to reach the milestone.

In 2000, the Yankees won both ends of a home and home, day-night double header against the New York Mets. Pitcher Dwight Gooden made his major league return and won the first game at Shea Stadium 4–2 while Roger Clemens won the nightcap by an identical score but beaned Met catcher Mike Piazza in the second inning at Yankee stadium.

9

Shortstop Roger Peckinpaugh hit safely in his 29th consecutive game to set a Yankee record in 1919. This mark stood until Joe DiMaggio broke the record in 1941 with 56 straight games with a hit.

Babe Ruth hit two home runs and two doubles for four extra-base hits in the 19–7 win in the first game of a doubleheader against the Detroit Tigers in 1927. The Yankees lost game two 14–4, the worst defeat of the season for the "Murderer's Row" team.

Ben Chapman became the first Yankee to hit three consecutive home runs, two of them inside-the-park, in a 14–9 victory at Yankee Stadium over the 1932 Detroit Tigers.

Joe DiMaggio hit for the cycle for

the first of two times in his career in 1937. With a single, double, triple, and two home runs, DiMaggio had four extra-base hits.

The Yankees traded Ed Whitson, a high priced free-agent, back to the San Diego Padres in 1986 for Tim Stoddard. New York fans turned on Whitson, causing manager Lou Piniella to pitch him only on the road.

The 11,000th home run in Yankee history was hit by catcher Matt Nokes in 1994.

10

Baltimore Orioles owner Jack Dunn sold Babe Ruth and two others to the new owner of the Boston Red Sox, Joe Lannin, for a reported $25,000 in 1914.

Ray Caldwell's 9⅔ innings of no-hit relief pitching helped the Yankees defeat the Browns in St. Louis, 7–5, in a 17-inning game in 1917.

At the Polo Grounds in 1934, the American League All-stars came back to beat the National League 9–7 in a game that featured Carl Hubbell striking out five in a row including Babe Ruth and Lou Gehrig.

In the 1956 All-Star Game in Washington, D.C., Mickey Mantle hit a home run, Yogi Berra went 2 for 2, Whitey Ford pitched one inning, and Billy Martin was an unsuccessful pinch-hitter. The National League won at Griffith Stadium, 7–3.

Hideki Irabu won his major league debut and received a standing ovation from the sellout crowd at Yankee Stadium. Irabu struck out nine in 6⅔

innings in a 10–3 win over the Detroit Tigers in 1997.

The Yankees had won 124 consecutive games when leading at the beginning of the 9th inning. New York Mets pinch-hitter Matt Franco singled off Mariano Rivera to give the Mets a dramatic, come from behind, Subway Series victory, 9–8, in 1999. Jorge Posada hit home runs from both sides of the plate for the second time in his career.

11

Vitautas "Vito" Tamulis, born in Cambridge, MA, in 1911, pitched for the Yankees 1934-35.

Making his major league debut, Boston Red Sox pitcher Babe Ruth beat the Cleveland Indians in 1914, 4–3. Ruth struck out in his first at-bat. Ruth had 490 career at-bats as a pitcher, batting .304 with 149 hits, 15 home runs and 73 RBIs.

The Yankee pitching staff suffered a blow when starter Rudy May went on the disabled list in 1974. May suffered a shoulder injury and finished the season with an 8–4 record.

Mickey Mantle's final public appearance was designed to increase awareness of organ donation programs in 1995.

12

Highlander Roy Hartzell became the first American League player to hit a home run and a double in the same inning of a game in 1911. Hartzell had 8 RBIs on the day.

Jack Warhop, the only Highlander pitcher in history to steal home, did it for the second time in his career in the 3rd inning against the St. Louis Browns in 1912.

Boardwalk Brown set a Yankees record by walking 15 Detroit Tigers in a nine-inning game in 1914. He compiled a 40–39 record over five seasons with the Philadelphia A's and New York.

Babe Ruth passed 19th century star Roger Conner with his 137th career home run, making him the undisputed career home run leader in 1921.

Bob Shawkey became the first Yankee to hit two doubles in the same inning in 1923. Shawkey also hit a double and a triple in the third inning. The pitcher was 16–11 with New York that season. He had four seasons in which he won at least 20 games.

Babe Ruth hit the 30th of his 60 home runs in the 1927 season off Indian Joe Shaute in Cleveland in a 7–0 Yankee win.

Allie Reynolds pitched the first of two no-hitters of the 1951 season, a 1–0 victory over the Indians, defeating Cleveland ace Bob Feller.

Yankee Mickey Mantle hit a three-run home run off Robin Roberts in the 1955 all-star game, won by the National League, 6–5 in 12 innings.

NBC used outfield cameras that zoomed in on the catcher's signs in a 1959 Yankees game against the Boston Red Sox. Baseball commissioner Ford Frick requested that the practice stop.

Yankee pitcher "Louisiana Lightning" Rod Guidry announced his retirement from baseball in 1989 with a career 170–91 record and 3.29 ERA. This ended his stint as Yankee team captain. Guidry was the 6th captain in the history of the franchise.

Chicago White Sox Melido Perez pitched a six-inning, rain-halted, no-hitter against New York, 8–0 at Yankee Stadium in 1990. Melido's brother Pascual Perez, pitched a five-inning no-hitter in 1988 and joined the Yankees in 1990.

In 2000, the Yankees acquired pitcher Denny Neagle and outfielder Mike Frank from the Cincinnati Reds for four minor league players.

13

Boston Red Sox pitcher Carl Mays walked off the mound against the Chicago White Sox in 1919. Because of his action, he was subsequently suspended, traded to the Yankees, and reinstated by American League directors.

In a 4–2 Yankee victory over the Detroit Tigers in 1934, Babe Ruth hit his 700th career home run off Tommy Bridges. Lou Gehrig left in the 1st inning of the game with a severe case of lumbago.

Pitcher Jack Aker was born in 1940 in Tulare, CA. Aker played eleven major league seasons including 1969–72 with the Yankees. Aker led the league in 1966 with 32 saves with the Kansas City A's.

Yankee pitcher Vic Raschi's no-hit

bid was spoiled by a home run by Detroit Tiger Joe Ginsberg in 1952. Raschi was 2–0 with a 1.59 ERA in the 1952 World Series win over the Brooklyn Dodgers.

New York hosted the 29th all-star game at Yankee Stadium with the National League defeating the American League 6–0 in 1960.

Tom Tresh hit home runs from both sides of the plate for the second time in his career in 1964.

Bobby Murcer's three home runs accounted for all of the runs in the Yankees victory over the Kansas City Royals in 1973, 5–0.

The Yankees retired Roger Maris' (#9) and Elston Howard's (#32) uniform numbers in 1985.

14

Jesse "Powder" Tannehill, born in 1874 in Dayton, KY, went 15–15 in his only year as a Highlander in 1903. He compiled a career 194–118 record over 16 seasons.

The largest margin of victory by a Highlander team was recorded in 1904 with a 21–3 victory over the Cleveland Indians. The Indians led the American League with 647 runs scored in 1904, the Yankees finished fourth with 598.

Pitcher John J. "Johnny" Murphy was born in New York City in 1908. Murphy was an all-star pitcher 1937–39. He played all but the final season of his 13-year career with the Yankees.

Lou Gehrig kept his consecutive game streak alive, after a severe case of lumbago, when he was listed as the shortstop, led off the game with a single, and left for a replacement in 1934.

In 1957, Yankee Bill "Moose" Skowron hit the second of his two career pinch-hit grand slam home runs, off Chicago White Sox pitcher Jim Wilson.

The Yankees prevailed in eleven innings, 7–6 over the Chicago White Sox behind Cliff Johnson's pinch-hit home run to tie the game in the 9th and Graig Nettles RBI single for the win in the 11th in 1978.

15

The Highlanders suffered their worst shutout defeat when they lost to the Chicago White Sox, 15–0 in 1907.

Alvin "Jake" Powell was born in Silver Springs, MD, in 1908. He played outfield for the Yankees 1936–40. The 11-year major league veteran had a career .271 average.

Babe Ruth tied his 1919 home run record with a game-winning home run, his 29th of the 1920 season, in the 13th inning to defeat the St. Louis Browns, 13–10.

Switch-hitting infielder Wilson Delgado was born in San Cristobal, Dominican Republic, in 1975.

In 1980, Johnny Bench surpassed Yogi Berra as the career home run leader for a catcher when he hit his 314th. Berra sent Bench a telegram saying, "Congratulations on breaking my record. I always thought the record would stand until it was broken."

In a battle of football players,

Kansas City Royal Bo Jackson hit three home runs, but separated his shoulder on a hit by Deion Sanders, which turned into an inside-the-park home run in the Yankees 10–7 loss in 1990.

16

Joe DiMaggio extended his record hitting streak to 56 games in 1941 off Cleveland Indians pitchers Al Milnar and Joe Krakauskas. DiMaggio went 3 for 4 with a double and three runs scored in the Yankees 10–3 win.

After returning from World War II, Red Ruffing, at age 41 and overweight by 30 pounds, pitched for the first time since 1942 for the Yankees, and won, in 1945.

Bobo Newsom won his 200th career game, his first win as a Yankee, in 1947. The Yankees extended their winning streak to 19 in the nightcap of a 1947 doubleheader behind Vic Raschi.

The Yankees defeated the Kansas City Royals, 9–4 in extra innings in 1966. Horace Clark hit his second major league home run, both grand slams.

Don Mattingly hit his fourth grand slam home run of the 1987 season, tying an American League record with home runs in six straight games.

17

The Yankees recorded 21 hits and St. Louis had 17 in a 1919 game, won by the Browns, 7–6 in 17 innings, on a squeeze bunt.

Babe Ruth broke his home run record, established the previous year when he hit 29, with his 30th and 31st of the 1920 season off Chicago White Sox pitcher Dickie Kerr.

Detroit defeated the Yankees 19–1 for the most lopsided loss in New York team history (which was matched in 1928). The Tigers scored 13 in the 6th. They led the American League with 903 runs scored while the Yankees were next to last with 706 in 1925.

Babe Ruth received his 2,000th career base on balls against the Indians in Cleveland in 1934. Ruth retired with a record 2,056 career walks.

Yankee Tony Lazzeri had four extra-base hits in a game for the first and only time in his career with a double and three home runs in 1935.

Joe DiMaggio's 56-game hitting streak was ended by the outstanding defensive work of Indian third baseman Ken Keltner before 67,000 fans in Cleveland in 1941.

Roger Maris hit a home run (potentially # 62) that was erased in 1961 due to a rain-out in the 5th inning.

Reggie Jackson ignored Billy Martin's orders to swing away and struck out on a foul bunt in the 10th inning in a 9–7 loss to the Kansas City Royals. Jackson was suspended for five games without pay in 1978.

In 1987, Yankee Don Mattingly became the first American League player to hit a home run in seven consecutive games.

In 1996, reliever John Wetteland

finally blew a save after recording 24 consecutive saves for the Yankees.

18

Yankee outfielder Ping Bodie became the first Yankee to hit two grand slam home runs in the same season with a bases loaded home run against the Chicago White Sox in an 8–4 win in 1920.

Leftfielder Elmer Smith became the first Yankee outfielder to turn an unassisted double play in New York's 4–1 win against the Detroit Tigers in 1923, grabbing a line drive and doubling off the baserunner on a hit and run play.

Joe Torre was born in 1940 in Brooklyn, NY. Torre was the 1971 National League MVP when he led the league with a .363 average. The successful Yankee manager won four World Championships through the 2000 season.

The Detroit Tigers ended a 19-game Yankee winning streak with a 2–0 shutout in 1947.

In 1961, Commissioner Ford Frick ruled that Babe Ruth's 1927 record of 60 home runs in 154 games "cannot be broken unless some batter hits 61 or more within his club's first 154 games." Thus the "Maris asterisk," until made moot by Mark McGwire in 1998.

Chicago White Sox player Mike Andrews hit a home run to break up a no-hit bid by Yankee pitcher Mike Kekich in 1971. Kekich lost the shutout and never pitched one for the Yankees in over five AL seasons.

Yankee Don Mattingly tied Dale Long's major league record by hitting a home run in his eighth consecutive game, a 7–2 loss to the Texas Rangers in 1987.

A partisan crowd booed Yankee pitcher Jack McDowell in 1995 after a bad outing. McDowell gave them "the finger" and was ordered by the American League president to buy them tickets. McDowell was fined $5000.

On Yogi Berra Day at Yankee Stadium in 1999, David Cone became the 16th pitcher in history, and the third Yankee, to toss a perfect game, beating the Montreal Expos 6–0. Don Larsen threw out the ceremonial first pitch.

19

Edward "Big Ed" Sweeney caught all but the final 17 games of his 644 game career with the Highlanders/ Yankees 1908–15. He was born in 1888 in Chicago, IL.

Robert "Long Bob" Meusel was born in San Jose, CA, in 1896. Long Bob played all but his final season with the Yankees (1920–29). He compiled a lifetime .309 average, batting .337 in 1927.

Yankee shortstop Mark A. Koenig was born in 1904 in San Francisco, CA. A member of the Murderer's Row Yankees, Koenig played six seasons for the Yankees 1925–30. He hit .500 in the 1927 World Series sweep of the Pittsburgh Pirates.

Brooklyn native Marius "Lefty" Russo, born in 1914, pitched his entire six-year career with the Yankees compiling a 45–34 record.

Buddy Rosar hit for the cycle for the only time in his Yankee career in 1940. Rosar was a Yankee during his first four seasons, 1939–42, making the American League all-star team in 1942, 1943, and 1946–48 as a member of the Philadelphia A's.

The Yankees obtained outfielder Elston Howard and pitcher Frank Barnes in 1950. They were the first black players signed by the Yankees, purchased from the Kansas City Monarchs.

Yankee catcher Thurman Munson hit a first-inning single in 1975. The hit and RBI against the Minnesota Twins were reversed when it was determined that the tar on his bat handle exceeded the 18-inch limit. Catcher Glenn Borgmann got the putout.

The All-Star Game was played at Yankee Stadium for the third time in history in 1977. Billy Martin managed and Willie Randolph, Graig Nettles, Thurman Munson, Sparky Lyle, and Reggie Jackson represented the Yankees in a 7–5 National League win.

Don Mattingly set an American League record with an extra base hit in his tenth consecutive game in 1987.

Dave Righetti surpassed Hall of Fame member Whitey Ford for the most career appearances by a Yankee pitcher in 1990 when he pitched in his 499th game for New York.

20

At a racetrack on Long Island, about 1,500 people became the first to pay to see a baseball game. The fans spent fifty cents to watch New York defeat Brooklyn, 22–18, in 1859.

Yankee Joe DiMaggio collected four extra-base hits in a game for the third time in his career, hitting three doubles and a home run in 1941.

Yankee pitcher Whitey Ford struck out six consecutive Kansas City A's in a 1956 game. It was the first of two times he achieved the feat. Ford was 19–6 and pitched a complete game win in Game 3 of the World Series against the Brooklyn Dodgers.

Pitcher Mel Stottlemyre hit an inside-the-park grand slam home run in a 6–3 win over the Boston Red Sox at the Stadium in 1965. He became the first pitcher to hit an inside-the-park grand slam since Deacon Phillippe of the Pittsburgh Pirates in 1910.

The Yankees swept a doubleheader from Chicago, 12–2 and 7–0, in 1973. White Sox Wilbur Wood became the last starting pitcher to start both games of a doubleheader. Wood took two losses on the day.

In 1987, Yankee first baseman Don Mattingly tied a major league record with 22 putouts in one game, matching Yankee Hal Chase's 1906 feat.

21

In 1921, the Yankees (7) and the Indians (9) combined for an American League record 16 doubles in the 17–8

Cleveland win, setting a franchise record for Cleveland.

Mike Hegan was born in 1942 in Cleveland, OH. Hegan played for the Yankees at first base and outfield 1964–67 and 1973–74. He struck out and walked, scoring a run, in two World Series plate appearances as a pinch-hitter in 1964.

Mickey Mantle and Roger Maris hit back-to-back home runs in the 1st inning off Bill Monbouquette, but it took a two-out, 9th inning pinch-hit grand slam by Johnny Blanchard to defeat the Boston Red Sox, 11–8, in 1961.

At an all-star banquet in Washington, D.C., in 1969, Babe Ruth was named the greatest baseball player in history and Joe DiMaggio was recognized as the greatest living player.

The Yankees swept a 1972 doubleheader from the California Angels with a 6–0 shutout by Fritz Peterson in the opener and a 3–0 shutout by Mel Stottlemyre in the second game.

Billy Martin was fired as the manager of the Texas Rangers in 1975.

Yankee Graig Nettles hit his 267th career home run to break Brooks Robinson's home run record for third basemen in a 3–0 shutout over the 1980 Milwaukee Brewers.

At a 1984 Yankee Stadium ceremony, the Yankees retired Roger Maris' number (#9) and honored him with a plaque.

The Seattle Mariners sent designated hitter Ken Phelps to the Yankees for outfielder Jay Buhner and first baseman/designated hitter Steve Balboni in 1988.

In 2000, the Yankees acquired outfielder Glenallen Hill from the Chicago Cubs for pitchers Ben Ford and Ozwaldo Mairena.

22

The Yankees purchased the contract of infielder Leo Durocher in 1925 and he began his major league career in October. Durocher played 17 seasons and went on to a successful career as a manager.

As a stunt, National Guard private Babe Ruth caught a baseball that was dropped from a plane at a reported altitude of 250 feet and traveling an estimated 100 MPH at Mitchell Field in New York in 1926.

Chicago White Sox pitcher Red Faber swung twice right-handed at Yankee pitcher Wilcy Moore pitches, then switched to the left side of the plate and hit a single to score the winning run in 1928.

Albert Walter "Sparky" Lyle was born in DuBois, PA, in 1944. He led the American League in saves with the Yankees in 1973 and 1976. He was the American League Cy Young Award winner in 1977.

Cliff Johnson was born in 1947 in San Antonio, TX. Johnson was a catcher, designated hitter, first baseman and outfielder in his 15-year major league career. He played for the Yankees 1977–79. He hit 22 home runs for the Toronto Blue Jays in 1983.

In an attempt to put more power in the lineup, Casey Stengel inserted Mickey Mantle at shortstop. His 10th inning home run gave the Yankees a 3–2 victory over the Chicago White Sox in 1954.

Catcher Johnny Blanchard was the hero of the Yankees 10–9 victory over the Boston Red Sox in 1961. Blanchard hit a home run to tie the score in the 9th, becoming the fifth player, and the third Yankee, to hit pinch-hit home runs in consecutive at bats.

Yankee first baseman Don Mattingly hits his 200th career home run in 1993.

In the 15,000th game in franchise history, the Yankees defeated the Tampa Bay Devil Rays, 5–4 in 1999 to raise their career record to 8,451–6,463 (.567) with 83 ties and three overturned protests.

23

The Yankees acquired third baseman Joe Dugan and outfielder Elmer Smith from the Boston Red Sox for outfielders Chick Fewster and Elmer Miller, infielder Johnny Mitchell, pitcher Lefty O'Doul, and $50,000 in 1922.

Lou Gehrig hit the first of his record 23 career grand slams as the Yankees beat the Washington Senators, 11–7, in 1925.

Yankees Bob Cerv and Elston Howard became the first teammates to hit pinch-hit home runs in the same inning when they connected in the 9th against the Kansas City A's in 1955.

Mickey Mantle hit for the cycle for the only time in his career in 1957

against the Chicago White Sox. His home run off Bob Keegan was the 199th of his career. Mantle added a stolen base in the 10–6 victory.

After his suspension by Billy Martin for loafing on a fly ball and national television confrontation, Reggie Jackson returned to the Yankees in 1978 as New York won their fifth straight game, 3–1 over the Chicago White Sox.

Kansas City Royal reliever Dan Quisenberry registered his 200th career save in his 409th appearance, the quickest in major league history to achieve the feat, in a 5–2 Yankee loss in 1984.

Born in South Adelaide, Australia, Yankee Mark Hutton became the first starting pitcher from "down under" when he defeated the California Angels, 5–2, in 1993.

The Yankees tied the Boston Red Sox and Toronto Blue Jays for first place. Don Mattingly singled in the 7th inning against the Angels in Anaheim to record his 2000th major league hit in 1994. He became the sixth Yankee to reach that plateau.

24

Detroit, MI, native Duane "Dee" Pillette, born in 1922, started his career with the Yankees, compiling a 2–4 record over two seasons, 1949-50. Pillette played eight major league seasons.

Pitcher Lefty Gomez became the first Yankee to strike out twice in the same inning, in the 7th inning of a 1932 game.

Billy Martin announced his resignation as Yankee manager in 1978 following his infamous "the one is a born liar and the other a convicted one" reference to George Steinbrenner and Reggie Jackson.

Ron Guidry set a Yankee record by pitching his ninth shutout of the season as he two-hit the Cleveland Indians, 4–0, in 1978. It was his third consecutive two-hitter.

The Yankees apparently won the infamous 1983 "pine tar" game when George Brett's home run was overturned for having too much pine tar on his bat. The league later overruled and the Kansas City Royals eventually won the game, concluded on August 18th.

In 1992, baseball commissioner Fay Vincent reduced George Steinbrenner's baseball ban to 30 months, reinstating him effective March 1, 1993.

Outfielder Glenallen Hill hit a home run in his Yankee debut to lead New York to a 4–3 win over the Baltimore Orioles in 2000.

Roger Maris hit home runs off four different pitchers, Frank Baumann, Don Larsen, Russ Kemmerer, and Warren Hacker, in a 1961 doubleheader sweep, 5–1 and 12–0, of the Chicago White Sox. Mickey Mantle hit a home run off Baumann. Maris led Mantle 40–38.

Douglas Dean Drabek was born in 1962 in Victoria, TX. Drabek started his career with the Yankees in 1986 and went on to win the 1990 National League Cy Young Award as a member of the Pittsburgh Pirates with a 22–6 record.

Yankee manager, and former player, Casey Stengel was enshrined in the Baseball Hall of Fame in Cooperstown, NY, in 1966.

The Yankees named Bob Lemon as Billy Martin's successor as manager in 1978.

Jim Bouton played in his first Old Timer's Day game at Yankee Stadium in 1998. Bouton had been scorned for his controversial baseball book "Ball Four."

25

In 1912, Outfielder Bert Daniels became the first Highlander to hit for the cycle.

The Boston Red Sox turned a triple-play but Babe Ruth's 35th home run of the season led the Yankees to an 8–2 win in 1920.

Yankee Atley Donald set an American League rookie pitching record when he registered his 12th consecutive victory, 5–1, over the St. Louis Browns in 1939.

26

Knuckleball pitcher Hoyt Wilhelm was born in 1923 in Huntersville, NC. He was the first relief pitcher inducted into the Hall of Fame (1985). He hurled a no-hitter against the Yankees in September 1958.

The Yankees scored nine runs in the 8th inning of a 12–3 win over the St. Louis Browns in 1927. Babe Ruth hit two home runs, his 32nd and 33rd, off Milt Gaston and Lou Gehrig added his 32nd of the season.

Bob Meusel hit for the cycle three times, a Yankee record. Meusel did it for the final time in his career in 1928.

The Yankees scored eleven runs in the 12th inning to defeat the Detroit Tigers, 12–1.

At age 18, Joe DiMaggio, playing for the San Francisco Seals of the Pacific Coast League, ended his first great hitting streak at 61 games in 1933. The son of a Hall of Famer, Oakland Oaks pitcher Ed Walsh, Jr., stopped him.

An unusual double play occurred when a line drive by Yankee Jesse Hill bounced off Senator pitcher Ed Linke's head to Washington catcher Jack Redmond, who threw to second to double off the runner in 1935.

Yankee catcher Bill Dickey hit three consecutive home runs in 1939.

Babe Ruth made his final public appearance at the New York premiere of the *The Babe Ruth Story* in 1948.

Mickey Mantle hit his first career grand slam home run in Detroit against Tiger pitcher Ted Gray in 1952.

Future Hall of Fame pitcher Jim Bunning two-hit the Yankees for a 3–2 Detroit Tiger win in 1957. One of the hits was Mickey Mantle's 200th career home run.

Johnny Blanchard hit his fourth consecutive home run over three games setting a major league mark. His two home runs on this date in 1961 paced the Yankees over the Chicago White Sox, 5–2.

Yankee catcher Elston Howard walked twice in the same inning, the 2nd, in a 1964 game.

The Minnesota Twins defeated the Yankees 3–2 in 18 innings in 1967.

The Yankees staged a dramatic 1977 win. Trailing by two runs, Cliff Johnson hit a two-run home run to tie it in the 9th and Reggie Jackson beat the Baltimore Orioles with a solo home run in the bottom of the 10th.

The Yankees trailed the Cleveland Indians 1–0 in the bottom of the ninth when Lou Piniella hit a three-run home run to cap a 3–1 win in 1978.

Jim "Catfish" Hunter, Billy Williams and Ray Dandridge were inducted into the Baseball Hall of Fame in Cooperstown, NY, in 1987. Hunter played his final five seasons with New York, leading the American League in wins, complete games, and innings in 1975.

27

Henry "Irish" McIlveen was born in 1880 in Belfast, Ireland. He played for the Highlanders 1908–09, hitting .212. He broke into the majors as a pitcher with the Pittsburgh Pirates.

Born in Niagara Falls, NY, in 1898, catcher Benny Bengough played for the Yankees 1923–30 as a part-time catcher.

Baseball icon Leo "The Lip" Durocher was born in W. Springfield, MA, in 1905. Durocher started his career as an infielder with the Yankees 1925–29.

Stanhope, NJ, native John Kucks was born in 1933. He enjoyed his most successful seasons with the Yankees (1955–59), going 18–9 in 1956.

The Chicago Cubs purchased pitcher Hank Borowy from the Yankees in an unexpected waiver deal in 1945. Borowy, 10–5 with New York, was put on waivers to solve a roster problem and was lost to the National League.

Yogi Berra began a string of 148 consecutive games without an error in 1947.

Yankee outfielder Earle Combs was inducted into the Baseball Hall of Fame by the Committee on Veterans in 1970.

Cleveland Indian second baseman Duane Kuiper became one of only three modern major league players to hit two bases loaded triples in one game. The Indians trounced the Yankees, 17–5, in 1978.

Tommy John committed three errors on one play in the Yankees 16–3 win over the Milwaukee Brewers in 1988. His dubious performance tied the major league record for errors in one inning by a pitcher.

Detroit Tiger Travis Fryman hit for the cycle in a 12–7 loss to the Yankees in 1993.

The Yankees designated infielder Dale Sveum for assignment in 1998.

28

The Highlanders turned a triple play in their 1906 win over the Cleveland Naps, 6–4. The Indians used the name "Naps" for several seasons while they were managed by Hall of Famer Napoleon Lajoie.

Bob Fothergill of the Chicago White Sox hit a home run and a triple in an 11-run 8th inning in the Yankees 14–12 loss in 1931.

Yankee Jimmie DeShong's no-hit bid was spoiled by a home run from Jimmie Foxx of the Philadelphia A's in 1934. DeShong was 6–7 for New York that season.

Myril Hoag and Joe DiMaggio were both knocked unconscious allowing Detroit Tiger Goose Goslin to hit an inside-the-park home run. Hoag was hospitalized with a concussion in 1936.

Yankee Charlie "King Kong" Keller hit three home runs in a 1940 victory over the Chicago White Sox, 10–9.

A combined team of Yankees and Cleveland Indians, called the "Yank-lands," lost a war benefit game against a North Carolina Pre-Flight navy team, 11–5. Babe Ruth coached the Yank-lands in 1943.

Mickey Mantle hit home runs from both sides of the plate for the sixth time in his career in 1958 against Kansas City A's pitchers Dick Tomanek and Ray Herbert.

Pitcher Waite Hoyt, a 237 game major league winner over two decades, was inducted into the Baseball Hall of Fame in 1969. Hoyt was a Yankee 1921–30, recording 22 wins in 1927.

California Angel catcher Tom Egan was charged with five passed balls and committed an error to allow the Yankees to score the winning run in a 6–5 win in 1970.

American League president Lee MacPhail decided George Brett's

1983 "Pine Tar" home run should count. The reminder of the game was played on August 18 with the Kansas City Royals defeating the Yankees, 5–4.

David Cone was traded by the Toronto Blue Jays to the Yankees in 1995 for pitchers Marty Janzen, Jason Jarvis and Mike Gordon.

Following liver transplant surgery, Mickey Mantle was readmitted to the hospital in 1995.

Darryl Strawberry hit his 300th career home run in the bottom of the 9th inning against the Kansas City Royals in 1996 to give the Yankees a 3–2 win.

29

Washington, D.C., native Walter Beall was born in 1899. He pitched for the Yankees 1924–27, compiling a 4–5 record.

The Cleveland Indians scored 17 runs in the first two innings to defeat the Yankees 24–6 at Dunn Field in 1928. The Indians set a record with 24 singles in one game. Johnny Hodapp got two hits in an inning twice. New York went on to win the 1928 World Series.

Lou Gehrig recorded four extra-base hits in a game for the second time in his career with the Yankees with a double, triple, and two home runs in 1930.

Mickey Mantle passed Lou Gehrig for sixth place in the all-time home run list with his 494th home run in a 2–1 Yankee win on a bases loaded walk to Elston Howard in 1966.

A surprise announcement at 1978 Old Timer's Day indicated that Billy Martin would return as Yankee manager in 1980, when Bob Lemon became general manager. Fans cheered wildly.

Yankee Stadium fans threw cups and blowup dolls at Oakland A's outfielder Jose Canseco in 1991.

The Yankees traded infielder Mariano Duncan to the Toronto Blue Jays for minor-leaguer Angel Ramirez and cash in 1997.

30

Charles "Casey" Stengel was born in 1889 in Kansas City, MO. He played six years for the Brooklyn Dodgers and three for the New York Giants. He managed the Dodgers (1934–36), Yankees (1949–60) and Mets (1962–65).

Born this day in 1914 in Springfield, MA, Steve Peek pitched one major league season, going 4–2 with the 1941 Yankees.

Gus Triandos, catcher/first baseman, was born in 1930 in San Francisco, CA. Triandos started his 13-year career with the Yankees in 1953-54. He was named to the all-star team three times in the 1950s with the Baltimore Orioles.

Jim Spencer was born in 1947 in Hanover, PA. Spencer was a 15-year major league veteran. He played first base for the Yankees 1978–81, collecting two hits in the 1978 World Series.

The Baltimore Orioles acquired pitcher Eddie Lopat from the Yankees in exchange for pitcher Jim Mc-Donald and cash in 1955.

Steve Trout was born in Detroit, MI, in 1957. He pitched in 12 seasons, spending part of 1987 with the Yankees where he lost all four of his decisions. Trout was 13–7 with the 1984 Chicago Cubs.

Catcher Ron Hassey was traded for the third time in eight months when the Yankees sent him to the Chicago White Sox for outfielder Ron Kittle, shortstop Wayne Tolleson, and catcher Joel Skinner in 1986.

Baseball Commissioner Fay Vincent permanently banned George Steinbrenner from day-to-day operations of the Yankees in 1990 because of dealings with a known gambler.

31

Allen "Rubberarm" Russell was born in 1893 in Baltimore, MD. Russell pitched for the Yankees from 1915–1919. He won a combined 17 games with New York and Boston in 1919.

Henry Bauer was born in E. St. Louis, IL, in 1922. He was a Yankee regular in the outfield 1948–59, hitting .320 in 1950.

Lou Gehrig recorded 8 RBIs in a game for the second time in the 1930 season. Gehrig drove in 174 runs that year to lead the American League for the third time in four years. He had more RBIs in only one season, 184 in 1931.

The Yankees traded pitcher Mark Hutton to the Florida Marlins for pitcher David Weathers in 1996. In 1993, Hutton had the distinction of becoming the first Australian-born pitcher to start a major league game.

The Yankees acquired slugger Cecil Fielder from the Detroit Tigers for Reuben Sierra in 1996. Fielder led the American League in RBIs three consecutive seasons with the Detroit Tigers 1989–91 after returning from a year in Japan.

Catcher Jim Leyritz was traded by the San Diego Padres to the Yankees for pitcher Geraldo Padua in 1999.

AUGUST

1

Babe Ruth hit his 42nd home run of 1928 season to put him four weeks ahead of his 1927 pace.

Lou Gehrig hit for the cycle for the second and final time of his career in 1937. Yankee pitcher Lefty Gomez broke the major league mark for walks in a shutout by walking eleven St. Louis Browns in a 9–0 victory in 1941.

Shortstop Phil Rizzuto set a Yankee franchise record with 10 putouts at shortstop in a 14-inning game in 1947. Rizzuto twice led the American League in fielding percentage, 1949-50.

Elston Howard, long-time Yankee catcher in the twilight of his career, was traded to the Boston Red Sox in 1967.

Thurman Munson and Carlton Fisk were involved in an altercation at Fenway Park. They came up swinging when Munson crashed into Fisk after a missed 9th inning bunt. The Boston Red Sox won in the bottom of the 9th over the Yankees, 3–2, in 1973.

Billy Martin became Yankee manager in 1975, replacing Bill Virdon, who was the Sporting News 1974 Manager of the Year.

Reggie Jackson was inducted into the Baseball Hall of Fame in Cooperstown, New York in 1993. Mr. October led the American League in home runs with 41 for the 1980 Yankees .

2

Joe DiMaggio made a spectacular catch off the bat of Detroit Tiger Hank Greenberg in 1939, reported to be the greatest catch in the history of Yankee Stadium.

Yankee catcher Thurman Munson, piloting a twin-engine Cessna Citation, missed the landing strip and crashed in Akron, OH, dying instantly in 1979.

Yankees rookie Kevin Maas hit his 10th home run in just 77 at-bats, marking the fastest that any player has ever reached the mark. New York lost in 11 innings, 6–5, to the Detroit Tigers in 1990.

Baseball Commissioner Bud Selig reduced Darryl Strawberry's suspension by one week in 1999. The Yankees announced Strawberry would join the Columbus Clippers on August 4.

3

Charlie Hemphill became the first Highlander to walk five times in a game in 1911, his final major league season. Hemphill hit .297 as a regular outfielder for New York in 1908.

Yankee catcher Les Nunamaker threw out three runners at second base in the 2nd inning against the Detroit Tigers in 1914. It marked the only time a major league catcher has thrown out three runners in one inning.

The Yankees were shut out for the first time in 309 games, dating back to August 2, 1931, as the Philadelphia A's Lefty Grove blanked New York in 1933, 7–0.

Shortstop Kevin Elster began his career with the New York Mets in 1986 before moving briefly to the Yankees in 1994-95. He was born in 1964 in San Pedro, CA.

The Yankees lost both ends of a doubleheader to the Chicago White Sox, 1–0 and 14–2, costing manager Gene Michael his job in 1982. Clyde King replaced him. George Steinbrenner rewarded 34,000 fans with free tickets for enduring the sweep.

Mike Oquist gave up 14 earned runs, becoming the first pitcher in 22 years to give up that many runs in an appearance as the Yankees crushed the Oakland A's in 1998, 14–1.

4

The Highlanders battery in this 1905 game had Doc (not a physician) Newton on the mound and Mike "Doc" (a physician) Powers behind the plate.

George "Tuck" Stainback, a career .258 hitter over 13 seasons, spent four years in the Yankees outfield in the 1940s. He was born in 1910 in Los Angeles, CA.

In a baseball statistical oddity, every player in the lineup of both the Cleveland Indians and the Yankees recorded a putout in this 1925 game.

George Dallas Green was born in 1934 in Newport, DE. Green managed the Yankees in 1989.

Yankee catcher Bill Dickey tied a major league record with a grand slam home run in his second consecutive game in 1937. Babe Ruth was the first Yankee to do it in 1927.

George Selkirk walked twice in the 5th inning of a 1938 game. It was the third, of a record four, times in his Yankee career that he achieved the feat.

Vic Raschi set a record for pitchers when he drove in seven runs in the Yankees 15–0 victory over the Detroit Tigers in 1953.

Nearing the end of his playing career in 1960, Cincinnati Reds infielder Billy Martin threw his bat at Chicago Cub pitcher Jim Brewer. Martin then punched Brewer and fractured his right orbital bone after Martin thought the pitcher was throwing at him.

In his first at-bat in two months after breaking his left foot, Mickey

Mantle hit a pinch-hit home run in the 9th inning off George Brunet to defeat the Baltimore Orioles, 11–10, in 1963.

Reliever Lindy McDaniel came into the game in the 2nd inning in relief of Fritz Peterson and allowed only one run in 13 innings to record a 3–2 victory for the Yankees over the Detroit Tigers in 1973.

Toronto police arrested Yankee outfielder Dave Winfield and charged him with cruelty to animals after one of his warm-up throws struck and killed a seagull before the 5th inning of a 3–1 Yankee win over the Blue Jays in 1983.

Phil Rizzuto Day was celebrated at Yankee Stadium in 1985. His uniform number (#10) was retired. Chicago White Sox hurler Tom Seaver became the 17th player in history to win 300 games in his career when he defeated the Yankees on six hits, 6–2.

Roberto Kelly hit a two-out 9th inning double to break up Toronto Blue Jay pitcher Dave Stieb's no-hitter in 1989. The Yankees lost 2–1 and managed only two hits. It was the third time Stieb lost a no-hitter with two out in the 9th.

The Yankees purchased the contract of Darryl Strawberry from the Columbus Clippers of the International League in 1995.

Yankee Darryl Strawberry hit a game-tying pinch-hit grand slam home run in the 9th inning of New York's 10–5 win. He became the second major leaguer to hit two pinch-hit grand slams in one season in 1998.

5

Highlanders first baseman Hal Chase had a record 38 putouts in a doubleheader versus the St. Louis Browns in 1905.

Babe Ruth hit two home runs, but was twice walked intentionally in extra-innings. The Yankees won in 13 innings, 9–8 in 1923, behind Bob Meusel's single.

Marilyn Monroe died, a victim of an apparent overdose at her Los Angeles, CA, home in 1962. Her former husband, Joe DiMaggio, took charge of funeral arrangements the following day and often left flowers at her grave.

American League President Lee MacPhail suspended Yankees manager Billy Martin for the second time of the 1983 season due to his continued abuse of umpires.

Lou Piniella Day was celebrated at Yankee Stadium in 1984. Piniella played for New York 1974–84, batting .330 in 1977 as a starting outfielder.

6

The Yankees defeated the Cleveland Indians 7–6, but the Indians successfully overturned the win by a protest in 1937.

Andy Messersmith was one of the first big free-agents in baseball. Born in 1945 in Toms River, NJ, Messersmith spent one disappointing season with the Yankees in 1978, failing to win a game after a spring training injury limited his play.

Anthony Michael "Tony" Lazzeri died at the age of 42 due to injuries suffered from an epileptic seizure in 1946. He was a member of the Yankees 1926–37 and is a member of the Baseball Hall of Fame.

Twins manager Billy Martin punched Minnesota pitcher Dave Boswell, sending him hospital to get twenty stitches in 1969.

Major league owners voted to split the 1981 season in half after a player's strike, the first split season since 1892. Therefore, the Yankees were guaranteed a playoff spot as first-half champions of the American League East.

The Yankees traded 1978 play-off hero Bucky Dent to the Texas Rangers for outfielder/first baseman Lee Mazzilli in 1982.

Veteran pitcher Dave LaRoche developed a version of the blooper pitch (the LaLob), which he used to strike out Lamar Johnson to end a 6–0 Yankee victory over the Texas Rangers in 1982.

Darryl Strawberry hit a home run in his first three at-bats and stole the spotlight from Cecil Fielder as the Yankees defeated the Detroit Tigers 9–2 in 1996. It was "The Straw's" 27th multi-home run game of his career.

In 1996, Darryl Strawberry became the first Yankee player to hit five home runs in a span of three regular-season games since Bill "Moose" Skowron did it in July 1956.

7

Babe Ruth hit the 200th grand slam home run in the history of the American League in 1929. It was his 12th career grand slam, 8th with the Yankees. Ruth had hit #199 the previous day.

Birthday of World Series perfect game hurler Don Larsen, born in 1929 in Michigan City, IN.

Hank Bauer tied a major league record against the Washington Senators, becoming the first Yankee to hit a leadoff home run in his second consecutive game in 1957.

Right-handed reliever Jason Grimsley was born in Cleveland, TX, in 1967. He appeared in 55 games for the Yankees in 1999 with a 7–2 record and one save.

The Yankees honored popular outfielder Bobby Murcer by giving him a day at the Stadium in 1983.

Ron Guidry retired the side on nine pitches (three strikeouts) in the 9th inning in 1984. Guidry became the second Yankee to complete the feat, which has happened only ten times in American League history.

For the second consecutive day, a major league player reached the 3000 hit plateau as former Yankee Wade Boggs, playing for the Tampa Devil Rays, became the first to achieve the feat with a home run, off Cleveland Indian Chris Haney in 1999.

The Yankees signed controversial designated hitter/outfielder Jose Canseco off waivers from the Tampa Bay Devil Rays and re-acquired infielder Luis Sojo from the Pittsburgh Pirates in 2000.

8

Detroit Tiger pitcher Howard Ehmke pitched a complete game shutout in one hour and 13 minutes, an American League record, in a 1–0 win over the Yankees in 1920.

Yankee Left-handers Whitey Ford and Bob Kuzava blanked the White Sox, 1–0 and 3–0 respectively in both ends of a doubleheader sweep in 1953. Kuzava gave up his only hit in the 9th inning of the second game.

On Old Timers Day at Yankee Stadium in 1970, New York retired Casey Stengel's uniform #37.

The Yankees signed a thirty-year lease in 1972 to play in new Yankee Stadium, beginning in 1976.

9

Ralph Houk played his entire career with the Yankees behind the plate on a part-time basis 1947–54. He managed the Yankees 1961–63 and 1966–72. He was born in Lawrence, KS, in 1919.

Bobby Veach flied out in 1925, the only time in the career of Babe Ruth that he was removed for a pinch-hitter.

Eli Grba, who pitched for the Yankees in 1959-60 was born in 1934 in Chicago, IL.

Yankee third baseman Red Rolfe began an 18-game scoring streak, scoring 30 runs over the span in 1939.

"Neon" Deion Sanders was born in 1967 in Fort Myers, FL. Sanders starred in the NFL and started his career with the Yankees as an outfielder

in 1989-90. Sanders led the National League with 14 triples in 1992 as an Atlanta Brave.

The Yankees staged a dramatic come from behind win in 1978. Trailing 7–3 in the bottom of the 9th inning, the Yankees tied it when Reggie Jackson was beaned and won it on Lou Piniella's suicide squeeze bunt.

Phil Rizzuto Hall of Fame Night was celebrated at Yankee Stadium in 1994.

The Yankees ended Minnesota Twins pitcher Brad Radke's winning streak at 12 consecutive starts when Luis Sojo doubled home an 8th inning run to lead the 4–1 victory in 1997.

For the first time in history, five grand slams were hit in a single day with Yankee Bernie Williams joining with four other major league players to set the record in 1999.

10

Highlander hurler Jack Chesbro was knocked out by the Chicago White Sox after pitching 30 consecutive complete games in 1904. Chesbro won 41 games and pitched 48 complete games out of 51 starts for the season.

Born in Newport, VA, in 1923, Erwin "Bob" Porterfield pitched his first four major league seasons for the Yankees 1948-51. He was 22–10 for the 1953 Washington Senators.

Babe Ruth announced that 1934 was definitely his final major league season as a regular player. He indicated his desire to manage and pinch-hit.

George Selkirk drove in eight runs for the first of two times in his Yankee career in 1935. Selkirk had 94 RBIs that season.

Mickey Mantle blasted a 460-foot home run off Ray Moore to become the first to clear the center-field hedge at Baltimore's Memorial Stadium in the Yankees' victory over the Orioles, 6–3 in 1957.

Andy Stankiewicz played infield in his first two major league seasons with the Yankees 1992-93. He hit .268 in 116 games in 1992. "Stanky" was born in 1964 in Inglewood, CA.

The Yankees hit three consecutive home runs (Bobby Murcer, Thurman Munson, and Gene Michael) in the 6th inning of a 5–1 win over the Oakland A's in 1969. It was Thurman Munson's first major league home run.

The 1981 season was played in two segments, due to a players' strike. Tommy John began the second season with a 2–0 win over the Texas Rangers. Oscar Gamble and Graig Nettles hit home runs at Yankee Stadium.

During Billy Martin Day, the Yankees retired his uniform #1 to honor the former player and manager in 1986. He was the 13th Yankee to have his number retired.

11

Hartsville, SC, native Louis "Bobo" Newsom was born in 1907. Newsom played major league baseball from 1929–48 and 1952-53. He played for the Yankees in 1947.

Pitcher John "Dusty" Rhodes was born in Salt Lake City, UT, in 1907. He pitched for the Yankees 1929–32, going 6–3 in 1931, his only winning major league season.

In Cleveland in 1929, Babe Ruth hit Willis Hudlin's first pitch of the 2nd inning over the fence to record his 500th career home run. He had over twice the amount of the second player on the list, Cy Williams of the Philadelphia Phillies, who had 237.

Joe DiMaggio, suffering through a 4 for 38 slump, was benched for the first time in his career in 1950.

Boston's Ted Williams singled off Yankee Bob Turley in 1955 for his 2,000th career hit.

Pitcher Mel Stottlemyre was called up from Richmond in 1964. He won nine games in the pennant stretch that season.

In the 2nd inning of a 1967 game, Al Downing became the first Yankee to retire the side on nine pitches (three strikeouts). This feat has happened only ten times in American League history.

Reggie Jackson hit his 400th career home run, off Britt Burns, as the Yankees defeated the Chicago White Sox 3–1 at Yankee Stadium with the help of a 9th inning home run by Aurelio Rodriguez in 1980.

In 1990, in 110 at-bats, Yankee Kevin Maas became the fastest player in major league history to record 13 home runs.

Boston Red Sox pitcher, and future Yankee, Roger Clemens recorded his 2,000th career strike out when he downed Danny Tartabull of the Yankees in 1993.

12

Making his farewell appearance as a Yankee at Fenway Park, Babe Ruth singled and doubled in the first game of a 1934 doubleheader loss to Wes Ferrell and the Boston Red Sox, 6–4. Ruth left the second game to a standing ovation after going hitless.

Hank Bauer scored five runs in a game for the 10th time in team history in 1953 against the Washington Senators. The Yankees recorded 28 hits in the game. Bauer led the Yankees in runs scored in the World Series that year, with six.

Mickey Mantle hit the longest home run at Yankee Stadium. Measuring 502 feet, the ball sailed over the 22-foot screen into the center-field bleachers off Chicago's Ray Herbert in a 7–3 Yankees win over the 1964 White Sox.

In Mel Stottlemyre's major league debut in 1964, Mickey Mantle hit two home runs, one right-handed and one left-handed for the 10th and final time in his career.

Mickey Mantle and Whitey Ford entered the Baseball Hall of Fame in 1974, becoming the first teammates inducted at the same time.

Members of the Major League Baseball Players Association went on strike in 1994, subsequently forcing the cancellation of the World Series.

13

After a train wreck, Yankee Everett Scott kept his consecutive game streak alive, as it neared 1,000, by spending $40 to hire a car to get to Chicago in time for a 1922 game against the White Sox.

Yankee pitcher Red Ruffing hit a home run for the only run of the game in a 1–0, ten-inning victory in 1932, matching the feat of Washington Senator Tom Hughes who also won 1–0 in ten innings in 1906.

Bill Stafford was born in 1939 in Catskill, NY. Stafford played his first six seasons with the Yankees 1960–65, enjoying back-to-back 14–9 seasons in 1961-62. He concluded his career with the Kansas City A's in 1966-67.

The Yankees shut out the Philadelphia A's 21–0 in game two of a 1939 doubleheader tying the American League record for the largest margin of victory in a shut out.

Joe DiMaggio drove in eight runs in a game for the second and final time of his career in 1940. He had 133 RBIs that season and twice led the American League in RBIs, 1941 and 1948.

Born in Louisville, KY, in 1964, Seattle Mariners slugger Jay Buhner started his career with the Yankees, appearing in 32 games 1987-88. Buhner hit 44 home runs for the 1996 Mariners.

George Weiss died in 1972. Weiss was general manager of the Yankees during a span when they won ten American League Pennants and seven World Series Championships.

Roy White hit home runs from both sides of the plate for the second time in his career in 1973.

The Baltimore Orioles led 3–0 after six innings in 1978. The Yankees scored five runs in the top of the 7th when heavy rains ended with the score reverting to the last completed inning, giving the Orioles the victory. This rule was changed in 1980.

Flags flew at half-mast at Yankee Stadium when legend Mickey Mantle died of liver cancer at the age of 63 in Dallas, Texas in 1995.

The Red Sox traded catcher/designated hitter Mike Stanley back to the Yankees in 1997 after spending 1996 and most of the 1997 season in Boston.

The United States Postal Service unveiled the "Roger Maris, 61 in '61" commemorative stamp in 1999 at Yankee Stadium.

14

Yankee Muddy Ruel hit into a triple-play in 1919. A catcher, Ruel played 19 major league seasons and hit .316 in the 1925 World Series as a member of the Washington Senators.

Brooklyn Dodger John Quinn, at age 49, became the oldest pitcher to win a major-league game. He entered the game in relief of Van Mungo in the top of the 9th and the Yankees lost 2–1 in the bottom of the inning in 1932.

Yankee Red Ruffing became the first pitcher in team history to hit a grand slam home run when he connected off Boston Red Sox pitcher Bob Weiland in 1933. Ruffing was also the first Yankee pitcher to hit two home runs in one game, in 1930.

The largest weekday crowd in history watched the Tigers sweep two at Yankee Stadium in 1934. It was the Detroit's 14th straight win.

The Yankees turned seven double plays in a 1942, 11–2, win over the Philadelphia Athletics to set a major league record, which was tied in 1969 by the Houston Astros.

The Yankees lost a 1960 double-header to Washington and fell to 3rd place in the American League. The clubs set major league records by playing 24 errorless innings and using 17 pinch-hitters, nine by the Yankees, in a doubleheader.

The Yankees pounded the California Angels 15–3 behind emergency starter Dick Tidrow. A three-run home run by Graig Nettles, and a lead off home run by Mickey Rivers led to victory in 1977.

15

Highlander Guy Zinn set a record by stealing four bases, including home twice, in the same game in 1912. The regular outfielder had 17 steals on the season.

Born in W. Wyoming, PA, in 1919, Joseph "Specs" Ostrowski pitched the last three years of his career with the Yankees 1950–52, going 9–7.

In Game 2 of a doubleheader, Mickey Mantle hit home runs from both sides of plate for the second time in his career in 1955 in Baltimore against Oriole pitchers Ray Moore and Art Schallock.

Oakland castoff Scott Brosius shined for the 1998 Yankees. Born in 1996 in Hillsboro, OR, Brosius was the 1998 World Series MVP.

Bob Costas delivered the eulogy, Bobby Richardson provided the sermon and Roy White sang at Mickey Mantle's 1995 funeral.

Darryl Strawberry was activated by the Yankees following a four-month stint on the disabled list and rehabilitation in Columbus in 1997.

16

The Detroit Tigers played a home game against the Highlanders in 1903 in Toledo, OH, won by New York, 12–8.

Ernest "Tiny" Bonham was born in Ione, CA, in 1913. Tiny was 21–5 with the 1941 Yankees, playing in New York 1940–46. He concluded his career with the Pittsburgh Pirates with a 103–72 record over ten major league seasons.

In 1914, Charlie Mullen became the fifth Yankee to record four stolen bases in a game. The first baseman had only 11 steals that season and 28 total stolen bases in five major league seasons.

In the only fatality recorded in a major league baseball game, Yankee pitcher Carl Mays beaned Indian shortstop Ray Chapman at the Polo Grounds in 1920. Chapman rose to his feet, but died the next morning of head trauma.

Gene Woodling was born in 1922

in Akron, OH. Woodling played six seasons with the Yankees 1949–54. He led the American League with a .429 on-base percentage in 1953. Woodling led the Yankees with a .429 average in the 1950 World Series.

In 1927, crushing a Tommy Thomas pitch, Babe Ruth became the first player to hit a home run over the roof of Chicago's old Comiskey Park in an 8–1 Yankee win.

Babe Ruth died of throat cancer at 8:01 P.M. at the age of 53 in 1948. His wife Claire and his two adopted daughters were at his side at Memorial Hospital in New York City.

The Yankees blew a 9–4 lead in the top of the 9th inning, but went on to defeat the Chicago White Sox, 11–10, in the bottom of the 9th inning in 1977.

Catcher Tom Pagnozzi was released by the St. Louis Cardinals in 1999 and was subsequently signed with by Yankees.

17

Fritz Maisel stole four bases in one game in 1915, including a steal of second, third, and home. The Yankee outfielder led the American League with 74 steals in 1914. He finished second (51) to Detroit Tiger Ty Cobb (96) in 1915.

On his way to a second consecutive American League home run championship, Yankee first baseman Wally Pipp hit his only grand slam home run of the 1917 season.

After being hit by a pitch from Yankee Carl Mays in 1920, Cleveland shortstop Ray Chapman became major league baseball's only fatality, dying early in the morning one day after being hit in the head by a pitch.

The Yankees purchased the contract of pitcher Lefty Gomez from the San Francisco Seals of the Pacific Coast League in 1929.

Everett Scott's consecutive game record of 1,307 games was broken by Yankee first baseman Lou Gehrig in 1933 when he played in his 1,308th straight game.

The Yankees recorded a 15–0 shutout win over the Philadelphia A's in 1942.

Johnny Lindell became the first Yankee to hit four consecutive doubles, in a 10–3 victory over the Cleveland Indians in 1944. Lindell drove in two runs and scored twice. He led the American League with 16 triples that season.

An estimated crowd of 100,000 fans passed by the body of Babe Ruth on display at Yankee Stadium in 1948. A day after Babe Ruth died, Yankee Tommy Henrich hit his fourth grand slam of the season tying one of Ruth's records.

Yankee catcher Yogi Berra turned the second unassisted double play of his career behind the plate in 1962. He first did it in 1947. Berra caught three no-hitters, two by Allie Reynolds in 1951 and Don Larsen's World Series perfect game in 1956.

Catcher Jorge Posada was born in Santurce, Puerto Rico, in 1971. Posada hit .333 in the 1998 World Series against the San Diego Padres and hit a home run in Game 2.

18

Hall of Fame pitcher Burleigh Grimes played for all three New York teams in his career, ending up with the Yankees in 1934. He won over 20 games five times. He was born in 1893 in Clear Lake, WI.

Highlander "Wee Willie" Keeler struck out for only the second time in the 1906 season, both by Chicago White Sox spitball pitcher Ed Walsh.

Bucky Harris, who managed the Yankees 1947-48, was inducted into the Baseball Hall of Fame in 1975. He served 40 years as a major league player, manager and baseball executive.

Roy White hit home runs from both sides of the plate for the fourth time in his career on this date in 1976.

The Kansas City Royals won the controversial "Pine Tar" game, 5–4, which was completed after dispute in 1983. It took 12 minutes to finish the game before only 1,245 fans at Yankee Stadium. Dan Quisenberry retired the Yankees in order in the 9th.

In 1989, Dallas Green became the 16th manager fired by George Steinbrenner. He was replaced by Bucky Dent.

19

Highlander pitcher Jack Chesbro allowed 11 hits but maintained a shutout over the Detroit Tigers in 1908, 8–0. He was 14–20 with three shutouts that season, his last full-time major league campaign.

Richard "Swampy" Donald was born in 1912 in Morton, MS. He pitched his entire major league career with the Yankees 1938–45, winning 13 games twice.

Bobby Richardson, Yankee infielder of the 1950s and 1960s was born in 1935 in Sumter, SC. He holds World Series records (1960) for RBIs in a series (12) and game (6) and most hits in a series (13).

Babe Ruth's funeral was held at St. Patrick's Cathedral in New York in 1948. He was buried at Gate of Heaven Cemetery in Hawthorne, New York.

Elston Howard drove in eight runs in a game in 1962, a personal best. The Hall of Fame catcher had 91 RBIs that season and won the American League MVP award in 1963.

Wade Boggs pitched one scoreless inning for the Yankees against the Angels in Anaheim in 1997. The 3000 hit club member pitched again for Tampa Bay in August 1999.

Former Yankee pitcher Steve Howe suffered collapsed lungs and a ruptured trachea in a 1997 motorcycle accident. Howe received eight suspensions for drug and alcohol abuse during his major league career.

grand slam home run of his career in the 1st inning off Philadelphia A's pitcher Buck Ross in an 11–3 Yankee victory in 1938.

Third baseman Graig Nettles was born in 1944 in San Diego, CA. Nettles played 11 seasons with the Yankees (1973–83). He led the American League with 32 home runs in 1976. Nettles played 22 major league seasons.

Manager Yogi Berra confronted harmonica-playing infielder Phil Linz on the team bus after the Yankees' fourth consecutive loss. The argument was credited with sparking the team's drive to the 1964 American League pennant.

Yankee slugger Bob Watson hit a baseball that bounced off the loudspeakers in Seattle's Kingdome for a triple, leading the 5–4 victory over the Mariners in 1980. It was the second night in a row he hit the speakers.

George Steinbrenner resigned as managing general partner of the Yankees in 1990. Gene Michael was named vice president and general manager, replacing Harding Peterson.

Yankee Kevin Mass became the fastest batter to reach 15 career home runs (in the least number of at-bats) in 1990.

20

In 1922, Babe Ruth became the first Yankee to score five runs in a game in a 7–5 victory over the Chicago White Sox.

Lou Gehrig hit the 23rd and final

21

Pitcher Murry Dickson was born in 1916 in Tracy, MO. Dickson pitched 18 major league seasons, including 1958 with the Yankees. He won 20 games in 1951 for Pittsburgh and was an all-star in 1953 with the Pirates.

Pitcher Gerry Staley was born in 1920 in Brush Prairie, WA. Staley enjoyed a 15-year major league career, briefly playing for the Yankees 1951-52. Staley led the American League with 67 appearances with the Chicago White Sox in 1959.

Babe Ruth's 600th career home run came off St. Louis Browns pitcher George Blaeholder in an 11–7 win in 1931. Lou Gehrig followed Ruth with his own home run. As teammates, they hit home runs in the same game 72 times and in the same inning 19 times.

Lou Gehrig hit his 17th career grand slam home run in 1935, establishing a major league record.

John Ellis, a 13-year major league veteran, was born in 1948 in New London, CT. Ellis played for the Yankees during his first four seasons, 1969–72. He hit .285 as a regular catcher and first baseman for the 1974 Cleveland Indians.

John Wetteland, Yankee closer of the 1990s, was born in 1966 in San Mateo, CA. Wetteland was the MVP of the 1996 World Series with four saves.

The Yankees defeated the Texas Rangers to cut the Boston Red Sox lead to ½ game in the 1977 American League East race. Graig Nettles hit a home run and a double to lead the 2–1 victory.

22

Urban Shocker was born in 1890 in Cleveland, OH. He pitched for the Yankees 1916-17 and 1925–28 and won more than 20 games four consecutive years with St. Louis, leading the American League with 27 wins in 1921.

George Selkirk walked twice in the 2nd inning of this 1940 game. Selkirk achieved the feat of walking twice in an inning four times in his career, this was his final time to achieve it.

Yankee pitcher Tommy Byrne tied a major league record by walking 16 batters in 13 innings against the Washington Senators in 1951. Byrne walked 150 in 1951.

Roger Maris hit his 50th home run of the 1961 season off pitcher Ken McBride, becoming the first player to hit 50 home runs by the end of August, in a 4–3 loss to the California Angels.

Mickey Mantle tied Jimmie Foxx for third place on the all-time home run list with a pinch-hit home run in Minnesota off Jim Merritt. The Yankees lost the game to the Twins, 3–1, in 1968.

The Yankees claimed infielder Luis Sojo off waivers from the Seattle Mariners in 1996.

23

Infielder Lonny "Junior" Frey was born in 1910 in St. Louis, MO. Frey played 14 seasons, leading the National League in stolen bases in 1940 with 22. He played for the Yankees 1947-48. He appeared in three World Series, going a combined 0 for 20.

Born in Burnsville, NC, in 1918, pitcher Ken Holcombe started his career with the Yankees in 1945. He played six major league seasons, winning 11 games in 1951 with the Chicago White Sox.

Babe Ruth hit his fourth and final grand slam home run as a member of the Boston Red Sox in 1919.

Sherm Lollar was born in Durham, AR, in 1924. Lollar played 18 major league seasons and was named to the all-star team seven times. Lollar caught for the Yankees 1947-48. He hit a home run in Game 4 of the 1959 World Series with the Chicago White Sox.

The Yankees acquired left-handed pitcher Tom Zachary on waivers from the Washington Senators in 1928. Zachary gave up Babe Ruth's historic 60th home run in 1927.

Zeke Bella was born in Greenwich, CT, in 1930. The outfielder started his brief major league career with the Yankees in 1957 and finished with the Kansas City A's in 1959.

The Yankees purchased shortstop Frank Crosetti from San Francisco of the Pacific Coast League in 1930. Crosetti played one more year for the Seals, then joined the Yankees for 17 major league seasons, 1932–48.

A pre-game attraction featuring Walter Johnson pitching to Babe Ruth drew 69,000 fans to Yankee Stadium to provide World War II relief funds. Ruth hit the fifth pitch into the right field bleachers in 1942.

The game between the Yankees and Detroit Tigers was suspended after 19 innings due to curfew in 1968.

The Yankees moved into first place in 1977 with an 8–3 win over the Chicago White Sox behind strong pitching from Mike Torrez and five hits from outfielder Mickey Rivers.

Captain Graig Nettles hit his 30th home run of the season.

The Yankees sent outfielder Gerald Williams and reliever Bob Wickman to the Milwaukee Brewers for reliever Graeme Lloyd and outfielder Pat Listach in 1996.

Jorge Posada hit home runs from both sides of the plate for the first time in his career in 1998.

24

Tony Lazzeri hit the fourth Yankee grand slam home run of the 1927 season in a 9–5 win over the Tigers in Detroit.

In 1964, in the second Mayor's Trophy Game, the Yankees defeated the New York Mets, 6–4.

In the eighth Mayor's Trophy Game, in 1972, the Yankees defeated the New York Mets, 2–1.

In his first major league game in 1981, Minnesota first baseman Kent Hrbek hit a 12th inning home run to give the Twins a 3–2 victory over the Yankees.

Yankee Don Baylor tied Minnie Minoso's major league record when he was hit by a pitch for the 189th time in his career in 1985.

Mickey Mantle's monument was dedicated at Yankee Stadium in 1996.

25

Slow Joe Doyle won his major league debut, 2–0, and Walter Clarkson won the nightcap 7–0 as the Highlanders kept the Cleveland Indians scoreless in a doubleheader sweep in 1906. Doyle became the first pitcher in franchise history to debut with a shutout.

Yankee pitcher Harry Harper tied a major league record by hitting three batters in one inning in 1921. Harper wasn't all bad, he finished a ten-year career with a 2.87 ERA. He was 14–10 with the 1916 Washington Senators.

Yankee hurler of the 1960's Horace "Dooley" Womack was born in 1939 in Columbia, SC.

Detroit Tiger Virgil Trucks threw his second no-hitter of the 1952 season blanking the Yankees, 1–0. Phil Rizzuto's 3rd inning at-bat was scored an error, changed to a hit, then reverted to an error in the 6th inning to make the no-hitter controversial.

To make room for Enos Slaughter, the Yankees gave Phil "The Scooter" Rizzuto his unconditional release in 1956. Thanks to Ballantine Beer, Rizzuto became a Yankee announcer the following season, replacing Jim Woods.

Outfielder Rocky Colavito, with the Yankees in his final season, pitched 2⅓ innings to earn his only major league win by beating the Detroit Tigers, 6–5 in 1968. Colavito led the American League with 42 home runs in 1959 as a Cleveland Indian.

The Yankees defeated the Minnesota Twins 5–4 in 19 innings in 1976. Second baseman Willie Randolph tied an American League record with 13 assists.

Waite Charles "Schoolboy" Hoyt died in Cincinnati, OH, at the age of 84 in 1984. Hoyt, a Hall of Fame pitcher, played 21 major league seasons, including 1921–30 with the Yankees.

26

The Yankees turned a triple play in a 10–6 victory over the 1916 St. Louis Browns.

To settle a 1918 dispute, the contract of spitball pitcher Jack Quinn was awarded to the Yankees from the Chicago White Sox. Quinn lost Game 3 of the 1921 World Series to the New York Giants in relief of Bob Shawkey.

Slow-footed Chicago first baseman Zeke Bonura stole home with two outs in the 15th inning to help the White Sox defeat the Yankees, 9–8, in 1935.

A combined team of New York Giants, Brooklyn Dodgers, and Yankees defeated a group of Army all-stars, 5–2, at the Polo Grounds in 1943 in a "war-bond" game.

The Yankees announced that they had reacquired Enos "Country" Slaughter from the Kansas City A's in 1956.

The Yankees and Cincinnati Reds exchanged starting pitchers when New York acquired Bill Gullickson for Dennis Rasmussen in 1987.

27

One of the Highlanders first pitching stars, Happy Jack Chesbro, made his final New York appearance in a 17–6 loss to the Detroit Tigers in 1909.

Highlander Jack Warhop became the first pitcher in team history to steal home when he achieved the feat in the 6th inning against the Chicago White Sox in 1910.

The Yankees acquired pitcher Dutch Ruether from the Washington Senators in a waiver transaction in 1926.

Yankee Lou Gehrig walked five times in one game in 1935, the fourth player in franchise history to achieve the feat, tying the team record for the most walks in a game.

Joe DiMaggio became the third Yankee to record three triples in one game in game one of a 1938 doubleheader, 8–7, over the Cleveland Indians. It was the first of two times in his career that he drove in eight runs in a game.

Yankee Monte Pearson pitched a 13–0 no-hitter against the Cleveland Indians in the second game of a 1938 doubleheader. This stretched his personal winning streak to ten games.

The Yankees swept a 1963 doubleheader from the Boston Red Sox with a 5–0 shutout by Jim Bouton in the first game and a 3–0 shutout by Ralph Terry in game two.

At Yankee Stadium, Rangers Bump Wills and Toby Harrah hit back-to-back inside-the-park home runs on consecutive pitches as Texas won, 8–2, in 1977.

Chris Chambliss and Graig Nettles each hit two home runs to power the Yankees over the Oakland A's, 6–2 in 1978 at Yankee Stadium. Catfish Hunter was the winning pitcher.

28

Outfielder Robert "Braggo" Roth played the final year of a ten-year career with the Yankees in 1921. The career .284 hitter was born in Burlington, WI, in 1892.

Yankee infielder from 1917–26 Aaron Ward was born in Booneville, AR, in 1896. He batted .306 in 1921.

Highlander John "Tex" Neuer became the second pitcher in franchise history to debut with a shutout, 1–0 over the Boston Red Sox in 1907. He went 4–2 in this, his only major league season.

Centerfielder Lee Magee recorded four assists to tie a major league record in a 1916 game against the Detroit Tigers. Magee played regularly with the Yankees in 1916, recording 45 RBIs and 29 stolen bases.

Babe Ruth started a record streak during which he recorded at least one extra-base hit in nine consecutive games in 1921.

The Washington Senators defeated the Yankees 11–6 in 1924, despite Babe Ruth's two home runs, to move into first place. The Senators went on to win the American League pennant over New York.

Yankee George Selkirk walked twice in the 2nd inning of a 1936 game, making him the first man in franchise history to record the feat twice.

Louis "Sweet Lou" Piniella was born in 1943 in Tampa, FL. Lou played for the Yankees 1974–84 and managed the Yankees from 1986–88. He was the 1969 American League Rookie of the Year.

Ronald Ames Guidry was born in

1950 in Lafayette, LA. Guidry pitched his entire 14-year career with the Yankees and won the 1978 Cy Young Award with a 25–3 record and nine shutouts.

The Milwaukee Braves sold pitcher Johnny Sain to the Yankees for $50,000 and a young pitcher named Lew Burdette in 1951. Burdette came back to haunt New York in the 1957 World Series with three complete game wins and a 0.67 ERA.

Yankee pitcher Ron Guidry faced only 28 men in shutting out the Texas Rangers in 1977, 1–0.

29

After a night on the town, Babe Ruth was late for batting practice. Miller Huggins suspended him and fined him $5,000 for disobeying orders on the field and breaking team rules off the field in 1925.

On Elston Howard Night, the Yankees swept a doubleheader from the Boston Red Sox, 10–2 and 6–1 in 1964. Joe Pepitone hit three home runs, including one grand slam. Roger Maris added six singles.

Mickey Mantle hit the 447th home run of his career in the opening game of a doubleheader against Boston Red Sox Earl Wilson, then tied Babe Ruth's career strikeout record with #1,330 in the nightcap in 1964.

The Yankees' longest day. The Boston Red Sox took the first game of a doubleheader, 2–1 in nine innings. The Yankees won the second game in 20 innings by a score of 4–3. Total time for both games was eight hours and 19 minutes in 1967.

After being fined $500 for leaving the bench during a game, Joe Pepitone quit the Yankees in 1969.

Bobby Murcer hit for the cycle for the only time in his career in 1972 for the Yankees.

Dave Winfield (inside-the-park), Bobby Murcer, and Reggie Jackson hit home runs in the Yankees 1981 victory over the White Sox at Comiskey Park in Chicago.

In 1985, Yankee Don Baylor was hit by a pitch by California Angel Kirk McCaskill. It marked the 190th time he was hit by a pitch in his career, breaking the American League record established by Minnie Minoso.

30

Highlander pitcher Jack Chesbro, who won 41 games in 1904, gave up the first major league hit to Ty Cobb, a double in a 5–3 Detroit Tigers win in 1905.

Slow Joe Doyle became the first pitcher to win his first two major league games by shutout with a 5–0 win over the 1906 Washington Nationals. Hal Chase hit three triples and a home run for the Highlanders.

Pitcher Tom Hughes tossed the first nine-inning no-hitter in Highlander history in 1910, only to lose the no-hitter on a one out hit by Cleveland's Harry Niles in the 10th inning. New York lost the game in the 11th, 5–0, to the Indians.

Babe Ruth was ejected in 1922 for arguing a third strike with umpire Tom Connolly. Ruth then went into the crowd after a heckler and earned his fifth suspension of the season.

Yankee shortstop Bucky Dent, upset over being hit by a pitch, tore ligaments in his hand sliding into second base. He was lost for the remainder of the 1981 season.

Yankees Tommy John (43) and Joe Niekro (41) became the first over–40 pitchers to start both ends of a doubleheader since 1933, John lost 1–0 and Niekro pitched five innings for a 3–0 victory over the 1986 Seattle Mariners.

The Yankees re-acquired third baseman Charlie Hayes from the Pittsburgh Pirates. Hayes went on to catch the final out, a foul pop-up, in the 1996 World Series.

31

The Yankees recorded 27 hits against the Washington Senators in a 1921 game.

Claudell Washington was born in 1954 in Los Angeles, CA. Washington has the distinction of hitting the 10,000th home run in New York Yankee history in 1988. He played for the

Yankees 1986–88 and concluded his major league career in New York in 1990.

Yankee second baseman Bobby Richardson announced his retirement at age 31 in 1966. Richardson was the 1960 World Series MVP despite the four games to three Pittsburgh Pirates Series win.

The Yankees set a franchise record with 31 hits against the Chicago White Sox in 1974.

Graig Nettles hit his second home run of the game in the bottom of the 9th to give the Yankees a 5–4 win over the Seattle Mariners in 1977. Sparky Lyle won his third consecutive game in relief, an American League record.

The Yankees acquired save leader Lee Smith from the St. Louis Cardinals in 1993. Smith appeared in eight career games with the Yankees, earning three saves. He led the American League in saves with 33 in 1994 with the Baltimore Orioles.

Before a crowd of 55,707, Don Mattingly's uniform #23 was added to the list of retired numbers on the wall at Yankee Stadium's Monument Park in 1997.

SEPTEMBER

1

The Highlanders swept a double-header for the third consecutive day at Hilltop Park, 5–4 and 5–3 over the Washington Nationals in 1906, defeating them six times in three days.

Babe Ruth refused to have his picture taken in 1928 with Republican presidential candidate Herbert Hoover. Ruth stated, "Nothing doing, I'm for Al Smith."

Lou Gehrig hit his third grand slam home run in four days in 1931 in a win over the Boston Red Sox. It was his sixth consecutive game with a home run and his 10th consecutive game with an RBI.

In 1945, outfielder Hersh Martin became the sixth Yankee to walk five times in one game. Martin played for the Yankees 1944-45, walking 65 times and hitting seven home runs in 1945.

Tom Tresh hit home runs from both sides of the plate for the first time in his career in 1963.

The Yankees purchased the contract of designated hitter-outfielder Darryl Strawberry from Columbus of the International League in 1999.

2

Marcellus "Hoot" Pearson pitched for the Yankees 1936–40. He was 19–7 in 1936. He was born in Oakland, CA, in 1909.

Marv Throneberry was born in 1933 in Collierville, TN. "Marvelous Marv" started his career with the Yankees 1955–59. He struck out in his only World Series at-bat, in 1958. Throneberry concluded his career with the expansion New York Mets.

Yankee pitcher Spud Chandler walked 10 St. Louis Browns in a nine-inning game in 1942. He only walked 74 batters in 200 innings that season and pitched a complete-game loss in Game 3 of the 1942 World Series against the St. Louis Cardinals.

Johnny Neun replaced Bill Dickey as Yankee manager in 1946. Neun managed the Yankees for the remainder of the season, compiling an

8–6 record. He managed the Chicago Cubs in 1947-48.

The Yankees swept a 1952 doubleheader from the Boston Red Sox behind a shutout in game one by Tom Gorman, 5–0, and another in game two, 4–0 by Ewell Blackwell.

In 1969 Ralph Houk signed a three-year contract to manage the Yankees. At $65,000 per season, he became the highest paid manager in either league.

Billy Martin was fired as Detroit Tigers manager in 1973, three days after he reportedly ordered his pitchers to throw spitballs to Cleveland Indian batters.

Dave Cone made a dramatic return to the mound after a May operation to his pitching arm by tossing seven no-hit innings as the Yankees defeated the Oakland A's 4–0 in 1996. Mariano Rivera gave up one hit in the 9th.

In his 11th professional season, Clay Bellinger hit his first major league home run in his 32nd career at-bat in a 9–3 Yankee win over the Oakland A's in 1999. Darryl Strawberry appeared in a major league game for the first time since 9/27/98.

3

The Highlanders swept their fourth doubleheader in five days to move into first place in 1906. A dispute in the second game caused the Philadelphia A's to leave the field with the score tied 3–3. The Highlanders were awarded a win by forfeit.

One of their first stars, first base-man Hal Chase, jumped the Highlanders to join the upstart California State League in 1908.

The Yankees scored 12 runs in the 6th inning against the Boston Red Sox in 1926.

The Yankees defeated the Boston Red Sox by forfeit in 1939, the fourth win by forfeit in team history.

The Yankees clinched their third straight American League pennant, on the earliest date in major league history, as they defeated the Boston Red Sox, 6–3, in 1941.

At Fenway Park, Tommy Henrich and Joe DiMaggio led the way with four hits apiece. The Yankees totaled 18 hits, all singles, defeating the Boston Red Sox, 11–2, in 1947.

Pitcher Eric Plunk was born in 1963 in Wilmington, CA. Plunk played for the Yankees 1989–91 after being acquired from the Oakland A's.

Ralph Houk announced his resignation as Yankee manager, effective at the end of the 1973 season. The Yankees finished fourth in the American League East for the third straight year.

Yankee Tony Fernandez hit for the cycle in 1995, his only season with the team. Fernandez led the American League with 17 triples in 1990 as a member of the Toronto Blue Jays.

4

The Highlanders swept their fifth doubleheader in six days with 7–0 and 1–0 shutouts by Walter Clarkson and Al Orth respectively over the Boston Pilgrims in 1906 in the midst of a 15-game winning streak.

Yankee "Sad" Sam Jones no-hit the Philadelphia Athletics 2–0 in 1923, allowing just one walk with one Yankee error. He was 21–8 that season and compiled a career record of 229–217 over 22 major league seasons.

Yankee infielder Joe Gordon hit two doubles and two home runs to account for four extra-base hits in a game for the only time in his career in 1938.

The Yankees completed a 1944 doubleheader shutout sweep of the Philadelphia A's. Monk Dubiel won game one 10–0 and Mel Queen won game two 14–0.

The Yankees became the first baseball team, and Casey Stengel the first manager, to win five consecutive American League championships with their 1953 pennant.

Yankee pitcher Ron Guidry won his 20th game of the season on the way to a 25–3 record and the 1978 American League Cy Young Award.

Pitcher Jim Abbott, in his first year with the Yankees in 1993, pitched a 4–0 no-hitter against the Cleveland Indians at Yankee Stadium. Abbott walked five and struck out three.

Darryl Strawberry was arrested for allegedly striking Charisse Simons, his 26-year-old live-in girlfriend, in 1993.

Bernie Williams hit home runs from both sides of the plate for the third time in his career on this date in 1998.

5

Born in Danville, IN, in 1872, Albert "Smiling Al" Orth pitched his final six seasons for the Highlanders 1904–09, going 27–17 in 1906.

Babe Ruth added nine more innings to his World Series scoreless streak as a pitcher with a shutout win over the Chicago Cubs and Hippo Vaughn, 1–0 in Game 1 of the 1918 World Series. Ruth completed 13 scoreless innings in his first Series in 1916.

Yankee outfielders set a record with five assists, four by Bob Meusel, in an 8–2 loss to the Boston Red Sox in 1921. Meusel led the American League in outfield assists in 1921-22.

The Yankees played their final home game at the Polo Grounds in 1922 after seven seasons using the stadium as their home field.

Yankee Earle Combs walked twice in the same inning of a game for the second time in his career in 1932.

Bill Mazeroski was born in Wheeling, WV, in 1936. He never played in New York, but broke a lot of Yankee's hearts with his lead-off home run in the 9th inning of Game 7 of the 1960 World Series for the Pittsburgh Pirates off pitcher Ralph Terry.

The Yankees acquired first baseman Johnny Hopp from the Pittsburgh Pirates for cash in 1950. Hopp, nearing the end of his career, was second in the National League with a .340 average at the time.

The Cleveland Indians broke an 18-game losing streak by sweeping a doubleheader from the Yankees in 1977 on "I Hate the Yankee Hanky Night."

Roy Smalley hit home runs from both sides of the plate in a 19–8 romp over the Kansas City Royals in 1982.

Both home runs came with two men on base.

The Baltimore Orioles defeated the Yankees 13–9 in 1997 in the longest nine-inning game in American League history.

The 1998 Yankees (100–38) reached the century mark in victories earlier than any other team in history, beating the Chicago White Sox, 11–6. The 1906 Cubs and 1954 Indians had accomplished the feat on September 9th.

6

All of the Yankee starters recorded at least two hits, except Benny Bengough who had one, in a 14–2 victory over the Boston Red Sox in 1927. Babe Ruth hit three home runs to raise his season total to 47. Lou Gehrig added his 45th.

The Yankees set a record using ten pinch-hitters in a 1954 game.

The Yankees sold Matty Alou to the St. Louis Cardinals and brother Felipe to the Montreal Expos in 1973.

After an outburst to the press, Gene Michael was fired and replaced by Bob Lemon as Yankee manager in 1981.

Baltimore Oriole infielder Cal Ripken broke Lou Gehrig's major league consecutive game streak at Camden Yards in 1995, playing in his 2,131 straight American League game.

7

Highlander pitcher John Deering walked 11 Boston Pilgrims in 10 innings in 1903. He struck out 28 and walked 42 in two seasons with New York and the Detroit Tigers.

Washington National (Senator) Walter Johnson pitched his third shutout in four days, a 4–0 victory over the Highlanders in 1908. New York managed only two hits.

Earle Combs became the second Yankee in history to walk twice in the same inning of a game in 1931.

Joe DiMaggio became the second Yankee in history to hit a triple and a double in the same inning in 1942. Bob Shawkey was the first in 1923.

In Washington, Johnny Mize pinch-hit a grand slam giving the Yankees a 5–1 victory over the Senators in 1952. Mize had hit home runs in the fifteen major league baseball stadiums in use at the time (Sportsman Park was shared by the Cardinals and Browns).

Whitey Ford became the fifth major league pitcher to record consecutive one-hitters, beating Kansas City, 2–1 in 1955. Jim Finigan's two-out single in the 7th inning was the A's only hit.

Tony Kubek tied a major league record against the Minnesota Twins in 1964 when he became the second Yankee to hit leadoff home runs in two consecutive games.

The Yankees finished 5th in 1968 but crushed the Washington Senators 16–2 and 10–0 at the Stadium. Jake Gibbs, Joe Pepitone, Roy White, Frank Fernandez and Rocky Colavito hit home runs in the doubleheader.

Boston Red Sox manager Eddie Kasko used an entirely different, ten-player, lineup in both ends of a doubleheader against the Yankees in 1971. New York won both games, 5–3 and 5–0, at the Stadium.

In 1974, Yankee third baseman Graig Nettles hit a 7th inning single that was disallowed when his broken bat revealed "superballs" hidden inside to make the ball go further.

The Yankees trailed the Red Sox by four games in the American League East when they arrived in Boston for a four-game series. The 1978 "Boston Massacre" started with a 15–3 New York win. Willie Randolph drove in five runs.

8

The Yankees surrendered home runs from both sides of the plate to switch hitting Philadelphia A's outfielder Wally Schang in 1916.

Boston Red Sox Babe Ruth hit his 26th home run of the 1919 season, off Yankee Jack Quinn, breaking Buck Freeman's home run mark of 25 set in 1899 with the National League Washington Senators.

Yankee Babe Ruth recorded an extra-base hit in his 11th straight game to set an American League record. Ruth had seven doubles, one triple, and three home runs over the 11-game span in 1921.

Italian Americans arranged "Tony Lazzeri Day" at Yankee Stadium in 1927. The Yankees defeated the St. Louis Browns 2–1.

Sam Byrd, substituting for Babe Ruth (who believed he was having an appendicitis attack), hit two home runs to lead the Yankees to a 5–4 win over the Detroit Tigers in 1932.

The Yankees trailed 6–1, but scored eight in the 9th inning to defeat the Boston Red Sox, 9–6 in 1937.

In 1939, the Yankees defeated the Boston Red Sox 4–1 in seven innings in a game that was called because of lightning.

Second baseman Joe Gordon hit for the cycle for the Yankees in 1940. He won the 1941 American League MVP award.

Infielder Fred Stanley became the last Yankee to hit a grand slam in old Yankee Stadium in 1973. It was Stanley's only home run of the season and his first for New York.

Billy Martin was named the manager of the Texas Rangers in 1973, and remained with the team until 1975 when he returned to the Yankees. Martin had started the 1973 season managing the Detroit Tigers.

Dave Winfield hit a home run in a 10–5 Yankee win over the Baltimore Orioles in 1982. Winfield became the 9th player to hit 30 home runs in a season in each league and the 5th Yankee right-hander to hit 30 in a season.

Outfielder Steve Kemp suffered a fractured cheekbone when he was hit by a batting practice line drive by Omar Moreno in Milwaukee, ending his 1983 season with the Yankees. It was his first year of a five-year, $5.45 million contract.

Danny Tartabull collected nine RBIs in a Yankee victory over the Baltimore Orioles in 1992, 16–4.

Cardinal first baseman Mark Mc-Gwire connected off Cub pitcher Steve Trachsel for a 341-foot line-drive home run to left field for his historic 62nd home run of the 1998 season, breaking Roger Maris' 1961 record of 61.

9

Birthday of former Yankee manager Frank Chance, born in Fresno, CA, in 1877. He managed the team 1913-14 and was elected to the Baseball Hall of Fame in 1946.

Ambrose Puttman pitched for the Highlanders 1903–05, compiling a 7–7 record. Puttman was born in 1880 in Cincinnati, OH.

Hall of Fame pitcher Waite "Schoolboy" Hoyt was born in Brooklyn, NY, in 1899. Hoyt pitched for the Yankees 1918–30. He compiled a career 237–182 major league record.

The Highlanders recorded a doubleheader sweep by shutout over the 1907 Washington Nationals with a 10–0 win in the first game by Tex Neuer and a 2–0 win in the second game by Jack Chesbro.

Babe Ruth tied the single-season home run record in 1921 by hitting his 54th in a 14–5 Yankee win over the A's. It was reported to be the longest ball hit at Philadelphia's Shibe Park.

Yankee Frank Crosetti tied a major league record and became the first Yankee to strike out twice in one inning, the 7th, in 1932. The first to do it was Lefty Gomez, just six weeks earlier. Crosetti played his entire 17-year career with New York. He led the American League in stolen bases in 1938 and hit a home run in Game 2 of the World Series. Lou Gehrig

drove in eight runs in a game for the third and final time of his career.

The Yankees celebrated their eighth American League pennant in 1936 sweeping a doubleheader from the Cleveland Indians, 11–3 and 12–9. They ultimately won the division by 19½ games, their largest margin ever, over the Detroit Tigers.

Mickey Mantle hit a two-run home run off Chicago White Sox pitcher Billy Pierce in a seven-run 5th inning, in a 9–3 win in 1953 at Yankee Stadium. Mantle was caught blowing a bubble in center field and earned a contract with the Bowman Gum Co.

The largest crowd in major league history (93,103) attended Roy Campanella Night at the Los Angeles Coliseum. The Yankees beat the Dodgers, 6–2, in an exhibition game in 1959.

The Rangers fired manager Whitey Herzog in 1973 and eventually replaced him with Billy Martin.

In the third game of the 1978 "Boston Massacre," the Yankees shutout the Boston Red Sox, 7–0.

The Oakland A's defeated the Yankees 7–3 to complete a 12-game sweep of the season series in 1990. It was the first time a team had won every game against the Yankees in a single season.

The Yankees officially clinched the 1998 American League East title on the earliest date in American League history by defeating the Boston Red Sox, 7–5.

James Augustus "Catfish" Hunter, born in Hertford, North Carolina, died on this date in 1999 of ALS, "Lou Gehrig's Disease."

Yankee Hideki Irabu opposed

Matt Suzuki in the first match-up of Japanese starting pitchers in American major league history in 1999.

10

Bob Meusel, Babe Ruth, and Lou Gehrig became the first Yankees to hit back-to-back-to-back home runs, in the 4th inning of a 1925 game.

Yankee pitcher Lefty Grove walked 10 Detroit Tigers in nine innings in 1932. Grove finished that season with a 24–7 record and pitched a complete game win in Game 2 of the World Series against the Chicago Cubs.

Roger Maris was born in Hibbing, Minnesota in 1934. His family moved to Fargo, North Dakota in 1942. Maris set the single season home run record, eclipsing Babe Ruth, with 61 in 1961. St. Louis Cardinal Mark McGwire hit 70 home runs in 1998.

In the first game of a 1939 doubleheader against Cleveland, Indian pitcher Ray Caldwell no-hit the Yankees, 3–0.

Joe DiMaggio became the first major league batter to hit three home runs in one game at Washington's Griffith Stadium in an 8–1 victory over the Senators in 1950. It was the second and final time of his career that DiMaggio hit three home runs in a game.

The Yankees completed a fourgame sweep of the Boston Red Sox in 1978 to take over first place in the American League East. The Yankees scored 42 runs on 67 hits in the series.

11

Born in Hopkins, MI, in 1869, Frank Kitson pitched ten major league seasons, finishing his career with the Highlanders in 1907 with a 4–0 record. Kitson was 22–16 with Baltimore of the National League in 1899.

William "Buffalo Bill" Hogg was born in 1881 in Port Huron, MI. Hogg pitched for the Highlanders 1905–08, going 14–13 in 1906.

Yankee Marty McHale pitched a 4–0 shutout over the St. Louis Browns in his first start for New York in 1913. He was 11–27 in three seasons with the Yankees 1913–15.

Babe Ruth had four extra-base hits in a game for the first time in his career as a Yankee with two doubles and two home runs in 1922.

Boston Red Sox star Ted Williams collected his 2000th career hit in a 5–3 loss to the Yankees in 1955.

Catcher Don "Sluggo" Slaught played for the Yankees 1988-89. The Long Beach, CA, native was born in 1958. He hit .283 for the Yankees in 1988.

John Miller became the first Yankee to hit a home run in his first major league at-bat, one of two hits in 23 at-bats in 1966, and his only home run for New York. Miller resurfaced in the majors with the Los Angeles Dodgers in 1969, and hit one more.

In a strike-shortened season, pitcher Dave Righetti struck out 11 Boston Red Sox for the win at Yankee Stadium in the first meeting of the two teams in 1981. Righetti went on to become American League Rookie of the Year.

12

Spurgeon "Spud" Chandler was born in 1907 in Commerce, GA. The right-hander pitched for the Yankees 1937–47 and won the 1943 American League MVP.

Roger Peckinpaugh, at age 23, became the youngest manager in major league history when he took over for Frank Chance with the 1914 Yankees. He returned in 1915 as a shortstop only with the team.

Charles "King Kong" Keller was born in Middletown, MD, in 1916. Keller was a Yankee 1939–49, 1952. He hit .334 in 1939.

Pitcher Mike Wallace made his only start in 23 Yankee games with a 3–0 combined shutout with Dick Tidrow over the Baltimore Orioles and Jim Palmer in 1974.

In 1979, Boston Red Sox Carl Yastrzemski recorded his 3000th career hit with a single off Jim Beattie in a 9–2 Yankees loss. Yastrzemski became the first American League player with 3000 hits and 400 home runs.

Yankee center fielder Bernie Williams had eight RBIs with two home runs, one from each side of the plate, and a single to help defeat the 1996 Detroit Tigers, 12–3.

13

Pitcher Walter "Dutch" Ruether pitched for the Yankees 1926-27. He was born in Altameda, CA in 1893. He was 21–12 with the 1922 Brooklyn Dodgers.

Babe Ruth hit two home runs and the Yankees swept a doubleheader, 5–3 and 5–3, from the Cleveland Indians to clinch the 1927 American League pennant.

Yankee pitcher Jim Bouton won his 20th game of the 1963 season, a 2–0 shutout over the Twins in Minnesota. The victory gave the Yankees their 28th American League pennant.

Outfielder Bernie Williams was born in San Juan, Puerto Rico, in 1968. Williams has played his entire major league career (through 2000) with the Yankees, joining the team in 1991.

Robert E. Nederlander was appointed managing general partner of the Yankees in 1990.

14

Frank Chance died in 1924. He managed the Yankees 1913-14 and was elected to the Baseball Hall of Fame in 1946.

Second baseman Gerry Coleman was born in 1924 in San Jose, CA. Coleman was a Yankee his entire career, 1949–57, and an all-star in 1950. He led the team with eight hits, batting .364, in the 1957 World Series, his final season.

The Yankees clinched the 1943 American League pennant, their 14th championship, against the Cleveland Indians with an 8–3 win. Ernie Bonham won his 20th game of the season and Joe DiMaggio had four hits.

Joe DiMaggio received a medical discharge due to a duodenal ulcer in 1945 following military service.

In 1948, Charlie "King Kong" Keller became the third American League batter, and the second Yankee, to hit home runs in consecutive pinch-hit at-bats.

The Yankees clinched their fifth straight American League pennant in 1953 with an 8–5 win over the Cleveland Indians behind second baseman Billy Martin's four RBIs.

The Yankees won their 24th American League pennant in 1958, their ninth under manager Casey Stengel. Stengel tied former Philadelphia A's manager Connie Mack for the most American League pennants won.

In 1974, Yankee Graig Nettles hit a 1st inning home run off Detroit's Mickey Lolich while his brother Jim of the Tigers hit one off Pat Dobson in the 2nd inning. Graig became the second Yankee to hit a home run in the same game as his brother (DiMaggio—1950).

The Yankees won in the 9th inning when Thurman Munson singled and Reggie Jackson hit a long home run to defeat the Boston Red Sox at Yankee Stadium in 1977.

Owners of the 28 Major League teams voted to cancel the remainder of the 1994 season, the Division Series, the League Championship and the World Series.

15

Highlander Pete Wilson became the third pitcher in franchise history to debut with a shutout in a 1–0 win over the 1908 Boston Red Sox. Wilson pitched only one other shutout and was 9–8 in two major league seasons with New York.

Manager Frank Chance resigned in 1914 after a 61–75 record. By report, he tried to punch team owner Big Bill Devery in a conflict over player personnel.

For the third consecutive season, Babe Ruth broke the single season home run record. Ruth hit his 55th home run against the St. Louis Browns at the Polo Grounds in 1921.

The Yankees clinched their 15th American League pennant in 1947.

For a record sixth time in his career, first baseman Johnny Mize hit three home runs in one game. The Yankees lost to the Tigers, in Detroit, 9–7 in 1950.

Yankee general manager George Weiss allegedly hired private detectives to follow his star players in 1958. They tailed Bobby Richardson and Tony Kubek to a YMCA, where they played ping pong.

1945 American League batting champion Snuffy Stirnweiss was killed in 1958 when a drawbridge was left open and a Jersey Central train plunged into Newark Bay.

Mickey Mantle hit home runs from both sides of plate for the seventh time in his career in 1959 at Comiskey Park against Billy Pierce and Bob Shaw of the White Sox.

Dave Kingman was purchased by the Yankees from the California Angels in 1977, making him the first player to wear uniforms in four different divisions in the same season.

Kingman joined Charlie Keller as Yankees with the nickname "King Kong."

Ron Guidry stretched the Yankees lead over Boston to 2½ games with a 4–0 victory over the Red Sox at Fenway Park in 1978.

In 1985, the Yankees traded minor league pitcher Jim Deshaies and two players-to-be-named-later to the Houston Astros for 40-year-old Joe Niekro. Joe joined brother Phil Niekro on the same team for the first time since 1974 with the Atlanta Braves.

16

The New York Yankees clinched their fourth consecutive American League pennant with a win over the Detroit Tigers in 1939.

In 1948, Joe DiMaggio hit his 300th career home run to join Babe Ruth, Lou Gehrig, Mel Ott, Jimmie Foxx, Rogers Hornsby, Chuck Klein and Hank Greenberg in the exclusive club at the time.

Hank Bauer and Yogi Berra hit 9th inning home runs to defeat the Boston Red Sox, 5–4, and take over first place in 1955. Mickey Mantle pulled a hamstring muscle running out a bunt.

Tim "Rock" Raines, born in 1959 in Sanford, FL, started his major league career in Montreal in 1979, went to the White Sox in 1991 and joined the Yankees for the 1996 season, hitting .214 in the World Series.

Outfielder Mel Hall was born in 1960 in Lyons, NY. He played for the Yankees 1989–92, hitting .285 in 141 games in 1991.

The Yankees, on their way to an improbable comeback to win the 1978 American League East title, defeated the Boston Red Sox for sixth time in two weeks, 3–2.

The Yankees held Catfish Hunter Day to honor the future Hall of Fame pitcher, who planned to retire at the end of the 1979 season at the age of 33. Twenty-year-old left-hander Dave Righetti made his Yankee debut.

17

Centerfielder Casey Stengel debuted with the Brooklyn Dodgers with four singles, a walk, two stolen bases, and two RBIs in a 7–3 win over the Pittsburgh Pirates in 1912. Although he never played for the Yankees, Stengel led them as manager 1949–60.

Right field spectators presented Earle Combs with a gold watch between games of a 1927 doubleheader at Yankee Stadium, a 3–2 and 8–1 sweep over the Chicago White Sox. Combs hit his sixth and final home run of the season in the second game.

Mickey Mantle recorded his 2,000th career hit, and his 450th career home run (off Bob Duliba), in a 6–2 Yankee win over the Los Angeles Angels in 1964. New York took over first place in the American League.

Yankee Stadium celebrated Bobby Richardson Day in 1966. Richardson, age 31, had announced his retirement at the end of the season. He played his entire twelve-year career with the Yankees.

The Detroit Tigers clinched the 1968 American League pennant with a 2–1 victory over the Yankees.

Dave "King Kong" Kingman hit his first home run as a Yankee and Reggie Jackson added two home runs in this 1977 game.

The Boston Red Sox finally defeated the Yankees, 7–3, after New York had embarrassed them repeatedly in September of 1978.

Chet "Red" Hoff passed away at the age of 107 in 1998 in Daytona Beach, FL. He was the oldest living Yankee at the time of his death. He pitched for the Highlanders/Yankees 1911–13.

The United States Postal Service officially issued the "Roger Maris, 61 in '61" commemorative stamp in 1999 in Green Bay, WI.

Despite losing a doubleheader in 1938, The Yankees clinched their 10th American League pennant.

Mickey Mantle hit his 50th home run of the season, the eighth player to achieve the milestone, in the 11th inning off Chicago's Billy Pierce. New York won 3–2 to clinch the 1956 American League pennant.

Mickey Mantle Day was celebrated at Yankee Stadium in 1965. Mantle played his 2000th major league game in front of over 50,000 New York fans.

In 1993, The Yankees trailed the Boston Red Sox 3–1 in the 9th inning when a fan ran on the field and time-out was called. A pitch was delivered and Mike Stanley hit a popup to left field, which didn't count. New York rallied for three runs and won, 4–3.

18

George "The Bull" Uhle, born in Cleveland, OH, in 1898, pitched two seasons for the Yankees in the 1930s. Uhle won 22 or more games three times for the Cleveland Indians in the 1920s.

Joe Bush stopped St. Louis Brown George Sisler's 41-game hitting streak in 1922. Ironically, Sisler started the streak against the Yankee pitcher in July.

The Yankees edged the St. Louis Browns, 7–6 in 10 innings. Pitcher Red Ruffing became the first pitcher in franchise history to hit two home runs in a game, while recording the victory in 1930. Ruffing batted .364 with 40 hits and 22 RBIs that season.

19

Ralph Young was a nine-year major league veteran who was born in 1889 in Philadelphia, PA. Young started his career with the Yankees in 1913 and went on to have seven successful seasons in the infield of the Detroit Tigers.

Born in Birmingham, AL, in 1909, Hersh Martin played his final two major league seasons in the Yankee outfield 1944-45. He once walked five times in a game for New York. He was a National League all-star in 1938 with the Philadelphia Phillies.

Nicholas Etten was born in 1913 in Spring Grove, IL. The first baseman played nine seasons, including 1943–46 with the Yankees. He led the

American League in home runs in 1944 with 22 and RBIs in 1945 with 111.

Yankee Lou Gehrig collected three doubles and one home run for four extra-base hits, the first time in his career, in 1926.

Birthday of former Yankee pitcher Bob Turley, a 21-game winner in 1958, born in 1930 in Troy, IL.

Jim Abbott was born in Flint, MI in 1967. Abbott started his career with the California Angels 1989–92 and played with the Yankees 1993-94. A one-armed pitcher, Abbot pitched a 4–0 no-hitter against the Cleveland Indians 9/4/1993.

Mickey Mantle claimed third place on the all-time home run list at the time with his 535th career home run off Denny McLain in Detroit to pass Jimmie Foxx in 1968.

20

The Highlanders set a franchise record with twelve errors in a 1911 doubleheader.

Red Sox outfielder/pitcher Babe Ruth tied Chicago White Stocking (National League) Ned Williamson's 1884 major league home run record, with his 27th of the season to defeat Chicago White Sox pitcher Lefty Williams in 1919 on Babe Ruth Day at Fenway Park. Ruth scored the winning run in both games of a doubleheader sweep by Boston, his last games as a Red Sox player at Fenway Park.

Lou Gehrig drove in four runs to break his previous RBI record of 175,

set in 1927. By the end of the 1931 season he totaled 184 RBIs.

Yankee infielder-outfielder of the 1960s, and 1962 American League Rookie of the Year, Tom Tresh, was born in 1937 in Detroit, MI.

Ford C. Frick, a former New York sportswriter and broadcaster, was elected as the third Commissioner of Baseball in 1951.

Baltimore Oriole knuckleball pitcher Hoyt Wilhelm no-hit the Yankees, 1–0 in 1958, behind a solo home run by Gus Triandos. Don Larsen took the loss for New York.

Roger Maris hit his 59th home run and barely missed his 60th in the 154th game of the 1961 season against Oriole Milt Pappas in Baltimore. The Yankees clinched their 26th American League pennant.

Mickey Mantle hit his 536th, and final, major league home run off Boston's Jim Lonborg at Yankee Stadium in 1968.

The Yankees added a plaque commemorating the career of catcher Thurman Munson to Memorial Park in 1980 at the Stadium.

In 1997, the Yankees clinched their 37th post-season appearance by making the playoffs for the third consecutive year.

21

Highlander first baseman Hal Chase tied an American League record with 22 put outs in a 1906 game.

Babe Ruth was the unanimous choice for the 1923 American League MVP Award by the baseball writer's committee.

Bob Grim won his 20th game of the season when the Yankees defeated the Washington Senators, 3–1 in 1954. Grim was later named the 1954 Rookie of the Year. His 20 wins were the second most by a Yankee rookie pitcher.

The Yankees set a record, stranding 20 men on base. Mickey Mantle hit a 500-foot home run off pitcher Frank Sullivan but the Boston Red Sox won, 13–9 at Fenway Park in 1956.

In 1961, baseball commissioner Ford Frick ruled that Roger Maris could only be listed as the record holder for home runs in a 162-game season after he failed to reach the record in 154 games, as Babe Ruth had.

Cecil Grant Fielder was born in Los Angeles in 1963. The first baseman/designated hitter produced 51 home runs for the 1990 Detroit Tigers. He was the American League MVP runner-up in 1990-91. Fielder played for the Yankees 1996-97.

Ron Guidry pitched seven shutout innings and Goose Gossage recorded the save as the Yankees beat the Boston Red Sox 3–0 in the 1980 pennant stretch.

Cecil Fielder hit his 300th career home run on his 34th birthday to lead the Yankees over the Toronto Blue Jays, 5–4 in 10 innings in 1997.

22

Yankee Ben Paschal hit two inside-the-park home runs in one game, an 11–6 win over the Chicago White Sox at Yankee Stadium in 1925.

Earle Combs became the second Yankee to hit three triples in one game in an 8–7 win over the Detroit Tigers in 1927.

Manager Miller Huggins turned the Yankees over to coach Art Fletcher, and died three days later from blood poisoning at the age of 49 at New York's St. Vincent Hospital in 1929.

A record low crowd of 413 at Yankee Stadium in 1964 saw the Chicago White Sox defeat New York 4–1. Broadcaster Red Barber insisted that television cameras show the empty seats, a decision that eventually cost the play-by-play announcer his job.

One night after scuffling with a patron in the bar of a Baltimore hotel in 1985, manager Billy Martin's right arm was broken by pitcher Ed Whitson in an early-morning brawl in the same bar.

Ron Guidry became the American League's first 20-game winner in 1985 when the Yankees beat the Baltimore Orioles, 5–4.

23

America's first baseball team, the New York Knickerbockers, was officially formed in 1845.

Manager George Stallings was forced to resign in 1910 amid controversy over Highlander first baseman Hal Chase.

The Yankees set an American League record with 106 victories in the 1927 season with a 6–0 win over the Detroit Tigers.

The Yankees lost 9–5 but clinched

the 1937 American League pennant when the Boston Red Sox defeated the Detroit Tigers.

The Yankees clinched the 1955 American League pennant by beating the Boston Red Sox, 3–2.

Reggie Jackson was knocked down by Cleveland Indian pitcher John Denny in 1981. Jackson hit a home run, circled the bases, and charged the mound.

In 1984, the Detroit Tigers defeated the Yankees 4–1. Sparky Anderson became the first major league manager to win more than 100 games in a season in each league.

The 1998 Yankees tied the 1927 team for the most wins in franchise history with a victory over the Cleveland Indians, 8–4. The win pulled them within one game of the American League record of 111 wins in a season by the 1954 Indians.

A crowd of 27,549 fans helped the 1999 Yankees break a record for New York City season attendance with 3,072,009. The New York Mets had held the record with 3,047,724 in 1988.

24

New York pitcher Joe Lake allowed just one hit, by Chicago White Sox Patsy Dougherty, in a 1909 victory. Lake posted a 14–11 record that season. Dougherty led the American League in runs scored in 1904, as a member of the Highlanders.

After the resignation of manager George Stallings in 1910, Hal Chase, reported to be the center of the con-troversy, replaced him. Chase signed as a player-manager for the Highlanders for the 1911 season.

Babe Ruth of the Boston Red Sox surpassed the 19th century home record of Ned Williamson with his 28th home run of the season off Yankee Bob Shawkey, over the roof of the Polo Grounds in 1919.

In 1929, Tom Zachary of the Yankees recorded his 12th win without a loss in a 5–3 over the Boston Red Sox, becoming the first pitcher to go 12–0 in a season. Zachary surrendered Babe Ruth's 60th home run of 1927 as a member of the Washington Senators.

Babe Ruth made his farewell appearance as a player at Yankee Stadium in the 1934 home finale against Boston. Ruth walked in the first, limped to first base, and left for a pinch runner in a 5–0 loss to the Red Sox.

The Yankees defeated the Red Sox, 9–6, in a crucial game of the 1948 pennant race. The Indians lost to the Detroit Tigers forcing a three-way tie for first place between New York, Boston and Cleveland, all with 91–56 records.

The Yankees tied a major league record when three pinch-hitters struck out in one inning in 1954.

The Yankees clinched the 1976 American League East title by beating the Detroit Tigers, 8–0.

Ron Guidry tied Babe Ruth's American League record for lefthanders with his ninth shutout of the season as the Yankees beat the Cleveland Indians, 4–0, on a two-hitter in 1978.

25

Glendale, Long Island, native Phil "Scooter" Rizzuto was a star infielder for the Yankees 1941–56 with three years off for military service. He was born in 1918 and went on to become an announcer.

The Yankees swept a doubleheader from the St. Louis Browns to clinch the 1926 American League pennant, their fourth.

Feisty Yankee manager Miller Huggins died of a rare skin infection at the age of 49 in 1929.

Lou Gehrig played his 1,500th consecutive game and hit his 48th home run of the 1934 season, a personal high.

The Boston Red Sox moved into a first place tie in the race for the 1949 American League pennant with a 4–1 victory over Yankee Allie Reynolds. Joe DiMaggio listened to the game from a hospital bed, suffering from pneumonia.

Casey Stengel notched the 10th and final American League Pennant of his career as manager of the Yankees with a 4–3 win over the Boston Red Sox in 1960.

Whitey Ford beat Washington 8–3 as the Yankees clinched the 1962 American League pennant. Ralph Houk became the fifth man to win the pennant in each of his first two seasons as manager.

David Weathers was born in 1969 in Lawrenceburg, TN. He pitched for the Yankees 1996-97. Weathers pitched seven scoreless innings in the 1996 post-season, winning two games.

The Yankees swept the Toronto Blue Jays in a 1977 doubleheader with a 15–0 shutout in the opener by Ron Guidry and a 2–0 shutout by Ed Figueroa in game two.

Rickey Henderson stole his 75th base of the 1985 season in the Yankees' 10–2 win over the Detroit Tigers. This broke the club record for steals set by Fritz Maisel in 1914 with 74.

Houston Astros coach Yogi Berra announced his retirement at the end of the 1989 baseball season, bringing to a close a 46-year career in major league baseball. Berra won three American League MVP awards as Yankee catcher.

Boston Red Sox third baseman Wade Boggs went 4 for 5 in a 7–4 win over the Yankees in 1989 to become the first player in major league history to record 200 hits and 100 walks in four consecutive seasons.

The 1998 Yankees set an American League record with their 112th win, 6–1 over the Tampa Bay Devil Rays. The 1906 Chicago Cubs hold the major league record with 116 victories in a season.

26

Babe Ruth hit his 57th and 58th home runs of the season to lead the Yankees to an 8–7 victory over the Cleveland Indians, increasing the Yankees lead to 2½ games in the 1921 American League pennant race.

Former Yankee pitcher, Bobby Shantz, who also played briefly in the outfield, was born in Pottstown, PA, in 1925. Shantz was the 1952 American

League MVP with the Philadelphia A's with a 24–7 record.

In the shortest doubleheader ever recorded, the Yankees lost 6–1 in 72 minutes and 6–2 in 55 minutes to the St. Louis Browns after New York had already clinched the 1926 American League pennant.

The Yankees clinched their 19th American League pennant, their fourth straight, with a 5–2 win in 11 innings over the A's in Philadelphia in 1952.

Art Ditmar of the Athletics defeated the Yankees 8–6 in the last game the franchise played in Philadelphia in 1954 before moving to Kansas City for 1955. Yankees catcher Yogi Berra played his only career game at third base, Mickey Mantle played shortstop.

Roger Maris tied Babe Ruth's major league record with his 60th home run of the 1961 season against Jack Fisher of the Baltimore Orioles at Yankee Stadium.

Bobby Murcer's 9th inning home run capped a come-from-behind win against the Baltimore Orioles, his third pinch-hit home run of the 1981 season.

The Yankees clinched their first American League East title since 1981 when they swept the Milwaukee Brewers in a 1996 doubleheader, 19–2 and 6–2.

David Cone set a major league record for the most years between 20-win seasons. The Yankees beat the Tampa Bay Devil Rays, 3–1, giving Cone his 20th victory in 1998. Cone was 20–3 in 1988 with the New York Mets.

27

Cleveland Indian second baseman Napoleon Lajoie collected his 3,000th major league hit against the Yankees in 1914 in a 5–3 New York loss.

Pitcher Bob Shawkey struck out 15 Philadelphia A's in a nine-inning game, establishing a Yankee record in 1919. That mark stood until Ron Guidry struck out 18 California Angels in a 1978 game.

Babe Ruth hit his 29th home run of the 1919 season, his first of the year in Washington. Ruth became the first player to hit a home run in every American League stadium in one season.

The Yankees beat the Cleveland Indians in 1921, 21–7 at the Polo Grounds.

Lou Gehrig hit his first major league home run off Bill Piercy of the Boston Red Sox in an 8–3 Yankee win at Fenway Park in 1923. Gehrig signed a June bonus of $1500 and had played for Hartford of the Eastern League prior to the call from New York.

Babe Ruth hit a 6th inning grand slam off Lefty Grove to raise his home run total to 57, with three games remaining in the 1927 season. Lou Gehrig hit his 46th home run in a 7–4 win over the Philadelphia A's at Yankee Stadium.

Lou Gehrig completed the 6th consecutive season in which he played in every game. Gehrig hit a home run, his 46th, to tie him for the 1931 American League title with Babe Ruth.

15 years to the day after he hit his

first major league home run, Lou Gehrig hit his 493rd and final home run off Washington Senators pitcher Dutch Leonard in 1938.

The Yankees, who had won eight straight games, lost to the Philadelphia A's 6–2 to eliminate them from the 1940 American League pennant race and keep them from the World Series for the first time since 1935.

Don Mattingly's 24-game hitting streak was ended by Detroit Tiger Jack Morris in a 1–0 Yankee loss in 10 innings in 1986.

The Yankees won seven straight games to end the 1998 season with a .704 winning percentage. They became the first team since the 1954 Indians (111–43) to play .700 baseball for the entire season.

Joe DiMaggio made his final public appearance at Yankee Stadium in 1998. Yankee owner George Steinbrenner presented him with replicas of nine World Series rings, which had been stolen from him over 30 years ago.

28

Highlanders Birdie Cree and Hal Chase became the first teammates in major league history to each steal four bases in a game in 1911. Cree finished third in the American League with 48 steals that season. Detroit Tiger Ty Cobb led with 83.

The Yankees recorded 30 base hits in a 1923 victory over the Boston Red Sox. Babe Ruth returned to Fenway Park with a 9–3 complete game win over the Boston Red Sox in the 1930 season finale. Lou Gehrig replaced Ruth in left field, ending 885 consecutive games at first base.

In the opening game of the 1932 World Series, Red Ruffing got the win and Lou Gehrig hit a home run against the Chicago Cubs in the 12–6 victory.

In 1933, Yankee Ben Chapman became the first centerfielder in major league history to record two outfield assists in one inning.

Allie Reynolds became the first Yankee to pitch two no-hitters, both in 1951, as he blanked the Boston Red Sox in the first game of a doubleheader at Yankee Stadium, 8–0.

The Yankees won Game 1 of the 1955 World Series, 6–5 over the Brooklyn Dodgers at Yankee Stadium behind a home run from Elston Howard and two home runs from Joe Collins, his only two hits in the Series.

Mickey Mantle's only hit against Boston was his 52nd home run of the 1956 season, off Bob Porterfield. The Yankees used 26 players and the Red Sox used 18 for a total of 44 players in the game, a new major league record.

Mickey Mantle's last official at bat in his final major league game came in 1968 with the Yankees.

29

Pitcher Edwin "Cy" Pieh spent his entire three-year pitching career with the Yankees, going 9–9 from 1913–15. He was born in 1886 in Wannikee, WI.

The Highlanders stole 15 bases and received 13 walks in a 16–12 victory over the St. Louis Browns in 1911. They set a major league record with six stolen bases in one inning.

Babe Ruth hit his 54th home run on the last day of the 1920 season, his first year as a Yankee, to set the major league record for home runs in a season with 25 more than his previous mark. The Yankees beat the Philadelphia A's 7–2.

Babe Ruth tied a major league record by hitting a grand slam home run in his second consecutive game, off Washington's Paul Hopkins, in a 15–4 victory over the Senators in 1927.

The Yankees with 17 and Detroit with 28 set a nine-inning record for the most base hits in a game by combining for 45 hits in a 1928 Tigers win, 19–10.

Earle Combs became the fifth player in Yankee history to score five runs in a game in 1930. He led the American League with 22 triples that season.

The Yankees took a two games to none lead over the Chicago Cubs in the 1932 World Series with a 5–2 win at the Stadium. Lefty Gomez got the win and Lou Gehrig had three hits.

After going hitless over the first four innings against Brooklyn Dodger Ralph Branca, the Yankees scored five 5th inning runs to win the opener of the 1947 World Series, 5–3.

The Yankees, while idle, clinched their second consecutive pennant under manager Casey Stengel when the Cleveland Indians defeated the Detroit Tigers, 12–2, to give New York the 1950 American League title.

The Yankees took a two games to none lead in the 1955 World Series with a 4–2 victory over the Brooklyn Dodgers at Yankee Stadium. Winning pitcher Tommy Byrne helped his team with a two-run single in the 4th inning.

Mickey Mantle was admitted to the hospital for a hip infection in 1961.

Casey Stengel died at the age of 85 in 1975 in Glendale, CA. The Hall of Fame member managed the Yankees to ten pennants and seven world championships 1949–60.

Yankee Don Mattingly set a major league record when he hit his sixth grand slam of the 1987 season. Mattingly connected off Boston Red Sox pitcher Bruce Hurst in a 6–0 Yankee victory.

New York defeated the Texas Rangers in Game 1 of the 1998 American League Division Series, 2–0 at Yankee Stadium.

30

The Yankees clinched their second consecutive American League pennant with a 3–1 victory over the Boston Red Sox in 1922 behind pitchers Waite Hoyt and Joe Bush.

Babe Ruth broke his own home run record by hitting his 60th of the 1927 season off Washington Senator pitcher Tom Zachary in the 8th inning of a 4–2 Yankee win.

Babe Ruth played in his last game as a Yankee in 1934.

In the opener of the 1936 World Series, Carl Hubbell scattered seven hits to lead the New York Giants over the Yankees 6–1. George Selkirk's solo home run was the only New York score.

In Game 1 of the 1942 World Series, the Yankees held on to defeat the St. Louis Cardinals, 7–4. Pitcher Red Ruffing allowed just one hit through 8⅓ innings before the Cardinals scored four in the 9th.

The World Series, sponsored by the Gillette Safety Razor Company and Ford Motor Company, debuted on television in 1947 in a 5–3 Yankee win over the Brooklyn Dodgers in Game 1.

The Yankees defeated the Brooklyn Dodgers in Game 1 of the 1953 World Series, 9–5. Hank Bauer tripled home three runs for New York. Joe Collins and Yogi Berra hit home runs.

In Game 3 of the 1955 World Series at Ebbets Field, the Brooklyn Dodgers defeated the Yankees, 8–3. Mickey Mantle hit a home run for New York.

Despite going 0 for 1 in the Yankees final game, Mickey Mantle won the 1956 American League Triple Crown with 52 home runs, 130 RBIs, and a .353 batting average.

The Yankees won their fourth career forfeit. After trailing 4–2 in the ninth with 2 outs, fans rushed the field in the final Washington Senators game in 1971. Umpires, unable to restore order, declared the Yankees winners by forfeit.

The final game was played in "old Yankee Stadium" in 1973, completing the 50th Anniversary season of the park. The Yankees shared Shea Stadium for two years before the new stadium re-opened in 1976. Ralph Houk resigned as manager.

Yankee pitcher Ed Figueroa became the first native Puerto Rican to win 20 games in the major leagues with a 7–0 shutout against Cleveland in 1978.

Yankee Don Mattingly won the American League batting title with a .343 average when he finished the 1984 season 4 for 5 in a 4–2 win over the Detroit Tigers. Mattingly edged teammate Dave Winfield (.340).

The New York Yankees and the Colorado Rockies became the first wild-card teams in the major league's reorganized 1995 playoff system.

The Yankees defeated the Cleveland Indians in Game 1 of the 1997 American League Division Series, 8–6. Tim Raines, Derek Jeter, and Paul O'Neill hit back-to-back-to-back home runs, a post-season first. Tino Martinez added a home run.

The Yankees won Game 2 of the 1998 American League Division Series against the Texas Rangers, 3–1. Shane Spencer and Scott Brosius hit home runs.

OCTOBER

1

Jack Chesbro pitched his final Highlander victory defeating Washington National pitcher Walter Johnson, 2–1 in 1908.

The Yankees clinched their first pennant in the first game of a doubleheader against the Philadelphia A's, 5–3. Babe Ruth came in to pitch in relief in the second game, blew the save but got the win in 11 innings in 1921.

The Yankees won the final game of the 1927 season, 4–3 over the Washington Senators, to raise their record to 110–44. Gehrig hit his 47th and final home run of the season on "Lou Gehrig Day," held at Yankee Stadium by United German Societies.

Babe Ruth played in his last World Series in 1932 and hit his final two post-season home runs. By report, he pointed to centerfield in the 5th inning then connected off Charlie Root to take Game 3 against the Cubs, 7–5 at Wrigley Field in Chicago.

Babe Ruth pitched a complete game 6–5 victory for the 1933 Yankees over the Boston Red Sox. It was Ruth's last appearance as a pitcher in the major leagues.

Red Ruffing pitched the Yankees to a 3–2 win over the Brooklyn Dodgers at Yankee Stadium in the opening game of the 1941 World Series. Joe Gordon hit a home run and an RBI single.

The Yankees rallied to tie the St. Louis Cardinals 3–3 in the top of the 8th inning of Game 2 of the 1942 World Series. Rookie Stan Musial singled in the bottom of the 9th to score Enos Slaughter for a 4–3 Cardinal win.

The St. Louis Browns had their first sellout in 20 years at Sportsman's Park, clinching the 1944 American League pennant on the final day of the season with a 5–2 win over the Yankees.

Allie Reynolds spaced nine hits in a 10–3 Yankee victory in Game 2 of the 1947 World Series. Tom Henrich hit a solo home run in the 5th inning to lead the Yankees to a 2–0 lead in the series.

Joe DiMaggio Day at Yankee Stadium in 1949 had Mel Allen as the master of ceremonies. DiMaggio donated his gifts to charity and stated, "I'd like to thank the Good Lord for making me a Yankee."

In Game 1 of the 1952 World Series, Brooklyn defeated the Yankees 4–2 at Ebbets Field. Reliever Joe Black, who started only two games the entire season, pitched the complete game win for the Dodgers. Gil McDougald hit a home run for New York.

Yankee pitcher Eddie Lopat beat Brooklyn Dodger Preacher Roe, 4–2, despite being out-hit by the Dodgers 9–5. New York took a two games to none lead in the 1953 World Series behind home runs from Billy Martin and Mickey Mantle.

The Brooklyn Dodgers tied the 1955 World Series with an 8–5 win in Game 4 over the Yankees. Duke Snider's three-run home run led the victory. Gil McDougald hit a home run for the Yankees.

In Game 1 of the 1958 World Series, the Milwaukee Braves defeated the Yankees behind Warren Spahn, 4–3 in 10 innings. Moose Skowron and Hank Bauer hit home runs for New York.

Coming out of retirement in 1961, former Yankee manager Casey Stengel agreed to manage New York's National League expansion team, the Mets.

Roger Maris established a new home run record, hitting his 61st of the 1961 season against Tracy Stallard in the 4th inning of a 1–0 win at Yankee Stadium. Maris' record was broken in 1998 by Mark McGwire.

Mrs. Babe Ruth was presented with home plate and Mrs. Lou Gehrig with first base from the old Yankee Stadium as two years of renovation were about to begin at the end of the 1973 season.

On the last day of the 1978 season, the Cleveland Indians beat New York 9–2 while Boston won their eighth straight to force a one-game playoff between the Yankees and the Boston Red Sox.

The 1980 Yankees established an American League regular season attendance record with 2,627,417 fans. The previous record was held by the 1948 Cleveland Indians.

Yankee closer Dave Righetti saved both games of a doubleheader to bring his major league record save total to 46 in 1986.

Yankee first baseman Don Mattingly established a team record by collecting his 232nd hit of the 1986 season, breaking the mark set by Earle Combs in 1927 with 231 hits.

Darryl Strawberry was diagnosed with colon cancer in 1998.

2

The Yankees closed the 1921 season by defeating the Boston Red Sox, 7–6. Babe Ruth hit his 59th home run of the season off Curt Fullerton.

Game 1 of the 1926 World Series was a 2–1 Yankee win over the St. Louis Cardinals. Herb Pennock got the win when Lou Gehrig drove in the deciding run with a 6th inning single.

Tony Lazzeri hit two home runs

and Earle Combs added one as the Yankees completed a 1932 World Series sweep of the Chicago Cubs with a 13–6 win at Wrigley Field.

Bill Dickey and Tony Lazzeri drove in five runs apiece to lead the Yankees to an 18–4 win over the New York Giants in Game 2 of the 1936 World Series. Lazzeri hit the first World Series grand slam home run since 1920.

Brooklyn Dodger ace Whit Wyatt defeated the Yankees, 3–2, to even the 1941 World Series at one game each.

The St. Louis Cardinals took a two games to one World Series lead in 1942 when Ernie White shutout the Yankees on six hits, 2–0. Arguments during Game 3 resulted in $200 fines for Joe Gordon and Frank Crosetti.

The Yankees swept their 14th doubleheader of the season, an American League record, with 5–1 and 7–6 victories over the St. Louis Browns in 1943. Bud Metheny hit the 100th home run of the season for the Yankees in the opener.

Yogi Berra and Joe DiMaggio hit home runs but the Yankees lost Game 3 of the 1947 World Series to the Brooklyn Dodgers, 9–8. Berra's home run was the first pinch-hit home run in World Series history.

The Yankees and Boston Red Sox entered the last day of the 1949 season tied. An estimated crowd of 70,000 at Yankee Stadium came to see the finale, a 5–3 New York win to clinch the American League pennant.

The Yankees tied the 1952 World Series behind Vic Raschi's nine-strikeout, three-hit win over the Brooklyn Dodgers, 7–1 in Game 2.

Dodger Carl Erskine established a World Series strikeout record with 14, striking out Mickey Mantle and Joe Collins four times each. Roy Campanella broke a tie in Game 3 of the 1953 Series with a solo home run in the 8th inning for a 3–2 Brooklyn win.

Brooklyn Dodger Roger Craig pitched six innings for the 5–3 win in Game 5 of the 1955 World Series to put them one win away from the title. Two home runs by Duke Snider led the win over the Yankees, who had home runs by Yogi Berra and Bob Cerv.

The Yankees defeated the Milwaukee Braves, and pitcher Warren Spahn, in Game 1 of the 1957 World Series, 3–1 at Yankee Stadium. Whitey Ford pitched the complete game, allowing just five hits.

The Milwaukee Braves scored seven runs in the 1st inning and defeated the Yankees, 13–5, in Game 2 of the 1958 World Series. Lew Burdette defeated New York for the fourth consecutive time and hit a three-run home run.

In the 1963 World Series opener, Sandy Koufax struck out the first five batters and finished with 15, a Series record. John Roseboro hit a three-run home run as the Los Angeles Dodgers won 5–2 at Yankee Stadium. Tom Tresh hit a home run for New York.

Billy Martin was named manager of the Detroit Tigers in 1970.

In a one-game playoff to decide the American League East at Fenway Park, the Yankees defeated the Boston Red Sox 5–4. Bucky Dent hit a decisive three-run home run off pitcher Mike Torrez. The Yankees once trailed by 14 games in the summer of 1978.

On the last day of the 1985 season, Yankee knuckleballer Phil Niekro notched his 300th career victory, blanking the Toronto Blue Jays, 8–0. Niekro became the oldest pitcher in major league history to throw a shutout, at age 46.

The Yankees won Game 2 of the 1996 American League Division Series with an unearned run in the 11th inning for a 5–4 win over the Texas Rangers. Cecil Fielder hit a home run for New York.

The Yankees swept the Texas Rangers in the 1998 American League Division Series with a 4–0 win in Game 3. Shane Spencer and Paul O'Neill hit home runs before a long rain delay due to violent storms in Arlington.

3

The St. Louis Cardinals won Game 2 of the 1926 World Series as Grover Cleveland Alexander defeated Urban Shocker, 6–2.

Lou Gehrig hit a home run to lead the Yankees to a 2–1 win in Game 3 of the 1936 World Series. The Yankees lost the first two games but rebounded to win the final four games over the New York Giants.

Brooklyn Dodger pinch-hitter Cookie Lavagetto doubled in two runs in the bottom of the 9th inning to break up a no-hitter by Yankee Floyd Bevens in a dramatic Game 4

win in the 1947 World Series, 3–2, over the Yankees at Ebbets Field.

Dave Winfield was born in 1951 in St. Paul, MN. Winfield started his career with the San Diego Padres, but played for the Yankees (1981–90) making the all-star team nine times. Winfield hit two home runs in the 1992 ALCS with the Toronto Blue Jays.

Brooklyn pitcher Preacher Roe won Game 3 of the 1952 World Series at Yankee Stadium, 5–3. Yogi Berra, who had hit a home run, allowed two Dodger runs to score in the 9th inning on a passed ball.

The Yankees defeated the Dodgers in Game 6 of the 1955 World Series with five runs in the 1st inning off Brooklyn pitcher Karl Spooner. Led by "Moose" Skowron's home run, Whitey Ford recorded the complete game win, 5–1, to force Game 7.

Sal Maglie of the Brooklyn Dodgers defeated the Yankees 6–3 in the opening game of the 1956 World Series. Billy Martin hit a home run for New York and Whitey Ford took the loss.

In Game 2 of the 1957 World Series, Lew Burdette won the first of three decisions over the Yankees to tie the Series at one game apiece. Bobby Shantz took the 4–2 loss. Hank Bauer hit a home run for the Yankees.

The Yankees entered the World Series with a 15-game winning streak after Dale Long's 9th inning home run gave New York an American League record 193 home runs and paced an 8–7 win over the Boston Red Sox in the final game of the 1960 regular season.

In Game 2 of the 1963 World Series, Johnny Podres scattered seven hits and Tommy Davis tied a World Series record with two triples in the Los Angeles Dodgers' 4–1 win over Al Downing. Moose Skowron accounted for the only Yankee run with a home run.

The Yankees clinched their fifth straight pennant, and 29th in club history, by defeating the Cleveland Indians, 8–3 in 1964.

Tony Kubek became the only Yankee to hit a home run in final major league at-bat in 1965. Whitey Ford notched his 232nd career victory to become the winningest pitcher in Yankee history.

The Yankees won Game 1 of the 1978 American League Championship Series with a 7–1 win over the Kansas City Royals. Reggie Jackson hit a home run. New York had 16 hits.

The Yankees won Game 1 of the 1995 American League Division Series against the Mariners, 9–6. Wade Boggs and Reuben Sierra hit home runs for New York. Ken Griffey hit two for Seattle.

Darryl Strawberry had surgery in 1998 to remove a tumor that nearly obstructed his intestine.

In Game 1 of the 2000 American League Division Series, the Yankees lost to the Oakland A's 5–3.

4

In Game 1 of the 1922 World Series, Bullet Joe Bush pitched a shutout into the 8th inning before the New York Giants scored three runs to win, 3–2. Babe Ruth drove in the first run of the Series, for the second year in a row, with a single in the 6th.

Babe Ruth hit a single, double and scored twice, Bob Meusel hit a home run and Lou Gehrig had two hits and two RBIs in Game 1 of the 1928 World Series. Winner Waite Hoyt (23–7) allowed the St. Louis Cardinals only three hits in the 4–1 win.

The Yankees set another attendance record at Yankee Stadium in a Game 4, 5–2 victory over the New York Giants in the 1936 World Series. Lou Gehrig hit a home run to lead the Yankee to a three games to one Series lead before a reported 66,669 fans.

In Game 1 of the 1939 World Series, Yankee Red Ruffing and Cincinnati Reds Paul Derringer engaged in a pitching duel. Yankee catcher Bill Dickey singled home the winning run in the bottom of the 9th inning for a 2–1 win at the Stadium.

In Game 3 of the 1941 World Series, Yankee pitcher Marius Russo broke Brooklyn Dodger pitcher Fred Fitzsimmons' knee with a line drive. The Yankees scored two 8th-inning runs off Hugh Casey to win, 2–1, and take the Series lead, two games to one.

The St. Louis Cardinals scored six runs in the 4th inning of Game 4 of the 1942 World Series. The Yankees rallied to tie the game with five runs in the 6th, but St. Louis scored three more to win, 9–6, behind 22 hits. Charlie Keller hit a home run.

Joe DiMaggio's home run led the Yankees to a 2–1 win in Game 5 of the 1947 World Series. Spec Shea recorded the win on the mound allowing only one run and four hits against the Brooklyn Dodgers.

Reliever Jim Konstanty of the Philadelphia Phillies started and lost Game 1 of the 1950 World Series to Yankee Vic Raschi, 1–0. Bobby Brown doubled and scored on a sacrifice fly for the only run.

In the opening game of the 1951 World Series, Monte Irvin stole home in the 1st inning and added four hits in the New York Giants 5–1 win. Allie Reynolds took the loss for the Yankees at the Stadium.

The Yankees evened the 1952 World Series behind Allie Reynolds, 2–0, in Game 4. First baseman Johnny Mize had a home run, single, double, and walk in four plate appearances against the Brooklyn Dodgers.

In Game 5 of the 1953 World Series, Mickey Mantle's grand slam home run off Russ Meyer helped the Yankees to an 11–7 win. They took a three games to two lead back to Yankee Stadium. Gene Woodling, Billy Martin, and Gil McDougald hit home runs.

Dodger outfielder Sandy Amoros doubled up Yankee Gil McDougald after making an outstanding catch of Yogi Berra's drive to help Brooklyn win their first World Series Championship in 1955. Johnny Podres shutout the Yankees, 2–0, in Game 7.

Yankees Don Larsen and Ryne Duren combined for a 4–0 shutout over the Milwaukee Braves in Game 3 of the 1958 World Series. Outfielder Hank Bauer drove in all of New York's runs, adding a decisive 7th-inning, two-run home run.

In Game 1 of the 1961 World Series, Yankee Whitey Ford extended his record scoreless inning streak in a 2–0 win in the opener against the Cincinnati Reds. Elston Howard and Moose Skowron hit home runs.

Willie Mays scored on a surprise bunt by Jose Pagan in Game 1 of the 1962 World Series against the San Francisco Giants to end Whitey Ford's consecutive scoreless inning streak at 33⅔ innings. Clete Boyer's 7th inning home run helped Whitey Ford notch his final Series victory as the Yankees defeated the San Francisco Giants, 6–2.

Dave Righetti saved both games in a doubleheader sweep of the Boston Red Sox to reach 46 saves in 1986. This set the major league record for saves in a season, previously shared by Bruce Sutter and Dan Quisenberry with 45.

Jim Leyritz hit a two-run home run in the 15th inning to lead the Yankees to victory in Game 2 of the 1995 American League Division Playoff Series against the Seattle Mariners. The win was the longest game in playoff history (5:13).

The Yankees rallied for two runs in the 9th inning to win Game 3 of the 1996 American League Division Series over Texas. Bernie Williams hit a home run and robbed Ranger Rusty Grier of a home run in centerfield to lead the 3–1 victory.

The Yankees won Game 3 of the 1997 American League Division Series, 6–1 over the Cleveland Indians at Jacobs Field. Paul O'Neill hit a grand slam home run off Chad Ogea. David Wells pitched the complete game victory, walking none and striking out one.

The Yankees evened the 2000 American League Division Series with the Oakland A's behind a 4–0 shutout from Andy Pettitte and Mariano Rivera.

5

The Highlanders played their final game after ten seasons at Hilltopper Park with an 8–6 win over the Washington Senators in 1912. The New York "Yankees" began the 1913 season using the Polo Grounds as their home field.

The first radio coverage of the World Series by a wireless station was set up in 1921 at the Electrical Show at the 71st Regiment Armory in New York City, and by station WJZ in Newark, NJ in the 3–0 Yankees win over the New York Giants.

In Game 1 of the 1921 World Series, Yankee Carl Mays pitched a two-hit shutout, 3–0, over the New York Giants. It was the Yankees' first World Series game, played at the Polo Grounds.

The Yankees' only post-season tie was in Game 2 of the 1922 World Series against the New York Giants, 3–3. A near-riot erupted when umpires George Hildebrand and Bill Klem called the game, due to darkness, after ten innings.

In Game 3 of the 1926 World Series, Jesse Haines shut out the Yankees on five hits for a 4–0 St. Louis Cardinal win. Haines hit a two-run home run to pace St. Louis to a two games to one lead.

Waite Hoyt (22–7) opened the 1927 World Series for the Yankees. Two walks and two Pittsburgh Pirate errors gave New York three runs in the 3rd inning and they held on for a 5–4 win.

In Game 2 of the 1928 World Series Lou Gehrig hit a first inning three-run home run to lead the Yankees to a 9–3 victory over the St. Louis Cardinals and Grover Alexander. George Pipgras recorded the complete game win for New York.

In Game 5 of the 1936 World Series, pinch runner Yankee Bob Seeds was caught stealing second base in the 10th inning in his World Series debut to give the series to the New York Giants.

In Game 1 of the 1938 World Series at Wrigley Field in Chicago, Red Ruffing scattered nine hits and the Yankees managed to scratch out three runs for a 3–1 win in the opener.

Babe Dahlgren, filling in for non-playing captain Lou Gehrig, hit a home run and a double to lead the Yankees to a 4–0 win in Game 2 of the 1939 World Series over the Cincinnati Reds behind Monte Pearson's two-hit, shutout pitching.

Mickey Owens' passed ball in the bottom of 9th with two outs and two strikes in Game 4 of the 1941 World Series turned a 4–3 Brooklyn Dodger lead into an improbable 7–4 Yankee win and a three games to one lead in the Series.

Rookie pitcher Johnny Beazley and the St. Louis Cardinals stunned baseball by beating the favored Yankees, 4–2 to win the 1942 World

Series in five games. Phil Rizzuto hit a home run for New York in their first Series defeat in 16 years.

Game 1 of the 1943 World Series was won by the Yankees, 4–2 over the St. Louis Cardinals. 1943 MVP Spud Chandler recorded the complete game victory with the help of a Joe Gordon home run.

The Brooklyn Dodgers forced a 7th game in the 1947 World Series with a victory in Game 6 over the Yankees. Outfielder Al Gionfriddo, in his last major league game, robbed Joe DiMaggio of a home run in the bottom of the 6th to preserve the 8–6 win.

Tommy Henrich broke up a scoreless duel with a home run in the bottom of the 9th inning to give the Yankees and Allie Reynolds the 1–0 victory over the Brooklyn Dodgers and Don Newcombe in the first game of the 1949 World Series.

The Yankees won Game 2 of the 1950 World Series against the Philadelphia Phillies, 2–1. Joe DiMaggio led of the top of the 10th with a home run to win it for New York. Allie Reynolds recorded the complete game win.

The Yankees won Game 2 of the 1951 World Series on Joe Collins home run and five-hit pitching by Eddie Lopat, 3–1, to even the Series at one game each with the New York Giants.

Brooklyn won Game 5 of the 1952 World Series in the 11th inning when Duke Snider doubled home Billy Cox. Carl Erskine pitched the complete game victory, which sent the Series back to Ebbets Field with a three games to two Dodger lead.

The Yankees won their fifth consecutive World Series in dramatic fashion. Billy Martin's 12th hit of the Series, in the bottom of the 9th inning, defeated the Brooklyn Dodgers in Game 6 of the 1953 World Series, 4–3.

Marilyn Monroe, using her legal name Norma Jeane DiMaggio, officially filed for divorce from Joseph Paul DiMaggio in Superior Court of the state of California in 1954, charging "grievous mental suffering and anguish."

Yogi Berra became the fourth Yankee to hit a World Series grand slam home run in a Game 2, 13–8, loss to Brooklyn in 1956. New York used seven pitchers in the game. The Yankees trailed the Dodgers two games to none.

The Yankees, behind two home runs from Tony Kubek and one from Mickey Mantle, won Game 3 of the 1957 World Series over the Braves, 12–3. Hank Aaron hit a home run for Milwaukee.

Bill Mazeroski hit a two-run home run off Yankee Jim Coates in the 5th inning of a 6–4 Pirate win in Game 1 of the 1960 World Series. It was Pittsburgh's first World Series victory since 1925. Roger Maris and Elston Howard hit home runs for New York.

Cincinnati won Game 2 of the 1961 World Series with a 6–2 win over New York at Yankee Stadium. Yogi Berra hit a home run for the Yankees. Joey Jay pitched a four-hit complete game and Gordy Coleman hit a home run for the Reds.

The Giants evened the 1962 World Series with a 2–0 win over the Yankees at Candlestick Park in Game 2. Jack Sanford pitched the three-hit complete game for San Francisco.

Los Angeles came within one game of sweeping the 1963 World Series over New York with a 1–0 victory in Game 3. The Dodgers scored a first inning run while Don Drysdale allowed just three Yankee singles and struck out nine for the complete game.

The Yankees finished the 1980 season with an American League attendance record (2,627,417 fans), breaking the previous mark set by the 1948 Cleveland Indians.

The Yankees defeated the Texas Rangers 6–4 in the 1996 American League Division Series, three games to one. Bernie Williams hit a solo home run from each side of the plate, the first ever to achieve the feat in post-season play, to lead the win in Game 4.

6

In Game 2 of the 1921 World Series, Yankee Waite Hoyt allowed only two singles while New York Giant Art Nehf allowed just three, setting the record for the fewest combined hits in a World Series game in a Yankee victory, 3–0.

Surprise starter Jack Scott pitched a four-hitter after Hugh McQuillan warmed up for the Giants. The Yankees hit 18 grounders while Frank Frisch's two RBIs led the 3–0 win in Game 3 of the 1922 Series. The Giants led two games to none (one tie).

Babe Ruth hit three home runs in

Game 4 of the 1926 World Series against the Cardinals in St. Louis to lead the Yankees to a 10–5 win and tie the Series at two games each.

Surprise starter George Pipgras gave the Yankees a 6–2 win in Game 2 of the 1927 World Series against the Pittsburgh Pirates. Mark Koenig had three hits to give New York to a two games to none Series lead.

The Yankees ended the 1936 World Series with a 13–5 victory over the New York Giants. Lefty Gomez won his second game of the Series. The Yankees outscored the Giants 43–23 in six games. Jake Powell hit a home run for the Yankees.

The New York Giants held a 1–0 lead over Lefty Gomez in Game 1 of the 1937 World Series until the Yankees scored seven runs in the 6th inning on five singles, three walks, and two errors. Tony Lazzeri hit a home run in the 8th inning for an 8–1 win.

Lefty Gomez set a record with his sixth career Series victory without a loss in a 6–3 Yankee win in Game 2 of the 1938 World Series against the Chicago Cubs. The Yankees returned to the Stadium with a two games to none lead.

The Yankees captured the final game of the 1941 World Series with a 3–1 victory over the Brooklyn Dodgers to take the series four games to one. Tommy Henrich hit a home run for New York.

Mort Cooper defeated the Yankees 4–3 in Game 2 of the 1943 World Series, stirring memories of 1942 when the Yankees lost four straight games after winning the opener. Marty

Marion and Ray Sanders hit home runs for the St. Louis Cardinals.

The Yankees defeated Brooklyn 5–2 to win the 1947 World Series in seven games. Joe Page recorded the win in relief. Dodger heroes Bill Bevens, Al Gionfriddo, and Cookie Lavagetto all played their final major league game.

Larry MacPhail resigned as general manager of the Yankees after the final game of the 1947 World Series. Co-owners Dan Topping and Del Webb later bought out MacPhail's one-third interest in the club for $2 million and George Weiss became general manager.

Brooklyn Dodger Preacher Roe led his team to a 1–0 shutout over the Yankees in Game 2 of the 1949 World Series. Roe allowed just six hits and Jackie Robinson scored the winning run.

The Yankees moved within one game of a sweep in Game 3 of the 1950 World Series with a 3–2 win over the Philadelphia Phillies. Gene Woodling, Phil Rizzuto, and Jerry Coleman hit singles to produce the winning run.

In Game 3 of the 1951 World Series, the New York Giants defeated the Yankees 6–2. Gene Woodling hit a home run for the Yankees, who trailed two games to one.

The Yankees forced a 7th and deciding game of the 1952 World Series with a 3–2 win over the Brooklyn Dodgers at Ebbets Field in Game 6. Yogi Berra and Mickey Mantle hit home runs for New York.

Marilyn Monroe publicly announced her separation from Yankee Joe DiMaggio in 1954.

Whitey Ford pitched a complete game victory over the Brooklyn Dodgers in Game 3 of the 1956 World Series behind home runs by Billy Martin and 40-year-old Enos Slaughter, 8–3.

Milwaukee tied the 1957 World Series with a 3–1 victory over the Yankees in Game 4. Warren Spahn pitched the complete game behind home runs by Hank Aaron, Frank Torre, and Eddie Matthews. Elston Howard hit a home run for New York.

The Yankees scored 16 runs on 19 hits in their 16–3 defeat of Pittsburgh in Game 2 of the 1960 World Series at Forbes Field. Mickey Mantle hit two home runs for New York. The Pirates used six pitchers.

The 1963 Los Angeles Dodgers completed a sweep of the Yankees. Sandy Koufax won his second game of the World Series, 2–1. Joe Pepitone's error led to the decisive run in the 7th inning. Whitey Ford took the loss, Mickey Mantle hit a home run.

The Yankees won Game 2 of the 1977 American League Championship Series, 6–2. Cliff Johnson hit a home run and Ron Guidry allowed only three Kansas City Royals hits in the complete game victory.

Despite three solo home runs by Royal George Brett, Yankee ace Catfish Hunter led the Yankees to a 6–5 win over Kansas City in Game 3 of the 1978 American League Championship Series.

Yankee Phil Niekro became the 18th pitcher in major-league history to win 300 career games, on the final day of the 1985 season against the

Toronto Blue Jays, 8–0. At age 46, he became the oldest modern major league pitcher to throw a shutout.

David Cone set a National League record by striking out 19 batters in a nine-inning game in 1991 while pitching for the New York Mets.

The Cleveland Indians completed a thrilling victory over the Yankees with a 4–3 win at Jacobs Field in Game 5 of the 1997 American League Division Series.

The Yankees won Game 1 of the 1998 American League Championship Series with a 7–2 win over the Cleveland Indians. Jorge Posada hit a home run for New York and David Wells pitched eight strong innings.

The Yankees won Game 3 of the 2000 American League Division Series, 4–2, to take a two games to one lead over the Oakland A's.

7

Pitcher Jack Chesbro defeated the Boston Pilgrims 3–2 to win his 41st game of the season, a modern record, as the Highlanders took a ½ game lead over Boston in 1904.

The New York Giants recorded 20 hits in a 13–5 win over the Yankees in Game 3 of the 1921 Series. The Yankees maintained a Series lead of two games to one.

Judge Landis insisted and Game 4 of the 1922 World Series was played despite heavy rain. A four-run 4th inning off Carl Mays was enough to lead the New York Giants to a 4–3 win over the Yankees to give the Giants a two games to one Series lead.

In 1923, Yankee shortstop Everett Scott ran his career consecutive games played streak to 1,138, establishing the major league record.

In Game 5 of the 1926 World Series, Mark Koenig singled, took second on a wild pitch, third on a sacrifice, and scored on Tony Lazzeri's long fly for a 3–2 win in 10 innings. The Yankees took a three games to two Series lead over the St. Louis Cardinals.

Herb Pennock took a perfect game into the 8th inning of Game 3 of the 1927 World Series before Pirate Pie Traynor hit a one-out single. Pennock finished a three-hit, 8–1 win over Pittsburgh to put the Yankees one game away from a sweep.

In Game 3 of the 1928 World Series in St. Louis, Lou Gehrig led off the 2nd inning with a home run and the Yankees completed a 7–3 win to put them one win away from a sweep of the Cardinals.

The Yankees defeated the New York Giants for the second straight day by an identical 8–1 score in Game 2 of the 1937 World Series. Red Ruffing struck out eight and drove in three runs with two hits.

In Game 3 of the 1939 World Series, at Crosley Field in Cincinnati, Bump Hadley got the win in relief of Lefty Gomez, 7–3 over the Reds. Outfielder Charlie "King Kong" Keller hit two home runs to put the Yankees one win away from the Series sweep.

The Yankees took a two games to one lead in the 1943 World Series with a 6–2 win in Game 3. Four St. Louis Cardinal errors helped New York to victory.

The Yankees won Game 3 of the 1949 World Series with three runs in the top of the 9th inning for a 4–3 win over the Brooklyn Dodgers. Johnny Mize's pinch-hit single drove in two runs. Joe Page got the win in relief of Tommy Byrne.

The Yankees completed a World Series sweep of the 1950 Philadelphia Phillies "Whiz Kids" with a 5–2 win at Yankee Stadium behind Yogi Berra's home run. Whitey Ford won his first World Series game.

Mickey Mantle hit his first post-season home run and Billy Martin lunged to snag Jackie Robinson's drive for the final out of the 1952 World Series, won by the Yankees in seven games over the Brooklyn Dodgers.

In Game 4 of the 1956 World Series, Tom Sturdivant held the Brooklyn Dodgers to six hits in a 6–2 Yankee win at the Stadium to tie the Series at two games each. Mickey Mantle and Hank Bauer added home runs.

Lew Burdette won his second game of the 1957 World Series with a 1–0 shutout over the Yankees in Game 5 to give the Milwaukee Braves a three games to two Series lead.

John Blanchard hit a pinch-hit home run to tie the game in the 8th and Roger Maris hit a home run in the 9th to pace a 3–2 Yankee victory New York in Game 3 of the 1961 World Series. The Cincinnati Reds trailed the Yankees two games to one.

At Yankee Stadium in Game 3 of the 1962 World Series, Yankee Bill Stafford and Giant Billy Pierce pitched six shutout innings. Ed Bailey's 9th-inning home run ended Stafford's shutout, but the Giants managed only four hits and the Yankees won, 3–2.

Whitey Ford struggled in the opener of the 1964 World Series, won by the St. Louis Cardinals 9–5 behind a Mike Shannon home run in the 6th inning. Ray Sadecki and Barney Schultz combined for the win. Tom Tresh hit a home run for the Yankees.

The Yankees won their third straight American League Championship in 1978, defeating the Kansas City Royals behind a 6th inning home run by Roy White in Game 4. Graig Nettles hit a home run.

In Game 1 of the only Eastern Division Championship Series in 1981, the Yankees defeated the Milwaukee Brewers, 5–3. Oscar Gamble hit a home run. The Series came about after a player strike had the first and second half division winners play each other.

Dallas Green was named Yankee manager in 1988 following the firing of Lou Piniella.

The Oakland A's remained alive in the 2000 American League Division Series with an 11–1 victory over the Yankees to tie the series at two games apiece.

8

For a second straight year, the entire 1922 World Series was played at the Polo Grounds with the Giants taking the title four games to none (one tie) with a 5–3 win in Game 5 over the Yankees.

The "Murderer's Row" Yankees completed a 1927 World Series sweep of the Pittsburgh Pirates with a 4–3 win. Johnny Miljus threw two wild pitches, the second scored Earle Combs with the winning run in the bottom of the 9th.

In Game 3 of the 1937 World Series, the Yankees took a three games to none lead with a 5–1 win over the New York Giants at the Polo Grounds. Monte Pearson started and got the win for the Yankees.

In Game 3 of the 1938 World Series, the Yankees came one win away from a Series sweep of the Chicago Cubs with a 5–2 win. Rookie Joe Gordon hit a home run to tie the game in the 5th and Bill Dickey added a home run in the 8th.

The Yankees swept the Cincinnati Reds in the 1939 World Series, scoring three runs in the top of the 10th inning in Game 4 for the 7–4 victory. Charlie Keller and Bill Dickey hit home runs for the Yankees.

The Yankees moved one win away from the championship with a 6–4 win in Game 4 of the 1949 World Series. Ed Lopat recorded the win for the Yankees.

The Yankees evened the 1951 World Series with a 6–2 win in Game 4. Allie Reynolds pitched the complete game win and Joe DiMaggio hit a home run.

Don Larsen pitched the only no-hitter, a perfect game, in World Series history, defeating the Brooklyn Dodgers, 2–0 in Game 5 of the 1956 Series. Mickey Mantle hit a home run for the Yankees to give them a three games to two lead.

The Yankees forced Game 7 of the 1958 World Series against the Milwaukee Braves when Hank Bauer hit his fourth home run of the Series to lead New York to a 4–3, 10th inning win in Game 6.

The Yankees defeated the Pittsburgh Pirates, 10–0 in Game 3 of the 1960 World Series. Bobby Richardson drove in a World Series record six runs with a grand slam and a single. Mickey Mantle added a home run. Whitey Ford pitched the four-hit shutout.

Whitey Ford broke Babe Ruth's record of 29⅔ consecutive World Series scoreless innings in Game 4 of 1961 Series with a 7–0 victory over the Cincinnati Reds to take a three games to one lead. Ford left with an ankle injury in the 6th inning.

San Francisco evened the 1962 World Series at two games each with a 7–3 win over the Yankees. Giant Chuck Hiller hit a grand slam to break a tie in the 7th inning. Tom Haller added a home run.

The Yankees defeated the St. Louis Cardinals 8–3 in Game 2 of the 1964 World Series. Phil Linz hit a home run for New York and Mel Stottlemyre pitched the complete game win.

The Yankees won Game 4 of the 1977 American League Championship Series against the Kansas City Royals to force a deciding Game 5. Sparky Lyle got the win in relief of Ed Figueroa and Dick Tidrow.

The Yankees won Game 2 of the 1981 American League East Division Playoff Series against the Milwaukee Brewers, 3–0, behind Dave Righetti.

Lou Piniella and Reggie Jackson hit home runs.

9

Infielder Joseph Sewell, born in 1898 in Titus, AL, played the final three years of a 14-year career with the Yankees compiling a career .312 average.

In Game 4 of the 1921 World Series, Babe Ruth hit his first career World Series home run in the 9th inning but the New York Giants tied the Series at two apiece with a 4–2 win over the Yankees.

St. Louis pitcher Grover Cleveland Alexander allowed eight scattered Yankee hits in Game 6 of the 1926 World Series. Cardinal hitting led a 10–2 victory over the Yankees to force a deciding Game 7.

Babe Ruth hit three home runs as the Yankees completed their second consecutive sweep with a 7–3 victory over the Cardinals in St. Louis in the 1928 World Series. Cedric Durst and Lou Gehrig added home runs.

The New York Giants avoided a sweep in the 1937 World Series with a 7–3 win in Game 4. Carl Hubbell recorded the complete game win. Lou Gehrig hit a home run for the Yankees.

The Yankees completed a sweep of the 1938 World Series with an 8–3 victory over the Chicago Cubs at Yankee Stadium. Red Ruffing won his second game of the Series. Tommy Henrich hit a home run for the Yankees.

Outfielder/first baseman Joe Pepi- tone was born in Brooklyn, NY in 1940. Pepitone, a colorful figure, played for the Yankees 1962–69, recording 28 home runs and 100 RBIs in 1964. He hit a grand slam home run in Game 6 of the 1964 World Series.

The Yankees defeated the Brooklyn Dodgers 10–6 to win the 1949 World Series in five games. Bobby Brown batted .500 in the Series and drove in five runs. For the first time, a portion of a Series game was played under the lights at Ebbets Field.

Gil McDougald's grand slam home run in Game 5 of the 1951 World Series led the Yankees to a 13–1 victory over the New York Giants. Phil Rizzuto hit a home run and drove in three runs.

The Brooklyn Dodgers bounced back in Game 6 of the 1956 World Series, one game after Don Larsen's perfect game. Clem Labine pitched a 1–0 victory over the Yankees in ten innings to force a seventh and deciding game.

Hank Bauer hit a home run off the foul pole to even the 1957 World Series at three games apiece against the Milwaukee Braves with a 3–2 win. Bob Turley pitched a four-hitter for the win. Frank Torre (Joe's brother) hit a home run for the Braves.

The Yankees appeared in nine and won seven of the past World Series. In 1958, they came back to win the final two games against the Milwaukee Braves. Moose Skowron's three-run home run led a four-run 8th inning to clinch the victory in Game 7.

The Pittsburgh Pirates came back to capture Game 4 of the 1960 World

Series, 3–2, at Yankee Stadium to tie the Series at two games each. Moose Skowron hit a home run for New York.

The Yankees won Game 5 of the 1961 World Series with a 13–5 win over the Cincinnati Reds. Yankee reserve outfielder Hector Lopez hit a triple and home run to clinch the championship. Johnny Blanchard added a home run.

In the Yankees first American League Championship game, they defeated the 1976 Kansas City Royals, 4–1 on a complete game in Game 1 by Catfish Hunter.

The Yankees rallied for three runs in the 9th inning to defeat the Kansas City Royals, 5–3, to clinch the 1977 American League Championship Series in the fifth and deciding game for their 31st pennant. Sparky Lyle got the win.

Bernie Williams led off the bottom of the 11th inning with a home run to power the Yankees over the Baltimore Orioles 5–4 in 1996. Derek Jeter hit a disputed home run that was caught by a young fan leaning over Tony Tarasco's glove in right field.

The Yankees declined to pick up the 1998 contract option on outfielder Tim Raines in 1997.

Doctors announced in 1998 that Darryl Strawberry would undergo chemotherapy after it was reported cancer had spread to a lymph node.

The Yankees won the decisive fifth game of the 2000 American League Division Series with a 7–5 victory over the Oakland A's.

10

The Highlanders were two games out of first place with two games remaining, a season-ending double-header against the Boston Pilgrims. Jack Chesbro, a 41-game winner for New York, lost the first game to deny them the 1904 pennant.

The New York Giants managed one unearned run in the 1st off Waite Hoyt. Babe Ruth surprised the infield with a perfect bunt and scored on a double by Bob Meusel in a 3–1 Yankee win in Game 5 of the 1921 World Series to take a three games to two lead.

New York Giants outfielder Casey Stengel hit an inside-the-park home run off Joe Bush in the 9th inning of Game 1 of the 1923 World Series, the first Series game played at Yankee Stadium. The Giants beat the Yankees 1–0.

In Game 7 of the 1926 World Series. Babe Ruth walked with two out in the bottom of the 9th inning and was caught stealing second base to end the Series. The Yankees lost the game 3–2 and the Series 4–3 to the St. Louis Cardinals.

The Yankees announced in 1930 that they signed Joe McCarthy to manage the team for four years. McCarthy led New York to eight pennants and seven World Series Championships before resigning in 1946. He had managed the Chicago Cubs 1926–30.

The Yankees won Game 5 of the 1937 World Series, 4–2. Joe DiMaggio's home run led to the championship, four games to one, over the

New York Giants. Lefty Gomez got the win on the mound.

Used sparingly during the regular season, pitcher Marius Russo led the Yankees to a 2–1 win in Game 4 of the 1943 World Series over the St. Louis Cardinals to take a three games to one lead.

Hank Bauer hit a bases-loaded triple in Game 6 of the 1951 World Series to lead the Yankees to a 4–3 win over the New York Giants for their third straight championship. In his final Yankee at-bat, Joe DiMaggio hit a double in his 51st World Series game.

The Yankees won Game 7 of the 1956 World Series over the Brooklyn Dodgers, 9–0. Bill "Moose" Skowron hit a grand slam and Yogi Berra added two home runs. Johnny Kucks got the shutout win, allowing just three hits.

Warren Spahn had the flu and Lew Burdette, pitching on two days' rest, won his third complete game and second shutout in Game 7 of the 1957 World Series to lead the Milwaukee Braves to the championship over the Yankees. Yogi Berra appeared in his 53rd World Series game, setting a record. It was the first time in eight years that a New York team had not won the World Series.

Pittsburgh Pirate Bill Mazeroski hit a two-run double and Roy Face relieved Harvey Haddox with hitless pitching to preserve a 5–2 win over the Yankees in Game 5 of the 1960 World Series. Roger Maris hit his second home run of the Series.

Following a rainout, Tom Tresh hit a three-run home run in the 8th inning off San Francisco's Jack Sanford to give the Yankees a 5–3 win in Game 5 of the 1962 World Series against the Giants, giving New York a three games to two lead.

Yankee Jim Bouton battled St. Louis Cardinal Curt Simmons to a 1–1 tie after eight innings in Game 3 of the 1964 World Series. Mickey Mantle's 16th career Series home run broke Babe Ruth's record on the first pitch in the bottom of 9th for a 2–1 win.

In the 75th World Series, Davey Lopes had two home runs and five RBIs to lead the Los Angeles Dodgers to an 11–5 victory over the Yankees in Game 1 of the 1978 World Series. Ed Figueroa took the loss, Reggie Jackson hit a home run.

Kansas City Royal George Brett hit an upper deck three-run home run off reliever Goose Gossage for a 4–2 victory and a three game sweep of the Yankees in the 1980 American League playoffs.

The Yankees won Game 4 to even the 1998 American League Championship Series, 4–0, behind Orlando Hernandez. Paul O'Neill hit a home run for New York.

The Seattle Mariners won Game 1 of the 2000 American League Championship Series, 2–0 over the Yankees.

11

In Game 2 of the 1923 World Series, Babe Ruth hit two home runs and Aaron Ward hit one while pitcher Herb Pennock allowed nine hits in a

4–2 victory over the New York Giants to tie the Series at one game each.

Lou Gehrig was named 1927 American League MVP. Gehrig had established a major league record with 175 RBIs in the season. Babe Ruth was not considered because former winners were not eligible at the time.

Bill Dickey's two-run home run led the Yankees to a 2–0 win in Game 5 of the 1943 World Series, defeating the St. Louis Cardinals four games to one to take their 10th World Series Championship.

Citing cruelty, Joe DiMaggio's first wife, Dorothy Arnold, filed for divorce in 1945.

In Game 4 of the 1964 World Series, Ken Boyer hit a 6th inning grand slam off Al Downing to give the St. Louis Cardinals a 4–3 victory over the Yankees. Boyer became the second National League batter to hit a post-season bases-loaded home run.

"El Duque" Orlando Hernandez was born in Villa Clara, Cuba, in 1969, or was it 1965? He debuted in 1998 with the Yankees and went 17–9 in 1999.

Billy Martin was named manager of the Minnesota Twins in 1968.

The Yankees defeated the Los Angeles Dodgers in Game 1 of the 1977 World Series, 4–3. Willie Randolph hit a leadoff home run in the 6th, then doubled and scored the winning run on Paul Blair's single in the bottom of the 12th inning.

The Los Angeles Dodgers took a two games to none lead in the 1978 World Series. Ron Cey and Reggie Jackson drove in all the runs. Bob Welch saved Burt Hooton's 4–3 win by striking out Reggie on a full count with two out in the 9th inning of Game 2.

The Yankees took the 1981 Eastern Division Championship series over the Milwaukee Brewers with a 7–3 win and three game sweep. Oscar Gamble and Rich Cerone hit home runs for New York and Dave Righetti got the win in relief.

With the 1996 American League Championship Series tied at one game each, and Game 3 tied at two, Baltimore third baseman Todd Zeile's error allowed the go-ahead run to score. Cecil Fielder followed with a home run in the 5–2 Yankee win over the Orioles.

The Yankees took a three games to two lead in the 1998 American League Championship Series with a 5–3 win over the Indians in Game 5. Chili Davis hit a home run for New York. Kenny Lofton and Jim Thome hit home runs for Cleveland.

The Yankees evened the 2000 American League Championship Series at one game apiece with a 7–1 victory over the Seattle Mariners led by a seven-run 8th inning rally.

12

In Game 7 of the 1921 World Series, Yankee Carl Mays and New York Giant Phil Douglas pitched a 1–1 game before the Giants scored a run in the bottom of the 7th for a 2–1 win to take a four games to three lead.

The largest crowd to watch a World Series game at the time (62,430) saw Casey Stengel hit his second home run of the 1923 World Series for a 1–0 New York Giants win in Game 3 over the Yankees.

Infielder Tony Kubek, born in 1936 in Milwaukee, WI, played his entire nine-year career with the Yankees. Kubek was an all-star three times and appeared in six World Series. He won the 1957 American League Rookie of the Year Award.

Casey Stengel was officially introduced as the manager of the Yankees at New York's "21 Club" in 1948. In his two previous trials as manager, with the Boston Braves and Brooklyn Dodgers, Stengel never finished higher than fifth place.

Joe DiMaggio turned down a one-year contract extension from the Yankees for $100,000 in 1951, signaling his impending retirement as an active player.

The Yankees pounded the Pittsburgh Pirates 12–0 on 17 hits in Game 6 of the 1960 World Series. Bobby Richardson tied a single game record with two triples. Whitey Ford pitched the shutout. Despite the score, there were no Yankee home runs.

St. Louis took a three games to two lead with a 5–2 victory in Game 5 of the 1964 World Series. Cardinal catcher Tim McCarver hit a three-run home run in the top of the 10th, after Yankee Tom Tresh had tied the game with a two-run home run in the 9th.

The Yankees won Game 3 of the 1976 American League Champi-

onship Series, 5–3 over the Kansas City Royals. Chris Chambliss hit a home run to give New York a two games to one lead.

Los Angeles defeated the Yankees 6–1 to even the 1977 World Series at one game each. Catfish Hunter, who had not pitched in over a month, gave up home runs to Ron Cey, Steve Yeager and Reggie Smith and left in the 3rd inning of Game 2.

The Yankees won Game 4 of the 1996 ALCS with an 8–4 win over the Baltimore Orioles. Darryl Strawberry hit two home runs while Bernie Williams and Paul O'Neill had one each.

Joe DiMaggio was admitted to a Florida hospital in 1998.

13

In a series played entirely at the Polo Grounds in New York, the Giants wrapped up a five games to three win in the 1921 World Series with a 1–0 shutout over the Yankees in Game 8. Roger Peckinpaugh's 1st inning error led to the only run.

The Yankees scored six runs in the 2nd inning of Game 4 of the 1923 World Series to lead Bob Shawkey to an 8–4 win over the New York Giants. Whitey Witt had three hits and two RBIs to even the Series at two games each.

In one of the biggest disappointments in Yankee history, Bill Mazeroski's dramatic bottom of the 9th inning home run to left field at Forbes Field off Ralph Terry broke a 9–9 tie and gave the Pittsburgh

Pirates the 1960 World Series in seven games.

Billy Martin, who won the division with a 97–65, was fired as manager of the Minnesota Twins after being swept by the Baltimore Orioles in the 1969 American League Championship Series.

The Yankees, trailing two games to none to the Los Angeles Dodgers in the 1978 World Series, returned to Yankee Stadium to win Game 3 behind Ron Guidry, 5–1. Roy White hit a home run for New York.

Tommy John led the Yankees to a 3–1, Game 1, victory in the 1981 American League Championship Series.

Bob Quinn resigned as vice president and general manager and was replaced by Harding Peterson in 1989.

The Yankees clinched their first World Series appearance since 1981 with a 6–4 win over the Orioles in Baltimore in Game 5 of the 1996 ALCS. Jim Leyritz, Cecil Fielder, and Darryl Strawberry hit home runs.

The Yankees reached the World Series for a record 35th time by defeating the Cleveland Indians 9–5 in Game 6 of the 1998 American League Championship Series. Scott Brosius hit a three-run home run.

The Yankees won Game 3 of the 2000 American League Championship Series, 8–2. Bernie Williams and Tino Martinez hit back-to-back home runs and Mariano Rivera extended his postseason scoreless string to 33⅓ innings to eclipse Whitey Ford's record.

14

The Yankees took a three games to two lead over the New York Giants in the 1923 World Series with an 8–1 win. Joe Dugan hit a home run and Joe Bush pitched a complete game three-hitter for the Yankees.

The Yankees won Game 6 of the 1964 World Series over the St. Louis Cardinals, 8–3, to force a seventh game. Roger Maris, Mickey Mantle, and Joe Pepitone hit home runs for New York. Jim Bouton recorded his second win.

The Yankees won their 30th pennant on Chris Chambliss' bottom of the 9th inning solo home run to defeat the Kansas City Royals, 7–6 in Game 5 of the 1976 American League Championship Series.

The Yankees won Game 3 of the 1977 World Series to take a two games to one lead over the Los Angeles Dodgers. Mike Torrez pitched the complete game win, 5–3.

The Yankees won Game 4 of the 1978 World Series at Yankee Stadium with a 10th inning single by Lou Piniella over the Los Angeles Dodgers, 4–3, to tie the Series. Goose Gossage got the win in relief.

The Yankees won Game 2 of the 1981 American League Championship Series against the Oakland A's behind a seven-run 4th inning, 13–3. Lou Piniella and Graig Nettles hit home runs to lead the Yankees to a two games to none lead in the series.

The Yankees took a three games to one lead over the Seattle Mariners in the 2000 American League Championship Series with a 5–0 win. Roger

Clemens pitched a one-hitter and struck out 15. Derek Jeter and David Justice each hit home runs for New York.

15

The Yankees won their first World Series Championship with a 6–4 win over the New York Giants in Game 6 of the 1923 World Series at the Polo Grounds. Herb Pennock got the win and Babe Ruth contributed a home run.

Rather than accept trade offers, the Yankees released future Hall of Fame infielder Tony Lazzeri in 1937, allowing him to make his own deal. He signed as a player-coach with the Chicago Cubs for the following season.

Roger Maris hit a home run but the Yankees were held to only three hits in Game 6 of the 1962 World Series, a 5–2 loss to San Francisco. Whitey Ford took the defeat.

Despite home runs by Mickey Mantle, Clete Boyer and Phil Linz, St. Louis Cardinal pitcher Bob Gibson defeated the Yankees, 7–5, and captured the 1964 World Series in seven games.

The Yankees won Game 4 of the 1977 World Series, 4–2 over the Los Angeles Dodgers to take a three games to one lead. Reggie Jackson hit a home run and a double while Ron Guidry struck out seven in a four-hit effort.

The Yankees recorded 18 hits in Game 5 of the 1978 World Series to win, 12–2, over the Los Angeles Dodgers. Bucky Dent, Mickey Rivers, and Brian Doyle each had three hits as the Yankees forged a three games to two Series lead.

Dave Righetti, Ron Davis and Goose Gossage combined to record a 4–0 win over the Oakland A's to complete a sweep of the 1981 American League Championship Series. Willie Randolph hit a home run to lead the Yankees to their 33rd American League pennant.

The Seattle Mariners remained alive in the 2000 American League Championship Series with a 6–2 victory over the Yankees in Game 5.

16

Defying a ban, Babe Ruth, Bob Meusel, and Bill Piercy started a barnstorming tour after the 1921 World Series, which resulted in fines and suspensions.

In the first structural change since the turn of the century, the National League voted in 1960 to admit Houston and New York into the Senior Circuit. The Yankees again had competition for fans in the Big Apple.

In the most elongated series, punctuated by rain in both cities, the Yankees completed a 1962 World Series win with a 1–0 victory in Game 7 at San Francisco over the Giants.

The Yankees lost Game 1 of the 1976 World Series to the Cincinnati Reds, 5–1. Doyle Alexander took the loss.

The Los Angeles Dodgers remained alive with a 10–4 win over the Yankees in Game 5 of the 1977

World Series. Thurman Munson and Reggie Jackson hit back-to-back home runs in the 8th inning for New York.

Darryl Strawberry was released from the hospital and joined his teammates in the victory parade to celebrate the Yankees' 1998 World Championship.

17

Infielder Robert "Red" Rolfe was born in 1908 in Penacook, NH. He played his entire career with the Yankees, 1931 and 1933–42. Rolfe led the American League in hits in 1939, batting .329.

Babe Ruth met 17-year-old Helen Woodford at Landers' Coffee Shop in Boston. They married on this date in 1914 at St. Paul's Roman Catholic Church in Ellicott City, Maryland.

Despite a regular season record of 99–63, the Yankees fired manager Yogi Berra after losing the 1964 World Series to the St. Louis Cardinals in seven games.

Pitcher John Rocker, who blasted New York in a *Sports Illustrated* article after the Atlanta Braves were swept in the 1999 World Series, was born in 1974.

The Yankees lost Game 2 of the 1976 World Series in the bottom of the 9th inning, 4–3, to the Cincinnati Reds on a throwing error, a walk, and Tony Perez's single. The Reds led two games to none.

The Yankees won Game 6 of the 1978 World Series over the Los Angeles Dodgers, 7–2, to clinch their second consecutive championship, four games to two. Catfish Hunter got the win while Reggie Jackson hit a home run and Series MVP Bucky Dent had three hits.

Lou Piniella was named Yankee manager, replacing Billy Martin in 1985.

Dallas Green replaced Lou Piniella as manager of the Yankees in 1988.

The Yankees won Game 1 of the 1998 World Series, defeating the San Diego Padres 9–6 behind a grand slam home run by Tino Martinez and a three-run home run from Chuck Knoblauch.

The Yankees won the 2000 American League Championship Series four game to two over the Seattle Mariners with a 9–7 victory in Game 6. The Yankees scored six runs in the 7th inning led by a three-run home run by David Justice to head to the World Series for the third straight year. The 2000 World Series was an unprecedented "Subway Series" matching the Yankees against the Mets.

18

Five days after their 1960 World Series loss to the Pittsburgh Pirates in Game 7, the Yankees fired 70-year old manager Casey Stengel, stating he had reached mandatory retirement age.

Reggie Jackson hit three home runs on three consecutive pitches to help the Yankees win their twenty-first World Championship, defeating the Los Angeles Dodgers, 8–4, in

Game 6 of the 1977 Series. Chris Chambliss added a home run for New York.

New York Yankees General Manager Gene Michael stepped down from his post to become the team's director of Major League Scouting in 1995.

The Yankees defeated the San Diego Padres, 9–3, in Game 2 of the 1998 World Series. Bernie Williams and Jorge Posada hit home runs for New York, which took a two games to none lead.

Orlando Hernandez (ALCS MVP) pitched a shutout into the 8th inning. Derek Jeter led the Yankees to a record 36th pennant with a two-run home run in a 6–1 win over the Boston Red Sox in Game 5 of the 1999 American League Championship Series.

19

Sandy Alomar Sr. was born in 1943 in Salinas, Puerto Rico. He played 15 major league seasons as an infielder, including 1974–76 with the Yankees. He was an all-star with the 1970 California Angels and the father of catcher Sandy Alomar Jr.

Wade Taylor was 7–12 and appeared in 23 games in his only major league season, 1991 with the Yankees. Taylor was born in Mobile, AL in 1965.

The Cincinnati Reds took a commanding three games to none lead in the 1976 World Series with a 6–2 victory over the Yankees. Jim Mason hit a home run for New York in his only at-bat in the Series.

Oakland A's president Roy Eisenhardt fired manager Billy Martin after refusing to extend his contract in 1982.

In 1987, Woody Woodward resigned as general manager of the Yankees. Lou Piniella was named general manager and Billy Martin was named Yankee manager for fifth time, replacing Piniella.

20

Baseball Hall of Fame member and Yankee great centerfielder Mickey Mantle was born in 1931 in Spavinaw, OK.

The Yankees began a 16-game exhibition in Japan in 1955.

In 1964, three days after resigning as manager of World Champion St. Louis Cardinals, Johnny Keane replaced Yogi Berra as Yankee manager.

The Yankees won Game 1 of the 1981 World Series with a 5–3 victory over the Los Angeles Dodgers. Bob Watson hit a home run for the Yankees and Ron Guidry recorded the win.

The Yankees lost Game 1 of the 1996 World Series, 12–1 to the Braves in Atlanta. It was New York's first Series appearance in 15 years. John Smoltz allowed just four hits.

The Yankees took a commanding lead in the 1998 World Series with their third consecutive win over the San Diego Padres, 5–4. Eventual Series MVP Scott Brosius hit two home runs for New York in Game 3.

21

Yankee great pitcher of the 1950's and 1960's Edward "Whitey" Ford was born in New York City in 1928. Ford won the World Series MVP and the Cy Young Award in 1961.

The Cincinnati Reds completed a 1976 World Series sweep over the Yankees for their second consecutive World Championship. Hall of Fame catcher Johnny Bench hit two home runs to lead the Reds. Thurman Munson tied a record with his sixth straight single.

Goose Gossage recorded his second consecutive World Series save preserving Tommy John's 3–0 win in Game 2 of the 1981 Series giving the Yankees a two games to none lead over the Los Angeles Dodgers.

The Yankees lost Game 2 of the 1996 World Series, 4–0, to the Atlanta Braves. Greg Maddux got the win. The Yankees trailed two games to one.

The 1998 Yankees swept the San Diego Padres to win their 24th World Series championship with a 3–0 victory. Series MVP Scott Brosius fielded a grounder for the final out. It was the 125th win of the season.

The Yankees won the longest game in World Series history over the New York Mets with a 4–3 win in 12 innings in Game 1 of the 2000 Subway Series. Jose Vizcaino won it with a bases-loaded RBI single at Yankee Stadium.

22

Myles Thomas of State College, PA pitched for the Yankees from 1926–29, compiling a 14–12 record. He was born in 1899.

Joe DiMaggio was hired in 1967 as executive vice president of the A's, who were being moved from Kansas City to Oakland by owner Charlie Finley.

In 1974, the Yankees traded outfielder Bobby Murcer to the San Francisco Giants for outfielder Bobby Bonds.

Walter Lainer "Red" Barber died in 1992. Barber, as a broadcaster, was named to the Hall of Fame. He was a popular Yankees announcer in the 1950s and 60s and a nationally recognized baseball voice.

The Yankees won Game 3 of the 1996 World Series, 5–2, behind strong pitching by David Cone. Bernie Williams had a home run and three RBIs.

The Yankees recorded their 14th consecutive World Series victory with a 6–5 win over the New York Mets in Game 2 of the 2000 Subway Series. In a memorable moment, pitcher Roger Clemens threw the broken barrel of Mike Piazza's bat at the Met catcher as he ran down the first base line. The benches cleared, but no brawl ensued. The Yankees owned a two games to none lead.

23

Yankee manager Billy Martin was involved in an altercation with a marshmallow salesman outside a Bloomington, MN, bar. Martin was fired five days later in 1979.

The Los Angeles Dodgers began their comeback in the 1981 World Series with a 4–3 victory over the Yankees in Game 3 despite New York home runs by Rick Cerone and Bob Watson. The Yankees led two games to one.

The Yankees named Bob Watson as general manager in 1995.

The Yankees came back from a six-run deficit to defeat the Braves 8–6 in 10 innings in Game 4 of the 1996 World Series. Jim Leyritz's three-run home run tied it in the 8th inning. It was the largest comeback in World Series history.

The Yankees won Game 1 of the 1999 World Series over the Braves, 4–1 in Atlanta. Paul O'Neill hit a two-run single in the 7th inning to spark a four-run rally. Orlando Hernandez recorded the win on the mound.

24

Joe DiMaggio was named 1939 American League MVP, 27 days later he married an actress from Duluth, MN, Dorothy Arnold.

Pitcher Rawly Eastwick was born in Camden, NJ, in 1950. Eastwick led the National League in saves in 1975 and 1976. He pitched for the Yankees in 1978.

Yogi Berra was named the Yankees manager in 1963 after 18 seasons as a catcher with the club. Berra played in only 64 games in 1963, managed during the 1964 season, and briefly attempted a comeback with the New York Mets in 1965, appearing in four games.

Billy Martin was named 1974 American League Manager of the Year with the Texas Rangers.

The Dodgers came from behind for an 8–7 win in Game 4 of the 1981 World Series, to tie the Series at two games each. Reggie Jackson and Willie Randolph hit home runs for the Yankees but poor outfield play aided Los Angeles.

The Yankees won Game 5 of the 1996 World Series, 1–0, behind a four-hitter by Andy Petite and John Wetteland (Series MVP), who recorded a record third save. Cecil Fielder hit a double to score Charlie Hayes with the only run.

The Yankees won Game 2 of the 1999 World Series over the Braves, 7–2 in Atlanta with the 18 living members of the All-Century Team present. Jim Grey's controversial interview with Pete Rose.

The New York Mets won Game 3 of the 2000 World Series, 4–2 at Shea Stadium. Pitcher "El Duque" Hernandez set a Yankees World Series record with 12 strikeouts but recorded his first loss in nine postseason decisions. The Mets ended the Yankees' record World Series winning streak at 14.

25

The Metropolitans of New York (American Association) lost to the Providence Grays (National League) in a precursor to the modern World Series in 1884, dropping three straight games in New York.

Lee MacPhail was born in 1917. He was general manager of the Yankees (1967–74) and served as American League president (1974–83).

Dr. Bobby Brown was born in 1924 in Seattle, WA. The cardiologist played eight seasons with the Yankees (1946–54) and went on to become the 6th American League President (1983–1994).

Yankee reliever Sparky Lyle was named the 1977 Cy Young Award winner. Lyle compiled a 13–5 record with a 2.17 ERA and 26 saves out of the bullpen.

Steve Yeager and Pedro Guerrero hit back-to-back home runs off Ron Guidry in the 7th inning to lead the Los Angeles Dodgers to a 2–1 victory over the Yankees in Game 5 of the 1981 World Series to take a three games to two lead.

Following a Game 5 loss to the Los Angeles Dodgers in the 1981 World Series, Yankees owner George Steinbrenner allegedly scuffled with fans in a hotel elevator and received a fat lip and broken hand.

The Yankees took a commanding three games to one lead in the 2000 World Series with a 3–2 win over the New York Mets. Derek Jeter hit a leadoff home run for the Yankees, who moved one game away from their third consecutive championship.

26

Miller Huggins signed a two-year contract in 1917 as manager of the Yankees, after five seasons managing the St. Louis Cardinals. He led the Yankees to their first championship in 1923.

George "Snuffy" Stirnweiss, a New York City native born in 1919, played infield for the Yankees from 1943–50. He was a career .268 hitter.

The Baseball Writers Association of American selected Yankee shortstop Phil Rizzuto as the 1950 American League MVP.

1999 World Series, Game 3, Chad Curtis hit his second home run, leading off the 10th inning. The Yankees beat the Braves 6–5 at the Stadium.

In the last World Series game of the 20th century, the Yankees defeated the New York Mets in Shea Stadium, 4–2, to record their third consecutive World Championship, their fourth in five years. Utility infielder Luis Sojo hit a two-run single in the 9th inning to lead the rally. Derek Jeter, the 2000 World Series MVP, hit a solo home run in the 6th inning.

27

Bolivar, NY, native Patrick Dougherty played outfield for the Highlanders 1904–06. Born in 1876, Dougherty played 10 major league seasons, hitting .335 for the 1902 Boston Pilgrims.

Joe DiMaggio's divorce from Marilyn Monroe became final in 1954. DiMaggio went 0–2 in the marriage category.

Ralph Houk was named manager of the Boston Red Sox in 1980 at the age of 61.

In 1985, Billy Martin was fired by the Yankees for the fourth time and was replaced by Lou Piniella, who had been the hitting instructor for New York since retiring as an outfielder in 1984.

After two one-sided losses at home, the Yankees won the final four games of the 1996 World Series, their first championship since 1978, with a victory over the Atlanta Braves in Game 6, 3–2. Reliever John Wetteland was Series MVP with a record four saves.

The Yankees picked up the 1998 option on the contract of outfielder Chad Curtis in 1997.

The Yankees completed a sweep of the Atlanta Braves with a 4–1 Game 4 victory before 56,752 at Yankee Stadium to claim their second consecutive World Series title and third in the past four years. Reliever Mariano Rivera was the 1999 World Series MVP.

28

Joseph "Fireman" Page pitched for the Yankees 1944–50, going 14–8 in 1947. He was born in Cherry Valley, PA, in 1917.

The "old redhead" Red Barber re-signed as a Brooklyn Dodger broadcaster and joined the rival New York Yankees in 1953.

Billy Martin was named 1976 American League Manager of the Year with the Yankees.

In 1979, George Steinbrenner fired manager Billy Martin because of his barroom fight with a marshmallow salesman. Dick Howser was picked to replace Martin as Yankee manager.

In Game 6, the final game of the 1981 World Series, the Los Angeles Dodgers defeated the Yankees 9–2, completing four straight wins after losing the first two games to New York. Willie Randolph hit a home run for the Yankees.

Owner George Steinbrenner apologized for his team's four straight losses to drop the 1981 World Series, four games to two to Los Angeles. Pitcher George Frazier tied a record with three losses.

On *The Late Show with David Letterman* in 1996, members of the Yankees, and their manager Joe Torre, visited with Letterman in New York after winning their first World Series championship in 15 years.

29

In retaliation for reinstating suspended pitcher Carl Mays, whom the Yankees obtained from the Boston Red Sox earlier in the 1919 season, the National Commission refused to recognize the Yankees' third-place finish and withheld money from the players.

Ed Barrow left the Boston Red Sox

and was appointed General Manager of the Yankees in 1920. The team won their first American League pennant the following season.

Jesse Barfield was born in 1954 in Joliet, IL. Barfield became the first Yankee to strike out 150 times in a season in 1990. He had struck out a combined 150 times in 1989 playing for New York and the Toronto Blue Jays.

William Nathaniel (Buck) Showalter III was named the Yankees' manager in 1991, replacing Stump Merrill.

The 1999 Yankees celebrated their 25th World Series Championship with a ticker-tape parade through the "Canyon of Heroes" in lower Manhattan.

30

Beaver Lake, MI, native Fred Curtis was born in 1880. His only major league season was 1905 with the Highlanders, when he played sparingly.

Pitcher Marty McHale was born in Stoneham, MA, in 1888. A six-year major league veteran, McHale played for the Yankees 1913–15, compiling a 6–16 record in 191 innings in 1914.

Jim Ray Hart played 12 major league seasons, ten with the San Francisco Giants and the final two with the Yankees 1973-74. Hart compiled over 90 RBIs in three consecutive National League seasons, 1965–67. He was born in Hookerton, NC, in 1941.

Born in 1962, San Juan, Puerto Rico, native Danny Tartabull played for the Yankees 1992–95.Tartabull crushed 31 home runs for the 1993 Yankees.

31

Mickey Rivers was born in 1948 in Miami, FL. Rivers played outfield for the Yankees 1976–79. He led the American League in stolen bases in 1975 as a member of the California Angels.

Infielder Mike Gallego played for the Yankees 1992–94. He hit .283 in 119 games in 1993. He was born in 1960 in Whittier, CA.

Mike Flanagan, who posted a 23–9 record for the Baltimore Orioles, was named the winner of the 1979 American League Cy Young Award. Yankee Tommy John finished second.

The Yankees exercised the 1999 option on catcher Joe Girardi in 1998.

NOVEMBER

1

Pitcher Carl Mays was born in Liberty, KY, in 1891. Infamous for beaning Ray Chapman, Mays was 27–9 for the 1921 Yankees and had five major league seasons with at least 20 wins.

Yankee outfielder Alex Barr, who had only appeared in one major league game, was killed in Europe in World War I, ten days before the armistice in 1918.

Yankee left-hander Ron Guidry unanimously won the 1978 American League Cy Young Award. Guidry posted a 25–3 record and a 1.74 ERA.

The Yankees made two big deals in 1979. They obtained Rick Cerone from the Toronto Blue Jays for Chris Chambliss and acquired Ruppert Jones and Jim Lewis from the Seattle Mariners for four players.

In 1997, the Yankees announced they would not pick up 1998 contract options on third baseman Wade Boggs and starting pitcher Dwight Gooden, ending Gooden's career in New York.

2

Traffic in Tokyo, Japan was snarled in 1934 when baseball fans rushed to the airport to see Babe Ruth, who was touring with an American League all-star team.

It was announced that Babe Ruth applied for the job of St. Louis Browns manager after being released as Brooklyn Dodgers coach in 1938.

At the age of 66, George Weiss resigned as general manager of the Yankees in 1960.

Yankee Roger Maris was named the 1960 American League MVP. Teammate Mickey Mantle finished a close second. It was the first of two MVP awards for Maris.

CBS became the first corporate owner in Major League Baseball by buying eighty percent of Yankees for $11.2 million in 1964.

Joe Torre was named manager of the Yankees after Buck Showalter's resignation in 1995.

The Yankees exercised the 2000 options on outfielder Paul O'Neill and designated hitter Darryl Strawberry in 1999.

3

1942 American League MVP Joe Gordon hit .322 with 18 home runs and 103 RBI for the Yankees, but led the league in strikeouts, hitting into double plays and errors at second base. Triple crown winner Ted Williams finished second in a controversial vote.

Mickey Mantle was operated on to remove a piece of torn knee cartilage in 1953 in Springfield, MO. Mantle returned home to Oklahoma after three days in the hospital.

Members of the Yankees' 1954 championship team toured Japan and drew a record crowd of 64,000 against the All-Japan Stars in Osaka. Andy Carey hit 13 home runs and Elston Howard hit .468 on the 25-game tour.

Yankee coach Jeff Torborg replaced Jim Fregosi as manager of the Chicago White Sox in 1988.

Yankee pitcher David Cone was granted free agency in 1995.

David Cone became the first member of the 1999 World Champion Yankees to file for free agency.

4

Miller Huggins was named manager of the St. Louis Cardinals in 1912, beginning his 17-year career as a major league manager that ended with the Yankees in 1929.

At New York's Plaza Hotel in 1976, the first free-agent re-entry draft was held. Reggie Jackson was one of the biggest prizes, signing later in the month with the Yankees.

The Cincinnati Reds traded outfielder Ken Griffey Sr. to the Yankees for pitcher Fred Toliver and minor-leaguer Brian Ryder in 1981.

Dwight Gooden was suspended by Major League Baseball for repeated drug violations in 1994.

Baltimore Orioles free agent outfielder Clay Bellinger was signed by the Yankees in 1996.

The Yankees declined to pick up the 1998 contract option on second baseman Pat Kelly in 1997.

5

Infielder Otis Johnson played one major league season, 1911 with the Highlanders, hitting three home runs. Johnson was born in 1883 in Fowler, IN.

Catcher Roxy Walters was born in San Francisco, CA, in 1892. Walters played 11 major league seasons without hitting a home run. He started his career with the Yankees 1915–18.

Born in Charlotte, NC, in 1924, pitcher Sonny Dixon led the American League in appearances in 1954 with the Washington Senators and Philadelphia A's. Dixon played for the Yankees in his final season, 1956.

Catcher Bobby Ramos was born in 1955 in Havana, Cuba. He played six seasons, five with the Montreal Expos with his fourth season spent with the

Yankees in 1982, where he hit one home run.

Yankee shortstop Derek Jeter was the unanimous choice for 1996 American League Rookie of the Year. He became the eighth Yankee, and the fifth unanimous winner in American League history.

6

John D. "Jack" Chesbro died on this date in 1931. The former Yankee and member of the Baseball Hall of Fame was born in 1874 in North Adams, MA. He is one of two players to record 40 victories in a season in the 20th century.

The three DiMaggio brothers, Joe, Vince, and Dom, played together in the outfield for the first time in a charity game on the West Coast in 1938.

Two Yankees, Frank Crosetti and Joe Gordon, were punished for arguing in the 1942 World Series. Crosetti was suspended for the first 30 days of the 1943 season and both players were fined $250.

Outfielder/designated hitter Chad Curtis was born in 1968 in Marion, IN. Curtis played for the Yankees 1997–99 before being traded to the Texas Rangers prior to the 2000 season. He hit 21 home runs for the 1995 Detroit Tigers.

The Yankees named Lee Mazzilli as manager of Norwich (AA) of the Eastern League in 1998.

7

Birthday of Dick Stuart, Yankee nemesis in the 1960 World Series. He was born in 1932 in San Francisco, CA. Stuart led the American League in RBIs in 1963 as a Boston Red Sox first baseman.

Yankee catcher Jerry "Jake" Gibbs was born in 1938 in Grenada, MS. Gibbs played his entire career with the Yankees, 1962–71. He was the starter in 1968.

Yankee Elston Howard was named the 1963 American League Most Valuable Player, with 28 home runs and 85 RBIs. He became the first black player to receive the honor.

Boston Red Sox outfielder Jim Rice won the 1978 American League Most Valuable Player Award over Yankee pitcher Ron Guidry, who had won the Cy Young Award.

Baltimore Orioles manager Johnny Oates and Yankee Joe Torre were named co-winners of the 1996 American League Manager of the Year award.

The Yankees traded pitcher Kenny Rogers to the Oakland Athletics for a player to be named later in 1997. Rogers pitched a perfect game for the Texas Rangers 7/29/94 against the California Angels, 4–0.

8

Catcher Yogi Berra won the first of his three American League MVP awards in 1951. Berra hit 27 home runs and drove in 88 runs with a .294 batting average.

Whitey Ford was voted the 1961 Cy Young Award winner over Warren Spahn. Ford was 25–4 in leading the Yankees to their 19th World Series Championship.

The Yankees signed free-agent first baseman/designated hitter Bob Watson and pitcher Rudy May to long-term contracts in 1979.

9

Infielder Roy Schalk was born in 1908 in Chicago, IL. Schalk started his career with the Yankees in 1932. He was out of major league baseball until 1944 when he resurfaced and played two seasons as the regular second baseman for the Chicago White Sox.

Outfielder Jerry Priddy was born in Los Angeles, CA, in 1919. Priddy began his career with the Yankees in 1941-42. The infielder hit .296 with the St. Louis Browns in 1948 and played 11 major league seasons.

Utility player Ted Sepkowski (born Sczepkowski) played briefly in the majors in three seasons, ending his career with the Yankees in 1947. He was born in Baltimore, MD, in 1923.

Dave Wehrmeister was born in 1952 in Berwyn, IL. Wehrmeister played six major league seasons with four teams, including the Yankees in 1981.

Dion James played 11 seasons in the major leagues, including 1992–96 with the Yankees. Born in 1962 in Philadelphia, PA, James hit .332 in 115 games with New York in 1993.

10

The Yankees purchased Joe DiMaggio from the San Francisco Seals of the Pacific Coast League in 1934 for $25,000 and five players.

Pitcher Kenny Rogers won a World Championship with the Yankees in 1996, going 12–8. He was born in 1964 in Savannah, GA.

Joe Torre was named National League MVP in 1971. Torre led the league in RBI (137) and hitting (.363). He went on to manage the Yankees to four World Championships through 2000.

The Yankees traded Sparky Lyle, Dave Rajsich, Larry McCall, Mike Heath and Domingo Ramos to the Texas Rangers for Dave Righetti, Paul Mirabella, Juan Beniquez, and Mike Griffin in 1978.

Roger Clemens became the first American League pitcher to win the Cy Young Award four times when he captured the honor as a member of the 1997 Toronto Blue Jays.

The Yankees re-signed free-agent third baseman Scott Brosius to a three-year contract in 1998.

11

Owen "Ownie" Carroll pitched eight major league seasons, including part of 1930 with the Yankees. He was 16–12 with the 1928 Tigers. The Kearny, NJ, native was born in 1902.

Yankee Spurgeon "Spud" Chandler was named the 1943 American League Most Valuable Player. Chandler was 20–4 with the Yankees and led the league in complete games (20), shutouts (5), ERA (1.64), wins (20), and winning percentage (.833).

Marking the first major rule change in 80 years, American League owners voted in favor of using designated hitters, 8–4, in 1973.

Wade Boggs was granted free agency by the Yankees in 1995. He re-signed with New York and played two more seasons before going to Tampa Bay in 1998.

The Yankees traded third baseman Charlie Hayes and cash considerations to the San Francisco Giants for outfielder Chris Singleton and pitcher Alberto Castillo in 1997.

The Yankees re-signed pitcher David Cone to a one-year contract in 1998.

12

Donald Johnson was born in Portland, OR in 1926. He pitched for the Yankees in 1947 and 1950, compiling a 5–3 record. He pitched in seven major league seasons.

The Yankees acquired their first farm team when owner Jacob Ruppert purchased the Newark Bears of the International League from publisher Paul Block in 1931.

Bob Turley won the 1958 Cy Young Award over last year's winner, Warren Spahn. He was 21–7 with 19 complete games, leading the Yankees to their 18th World Series Championship.

Yankee coach Don Zimmer was named manager of the Texas Rangers in 1980, becoming the 10th manager in the club's nine-year history.

Billy Martin was named 1981 American League Manager of the Year with the Oakland A's.

In 1992, Yankee pitcher Steve Howe was reinstated by arbitrator George Nicolau following his eighth suspension for repeated drug offenses.

Hall of Fame catcher Bill Dickey died in 1993 at the age of 86 in Little Rock, AR. Dickey played his entire career with the Yankees 1928–43 and managed the team in 1946.

Pat Hentgen became the first player on a Canadian team (Toronto Blue Jays) to win the Cy Young Award in 1996. Andy Pettitte (21–8) of the Yankees finished second (by six votes) and reliever Mariano Rivera placed third.

13

The Baltimore Orioles, who later moved to New York to become the Highlanders or Hilltoppers and eventually the Yankees, entered the American League in 1900.

Former Yankee hurler and pitching coach Mel Stottlemyre was born in 1941 in Hazelton, MO. Stottlemyre won 20 games three times in the 1960s.

The Yankees signed free-agent pitcher Luis Tiant to a two-year, $875,000 contract in 1978. Tiant went on to a 13–8 record with New York in 1979.

In 1985 as a New York Met, Dwight Gooden became the youngest pitcher to win the Cy Young Award.

The Yankees signed free-agent pitcher Ramiro Mendoza.

14

"Handsome Harry" Howell pitched for the Baltimore Orioles 1901-02 and moved with the Highlanders to New York in 1903, going 10–7. Howell pitched in 13 major league seasons. The Brooklyn, NY, native was born in 1876.

Born in 1885 in Chicago, IL, outfielder Jack Lelivelt played six major league seasons. He was a Highlander/Yankee 1912-13 and hit his only two career home runs with New York in 1912.

Mickey Mantle became the second person in history to unanimously win the American League MVP award in 1956. Mantle garnered all 24 first-place votes. Catcher Yogi Berra finished second.

15

Born in West Wyoming, PA, in 1916, pitcher Joe "Specs" Ostrowski played five major league seasons, including 1950–52 for the Yankees. He pitched two scoreless innings in the 1951 World Series.

Yankee Gil McDougald was named the 1951 American League Rookie of the Year. The White Sox objected in favor of their candidate, Minnie Minoso, who would set a career major league record for being hit by a pitch.

Roger Maris was named the American League MVP for the second consecutive year in 1961 after establishing a new single-season home run record with 61. He won by four votes over teammate Mickey Mantle.

16

Dwight "Doc" Gooden was born in 1964 in Tampa, FL. Gooden was a member of three New York World Championship teams, the 1986 New York Mets and the 1996 and 2000 Yankees. Gooden was 24–4 in 1985.

In 1998, the Yankees acquired pitcher Dan Naulty from the Minnesota Twins for minor-league third baseman Allen Butler.

Yogi Berra had knee replacement surgery in 1999.

17

Pitcher Lee Stine was born in 1913 in Stillwater, OK. He played four seasons in the American League, finishing his career in 1938 with the Yankees.

Joe DiMaggio had two small bone particles removed from his throwing elbow at Johns Hopkins Hospital in Baltimore, MD, after suffering a "dead arm" for most of the 1947 season.

Pitcher Jeff Nelson was born in Baltimore, MD, in 1966. The right-handed reliever started his career in Seattle in 1992 before coming to New York in 1996.

18

The Yankees received pitchers Don Larsen, Bob Turley, Mike Blyzka, catcher Darrell Jonson, first baseman Dick Kryhoski, shortstop Billy Hunter and outfielders Tim Fridley and Ted del Guercio from Baltimore over 15 days of negotiating that started on this date in 1954. The Orioles received pitchers Harry Byrd, Jim McDonald, Bill Miller, catchers Gus Triandos and Hal Smith, second baseman Don Leppert, third baseman Kal Segrist, shortstop Willy Miranda and outfielder Gene Woodling from New York.

Baltimore third baseman Brooks Robinson was named American League Most Valuable Player over second place finisher Mickey Mantle in 1964.

Infielder Clay Bellinger was born in Oneonta, NY, in 1968. He hit his first major league home run on 9/2/99 in a 9–3 Yankee win over the Oakland A's.

Pitcher Allen Watson was born in New York City in 1970. Watson attended Christ the King High School in Queens, NY.

In 1986, Roger Clemens became the first starting pitcher since Vida Blue in 1971 to win the American League Most Valuable Player Award. Yankee Don Mattingly finished second.

19

A veteran of 14 major league seasons, Lewis "Deacon" Scott was a Yankee shortstop from 1922–25, playing in every game in 1922 and batting .269. He was born in 1892 in Bluffton, IN.

Joseph "Gabby" Glenn was born in Dickson City, PA, in 1908. Glenn caught part-time for the Yankees 1932–38. His real last name was Gurzensky.

Joe DiMaggio married actress Dorothy Arnold (Dorothy Arnoldine Olson) at St. Peter and Paul Cathedral in San Francisco, CA, in 1939. DiMaggio met Ms. Arnold while filming a bit part in the movie "Manhattan Merry-Go-Round."

Yankee pitcher Stan Bahnsen (17–12, 2.05, 162 strike outs) was named 1968 American League Rookie of the Year.

20

Clark "Old Fox" Griffith was born in 1869 in Stringtown, MO. Griffith pitched and managed the Highlanders 1903–07. He is a member of the Hall of Fame, winning over 20 games six times in his career.

Long Beach, CA, native Louis Berberet was born in 1929. He caught briefly for the Yankees 1954-55. He enjoyed a career .230 average over 448 games with four teams.

Seventeen-year-old Eiji Sawamura surrendered a home run to Lou Gehrig, the only American hit. Japan beat a United States all-star team in Japan, 1–0 in 1934. Sawamura struck out future Hall of Fame members Gehringer, Ruth, Foxx, and Gehrig in succession.

In 1945, Joe DiMaggio, who spent the past three years in military service, officially signed his 1946 contract with the Yankees.

Mickey Mantle was named the 1962 American League Most Valuable Player. Mantle hit .321 with 30 home runs and 89 RBIs to earn his third, and final, MVP honor.

In 1985, Yankee Don Mattingly became the first member of a non-championship team since 1978 to win the American League Most Valuable Player Award. Mattingly hit .324 with 35 home runs and 145 RBIs.

The Yankees obtained catcher Joe Girardi from the Colorado Rockies in 1995.

In 1998, the Yankees purchased the contracts of shortstop D'Angelo Jimenez and pitcher Luis DeLosSantos from the Columbus Clippers of the International League (AAA).

21

After a sixth place finish in 1911, Hal Chase resigned as New York Highlanders manager, remaining on as a player until he was traded in 1913. Harry Wolverton replaced Chase as manager for the 1912 season.

Right-handed reliever Todd Erdos was born in Washington, PA, in 1973.

Dick Howser resigned as Yankee manager despite leading the Yankees to a 103–59 record in 1980. Howser also managed one Yankee game, a win, in 1978. He managed the Kansas City Royals 1981–86.

22

Selva "Lew" Burdette, who started his career with the Yankees but went on to have back-to-back 20 win seasons with the Milwaukee Braves in the 1950s was born in 1926 in Nitro, WV.

Mickey Mantle edged Ted Williams by 24 votes to win the 1957 American League Most Valuable Player Award in a controversial year. Williams led the league in hitting (.388), hit 38 home runs, and had a .731 slugging percentage.

Reliever Lee Guetterman was born in 1958 in Chattanooga, TN. He pitched for the Yankees 1988–1992, appearing in 70 games out of the bullpen in 1989.

Outfielder Ricky Ledee was born in 1973 in Ponce, Puerto Rico, starting his Yankee career in 1998.

The Yankees traded pitcher Pat Dobson to the Cleveland Indians in exchange for outfielder Oscar Gamble in 1975.

The Yankees signed premier free-agent reliever Rich Gossage from the Pittsburgh Pirates to a six-year, $2.75 million contract, less than a month after Sparky Lyle won the 1977 Cy Young Award for New York.

The Yankees signed free-agent pitcher Tommy John in 1978 after a 17–10 season with the Los Angeles Dodgers.

Don Rowland, a national scout for the Yankees since 1995, was hired as director of scouting and player personnel by the Anaheim Angels in 1999.

23

Luis Tiant won 20 or more American League games in four seasons, leading the league in shutouts twice (1966 and 1968). He played two of his 19 seasons with the Yankees 1979-80. He was born in Marianao, Cuba, in 1940.

Frank Tepedino was born in 1947 in Brooklyn, NY. Tepedino started his major league career with the Yankees (1967–71, 72), playing first base and outfield.

Dale Sveum played for the Yankees in 1998. Sveum had a promising career interrupted by injury in 1988. Sveum hit 25 home runs and drove in 95 with the 1987 Milwaukee Brewers. He was born in Richmond, CA, in 1963.

Free-agent second baseman Steve Sax signed a three-year deal with the Yankees, leaving the 1988 World Champion Los Angeles Dodgers.

24

Pitcher Bob Friend concluded a 15-year career with both the Yankees and the New York Mets in 1966. He was born in 1930 in Fayette, IN.

Fred Beene was born in Angleton, TX, in 1942. He played seven major league seasons and played for the Yankees 1972–74, posting a 6–0 record in 1973.

Randy Velarde played infield for the Yankees during the first nine of his 12 major league seasons, 1987–95. Velarde hit .285 with 14 home runs as the regular second baseman for the 1996 California Angels. He was born in 1962 in Midland, TX.

In 1986, the Yankees traded several prospects including pitchers Doug Drabek (the 1990 National League Cy Young Award winner), Brian Fisher, and Logan Easley to the Pittsburgh Pirates for veterans Rick Rhoden, Cecilio Guante and Pat Clements.

25

Giuseppe Paolo (Joe) DiMaggio was born, the son of a fisherman, in Martinez, CA, in 1914.

Ted Williams, who nearly won the Triple Crown (lost the batting title by .0002 to George Kell), won the 1949 Most Valuable Player Award. Yankees Phil Rizzuto and Joe Page finished second and third respectively.

Russell Earl "Bucky" Dent was born in 1951 in Savannah, GA. Dent hit a heroic home run in the 1978 American League East playoff game against the Boston Red Sox. He managed the Yankees 1989-90.

Lou Piniella was named 1969 American League Rookie of the Year as a Kansas City Royal. Piniella went on to play the final eleven major league seasons with the Yankees (1974–84) and managed the team 1986–88.

Yankee catcher Thurman Munson was named 1970 American League Rookie of the Year, receiving twenty-three of twenty-four votes.

In 1980, Gene Michael became the 25th Yankee manager, succeeding Dick Howser.

The Yankees signed free-agent infielder Dale Sveum, who was a member of the 1997 "Freak Show Pittsburgh Pirates" to a two-year, $1.6 million deal.

The Yankees extended the deadline to exercise the 1999 option on outfielder-designated hitter Darryl Strawberry for an undefined period and signed outfielder Bernie

Williams to a seven-year contract in 1998.

26

Thomas "Long Tom" Hughes was born in 1878 in Chicago, IL. He pitched for the Highlanders in 1904, going 7–11 after his best major league season with the Boston Pilgrims, going 21–7 in 1903.

Hall of Fame pitcher Vernon "Lefty" Gomez pitched all but his final major league loss with the Yankees 1930–42. He won 20 games four times. He was born in Rodeo, CA, in 1908.

Jay Howell was born in 1955 in Miami, FL. He pitched for the Yankees 1981–84, appearing in 61 games in 1984. Howell was an all-star once in each league and recorded 29 saves with the 1989 Oakland A's.

The Yankees traded first baseman Bill "Moose" Skowron (.270, 23, 80) to the Los Angeles Dodgers in return for pitcher Stan Williams (14–12, 4.46) in 1962. The trade paved the way for Joe Pepitone to play first base.

Clyde King was named manager of the Yankees in 1982.

27

The New York Times dubbed baseball "The National Game" in an 1870 article.

Triple Crown winner Ted Williams (.343, 32, 162) was edged by Yankee Clipper Joe DiMaggio (.315, 20, 97) by one point for the 1947 American League MVP. His 56-game hitting streak helped him to defeat Williams.

The Yankees completed a six-player trade with the Cleveland Indians in 1972 that sent John Ellis, Jerry Kenney, Rusty Torres, and Charlie Spikes to the Indians for Jerry Moses and Graig Nettles.

George Steinbrenner was fined $15,000 and later suspended for two years in 1974 for illegal contributions to Richard Nixon's campaign.

28

Shortstop Wilbur "Roxy" Roach played in 82 games for the Highlanders in 1910-11. He was born in Morrisdale Mines, PA, in 1884.

Yankee pitcher Dave Righetti was born in 1958 in San Jose, CA. He was a Yankee 1979–90. Righetti was the 1981 American League Rookie of the Year and set a major league record with 46 saves in 1986. He was an all-star two times.

Baseball Commissioner Bowie Kuhn suspended Yankee owner George Steinbrenner for two years in 1974.

Yankee manager Billy Martin was involved in a fight with a Reno, NV, reporter in 1978. The incident was later settled out of court.

29

The Yankees traded utility player Phil Linz to the Philadelphia Phillies for Ruben Amaro in 1965.

Yankee third baseman Clete Boyer was traded to the Atlanta Braves for outfielder Bill Robinson and a player to be named later (Chi Chi Olivo) in 1966.

Right-handed reliever Mariano Rivera was born in 1969 in Panama City, Panama.

The Yankees signed free-agent Reggie Jackson to a five-year, $2.93 million contract in 1976. Reggie had a candy bar named after him and he won two World Series titles in New York on his way to the Hall of Fame.

In 1995 Charlie Smith, the player traded to the Yankees from the St. Louis Cardinals for Roger Maris in 1967, died at the age of 57.

The Yankees re-signed free-agent pitcher Mike Stanton to a three-year contract in 1999.

30

Pitcher Steve Hamilton was born in 1935 in Columbia, KY. Hamilton played for the Yankees 1963–70 and appeared in three World Series games in relief 1963-64.

In 1952, on a local New York television show, Jackie Robinson accused the Yankee organization of being racist due to its failure to have a black player on the club.

Yankee left-hander Dave Righetti won the 1981 American League Rookie of the Year Award. Righetti recorded 252 career saves, 224 as a Yankee. He played 11 of his 16 major league seasons with the Yankees.

The first merger of a baseball and basketball team won final approval in 1999, clearing the way for the Yankees and the New Jersey Nets to complete their merger.

DECEMBER

1

Cecil Perkins was born in Baltimore, MD, in 1940. Perkins had a brief major league career that included only one start, and one loss, with the Yankees in 1967.

The Yankees and Baltimore Orioles completed the largest trade in MLB history as 17 players, including Don Larsen, Gene Woodling, and Bob Turley, changed teams. The first phase of the transaction began November 18th and was concluded on this date in 1954.

Free-agent outfielder Don Baylor signed with the Yankees in 1982 near the end of his career. Baylor went on to become a successful manager in the major leagues.

The Yankees released designated hitter Chili Davis in 1999 after two seasons in New York.

2

Born in 1899 in Terrell, TX, Ray Morehart was a backup second baseman for the 1927 Yankees, hitting one home run in his final major league season.

Pitcher Don Brennan was born in 1903 in Augusta, ME. He played five major league seasons, starting his career as a Yankee in 1933. He pitched three scoreless innings against the Yankees with the New York Giants in the 1937 World Series.

Bob Kammeyer pitched for the Yankees in 1978-79, his only major league exposure. He was born in 1950 in Kansas City, KS. Kammeyer has the distinction of having an ERA of infinity in 1979, allowing two home runs, seven hits, and recording no outs.

The Yankees traded pitcher Stan Bahnsen to the Chicago White Sox in 1971 for infielder/outfielder Rich McKinney. Bahnsen won 21 games for the 1972 White Sox while McKinney appeared in only 37 games.

The Yankees did not exercise their option on Darryl Strawberry, making him a free-agent in 1995.

3

Charles "Butch" Wensloff was born in 1915 in Sausalito, CA. He pitched three major league seasons, starting his career with the Yankees 1943 and returning in 1947. Wensloff pitched two shutout innings in Game 6 of the 1947 World Series.

Joseph Collins was born in Scranton, PA, in 1922. Collins played for the Yankees his entire major league career, 1948–57, hitting .280 in 1952.

Harry Simpson, born in 1925 in Atlanta, GA, played three seasons for the Yankees in the 1950s. He was a career .266 hitter over 888 games with five teams.

Pitcher Gene Nelson started his 13-year major league career in 1981 with the Yankees. Nelson was born in Tampa, FL, in 1960. He won two games in relief for the Oakland A's in the 1988 American League Championship Series.

4

Born in Brookville, PA, in 1890, James "Bob" Shawkey pitched 13 seasons with the Yankees (1915–27) and won over 20 games four times. He also managed the Yankees in 1930.

Billy Bryan played over five seasons with the Kansas City A's before moving to the Yankees in 1966, where he played minimally the following two seasons. He was born in Morgan, GA, in 1938.

Infielder Tucker Ashford played for the Yankees in 1981, in the middle of his seven-year major league career. Ashford was born in Memphis, TN, in 1954.

Pat Sheridan played outfield for nine seasons with four teams, ending his career in 1991 with the Yankees. He was born in Ann Arbor, MI, in 1957. Sheridan hit a home run in Game 3 of the 1987 American League Championship Series as a Detroit Tiger.

Stan Jefferson played outfield in six major league seasons, including part of 1989 with the Yankees. Jefferson was born in 1962 in New York City. He stole 34 bases as a regular outfielder with the 1987 San Diego Padres.

The last trade of the decade sent popular first baseman Joe Pepitone to the Houston Astros for outfielder-first baseman Curt Blefary in 1969. Both players were born in Brooklyn, NY.

5

Baseball Commissioner Landis handed down six-week suspensions for Babe Ruth, Bob Meusel, and Bill Piercy for participating in an unauthorized barnstorming tour after the 1921 World Series.

In 1958, the Phillies, hoping to fill the New York void caused by the west coast departure of the Giants and Dodgers, dropped plans for 1959 broadcasts into the city after the Yankees threatened to broadcast into Philadelphia.

Los Angeles Dodger pitcher Steve Howe was suspended for one year by Major League Baseball in 1983 for cocaine use.

The Yankees obtained base-stealing outfielder Rickey Henderson and pitcher Bert Bradley from the Oakland A's in exchange for pitchers Jay Howell and Jose Rijo, outfielder Stan Javier, and minor leaguers Tim Birtsas and Eric Plunk. In their second trade on this day in 1984, the Yankees traded catcher Rick Cerone to the Atlanta Braves for pitcher Brian Fisher.

Free-agent Wade Boggs was re-signed by the Yankees in 1995. Catcher Jim Leyritz, star of the 1996 post-season, was traded by the Yankees to the Anaheim Angels for two players to be named later in 1996.

6

Tony "Poosh 'Em Up" Lazzeri was born in San Francisco, CA, in 1903. He played for the Yankees 1926–37, batting .354 in 1929. The Hall of Fame member also played for the Chicago Cubs, Brooklyn Dodgers and New York Giants.

Catcher Constantine "Gus" Niarhos was born in Birmingham, AL, in 1921. He started his career with the Yankees 1946–50 and ended up with a lifetime .252 batting average.

Hall of Fame pitcher Burleigh A. Grimes died in 1985 at the age of 92 in Clear Lake, WI. Grimes was the last of the "spitballers," who played for the Yankees in his final season, 1934. Grimes won 20 or more games in five of his 19 major league seasons.

Major League Baseball suspended Darryl Strawberry for 60 days after he tested positive for cocaine. The San Francisco Giants, citing a clause in his contract, terminated his deal and released him in 1995.

The Yankees re-signed free-agent pitcher David Cone to a one-year contract in 1999.

7

Lou Gehrig was elected to the Hall of Fame on this date in 1939. The five-year waiting rule was waived after the "Iron Horse" was diagnosed with amyotrophic lateral sclerosis (ALS).

Yankee first baseman Tino Martinez was born in Tampa, FL, in 1967. He joined the Yankees in 1996 following six years with the Seattle Mariners.

The Kansas City Royals traded outfielder Lou Piniella and pitcher Ken Wright to the Yankees for pitcher Lindy McDaniel in 1973.

Tino Martinez was traded from the Seattle Mariners to the Yankees along with relief pitcher Jeff Nelson and a minor leaguer for pitcher Sterling Hitchcock and infielder Russell Davis in 1995. Martinez's wife gave birth and he signed a $20.25 million dollar contract on the day of his trade.

The Yankees re-signed free-agent pitcher Allen Watson to a two-year contract in 1999.

8

The Yankees traded slugger Roger Maris to the St. Louis Cardinals for third baseman Charlie Smith in 1968.

Maris, contemplating retirement, played two successful seasons in St. Louis.

Team owners elected former Yankees infielder Dr. Bobby Brown as president of the American League in 1983.

Darryl Strawberry and his agent Eric Goldschmidt were indicted on federal tax evasion charges in 1994, alleging that Strawberry failed to report over $500,000 in income earned from 1986 through 1990.

The Cleveland Indians signed Yankee free-agent pitcher Dwight Gooden in 1997.

9

One day after the announcement that manager Bob Lemon would return in 1982, the Yankees announced former manager Gene Michael, whom Lemon replaced, would return as manager for the 1983 season.

The Yankees signed free-agent outfielder Steve Kemp and pitcher Bob Shirley. They also obtained pitcher Dale Murray from the Toronto Blue Jays for outfielders Dave Collins and Fred McGriff and pitcher Mike Morgan in 1982.

The Yankees signed a twelve-year television contract, to run through the year 2000, with the Madison Square Garden Network in 1988. The deal was worth a reported $500 million.

To complete the Jim Leyritz trade, the Yankees acquired third baseman Ryan Kane and pitcher Jeremy Blevins from the Anaheim Angels in 1996.

10

Traveling to Chicago for Major League Baseball meetings in 1923, New Haven manager Wild Bill Donovan was killed in a train wreck. Donovan was a pitcher for the Detroit Tigers and managed the Yankees and the Philadelphia Phillies.

The American League continued a rule that was designed to "break up the Yankees" in 1940. The rule prohibited a championship team from trading with any other club.

The Yankees signed free-agent first baseman George McQuinn in 1946. He was released by the Philadelphia A's at the end of the season. The Yankees had released McQuinn in the 1930s.

The Yankees sent $100,000, catcher Sherm Lollar and two players to St. Louis for Fred Sanford and Roy Partee in 1948.

The Chicago Cubs bought catcher Charlie Silvera from the Yankees in 1956.

The Yankees signed free-agent pitcher Jimmy Key in 1992. The Kansas City Royals signed David Cone to an $18 million contract.

The Yankees agreed to terms with free-agent designated hitter Chili Davis, who had been with the Kansas City Royals in 1997.

Tony Tarasco, known as the Baltimore Oriole outfielder who had a fly ball taken away by a 12-year-old boy in the 1996 American League Championship Series, signed a two-year contract to play in Japan in 1999 after a brief stint with the Yankees.

11

Joe DiMaggio in 1951 announced his retirement: "When baseball is no longer fun, it's no longer a game. And so, I've played my last game." DiMaggio played 13 seasons with the Yankees.

The Yankees traded Hank Bauer, Marv Throneberry, Don Larsen and Norm Siebern to the Kansas City A's for outfielder Roger Maris and two others in 1959.

The Yankees pulled off two blockbuster trades, sending Bobby Bonds to the California Angels for Mickey Rivers and Ed Figueroa and trading pitcher George "Doc" Medich to the Pittsburgh Pirates for pitchers Dock Ellis and Ken Brett in 1975.

Darryl Strawberry was charged in California with failing to make child support payments in 1995.

The Yankees signed relief pitcher Mike Stanton, who had played with the Boston Red Sox and the Texas Rangers in 1996. Stanton had 27 saves for the 1993 Atlanta Braves.

12

Frank Truesdale was born in 1885 in Kirkwood, MO. He played 77 games at second base for the Yankees in 1914.

Born in Birmingham, AL, in 1902, Paul "Pee-Wee" Wanninger started his career with the Yankees in 1925 as the regular shortstop, hitting his only career home run.

Pedro Gonzalez started his career with the Yankees in 1963 and recorded one World Series at-bat in 1964. Born in 1937 in San Pedro De Macorís, Dominican Republic, Gonzalez played five major league seasons.

Steve Farr pitched 11 major league seasons, including 1991–93 with the Yankees. He appeared in 60 games in 1991. Farr was born in 1956 in LaPlata, MD.

Mike Buddie debuted with the Yankees in 1998 with a 4–4 record in 24 appearances. Buddie was born in 1970 in Berea, OH.

After receiving his last rites, Joe DiMaggio made a miraculous recovery, defying doctors' dire predictions in 1998.

13

The *New York Clipper* reported in 1856 that "the game of Base Ball is generally considered the National game amongst Americans."

Henry "Heeney" Majeski was born in Staten Island in 1916. Majesky played one season with the Yankees (1946). He hit .310 for the 1948 Philadelphia A's.

Infielder Dale Berra was born in 1956 in Ridgewood, NJ. Berra broke in with the Pittsburgh Pirates and played with the Yankees 1985-86. He is the son of Hall of Fame catcher Yogi, who managed him briefly in New York.

In 1961, Mickey Mantle signed a 1962 contract for $82,000. Only Joe DiMaggio had been paid more by the Yankees at the time.

Catfish Hunter won his claim against A's Charlie Finley and was declared a free agent by arbitrator Peter Seitz in 1974.

The Yankees and the federal government agreed on a plan to reserve additional seats for disabled fans and provide greater access at Yankee Stadium in 1999.

Outfielder Chad Curtis was traded by the Yankees to the Texas Rangers for pitchers Brandon Knight and Sam Marsonek in 1999.

14

The Yankees lost several players in the 1960 expansion draft to fill the Senators and Angels rosters. Infielder Gil McDougald, outfielder Bob Cerv and pitcher Eli Grba were drafted by Los Angeles while Washington selected pitcher Bobby Shantz.

Roger Maris died of cancer at the age of 51 in 1985.

The Yankees traded pitcher Dan Naulty to the Los Angeles Dodgers for first baseman Nicholas Leach in 1999.

15

First baseman William "Eddie" Robinson was born in Paris, TX, in 1920. He played three seasons for the Yankees (1954–56). He hit .311 for the 1950 Chicago White Sox.

The Yankees acquired future Hall of Fame pitcher Waite Hoyt, Harry Harper, Mike McNally, and Wally Schang from the Boston Red Sox for Del Pratt, Muddy Ruel, Hank Thormahlen, and Sammy Vick in 1920.

Edward G. Barrow died in 1953. He was regarded as baseball's first real general manager and was the man behind the New York Yankee dynasties of the 1920s and 1930s.

The Yankees signed coveted free-agent Dave Winfield to a ten-year contract reportedly worth $15 million in 1980. He had played with the San Diego Padres. Winfield hit 32 home runs in 1982 for New York, playing 1980–90 for the Yankees.

Free-agent Ron Guidry re-signed with the Yankees in 1981 to a four-year $3.6 million contract.

Wade Boggs was signed by the Yankees as a free agent in 1992 after 11 years as a Boston Red Sox infielder. He led the American League in hitting 1983 and 1985–88.

16

The Yankees made an 11-player trade with the Philadelphia A's in 1953. Among mostly minor players, the Yankees acquired Eddie Robinson, who became a valuable pinch-hitter, and gave up prospect Vic Power.

The Yankees hired Yogi Berra to manage the team for the second time, replacing Billy Martin in 1983.

In 1996, the Texas Rangers signed Yankee reliever and 1996 World Series Most Valuable Player John Wetteland.

17

The 1924 Yankees traded pitchers Joe Bush, Milt Gaston and Joe Giard to the Browns to get Urban Shocker back to New York, a pitcher they had traded to St. Louis in 1918.

Roland Sheldon was born in 1936 in Putnam, CT. He pitched for the Yankees 1961–65. Sheldon pitched 2 2/3 shutout innings against the St. Louis Cardinals in the 1964 World Series.

The Yankees received American League approval to sell Yankee Stadium to wealthy Chicago businessman Arnold Johnson in 1953. Johnson leased the Stadium back to the Yankees.

The Yankees fired long time television and radio voice Mel Allen in 1964 … "going, going, gone."

18

Yankee slugger 1954–62, William "Moose" Skowron was born in Chicago, IL, in 1930. Skowron played 14 major league seasons with a career .282 average and 211 home runs.

Phil "Scooter" Rizzuto, former Yankee shortstop and member of the Baseball Hall of Fame, signed a contract in 1956 to announce Yankee games on radio and television.

The Yankees announced that they signed manager Dick Williams, which led to a conflict with Oakland A's owner Charlie Finley. Two days later, American League President Joe Cronin ruled that the deal was void.

Darryl Strawberry and his agent plead not guilty to tax evasion charges in U.S. District Court in White Plains, NY, in 1994.

19

Mickey Witek was born in 1915 in Luzerne, PA. He played seven major league seasons in New York, mostly with the Giants. He singled in his only at-bat as a Yankee in 1949.

Outfielder Gordie Windhorn was born in 1933 in Watseka, IL. He played for the Yankees in 1959 and went on to play two more major league seasons, ending his career with the Los Angeles Angels in 1962.

The Yankees sent Ed Farrell, Jim Densmore, Floyd Newkirk, Les Powers, and Ted Norbert to the San Francisco Seals to complete the acquisition of Joe DiMaggio in 1934.

Walt "No Neck" Williams was born in 1943 in Brownwood, TX. No Neck played 10 major league seasons, including his final two with the Yankees 1974-75. He hit .304 with the 1969 Chicago White Sox.

Rob Gardner was born in 1944 in Binghamton, NY. Gardner pitched in eight major league seasons, including two stints with the Yankees 1970 and 1971-72. He was 8–5 in 1972.

The Yankees were among the first arrivals at the Ahoskie, NC, law offices of Cherry, Cherry, and Flythe in the race to sign Jim "Catfish" Hunter in 1974 after he was declared a free-agent.

The Toronto Blue Jays signed free-agent, and former Yankee designated hitter/outfielder, Dave Winfield in 1991.

20

James Williams, Highlander second baseman from 1903–1907, was born in 1876 in St. Louis, MO.

Watertown, WI, native Fred Merkle was born in 1888 and played his final two seasons with the Yankees, 1925-26. Merkle enjoyed his heyday with the New York Giants, hitting .309 in 1912 but is mostly remembered for his infamous baserunning goof.

George Pipgras was born in Denison, IA, in 1899. He pitched for the Yankees 1923–33, going 24–13 in 1928.

Siding with Oakland, American League president Joe Cronin ruled the Yankees could not sign manager Dick Williams in 1973. The Yankees had announced a deal with the A's manager two days earlier.

The Yankees signed designated hitter/catcher Jim Leyritz to a one-year contract in 1999.

21

The Boston Red Sox traded pitchers Dutch Leonard and Ernie Shore and outfielder Duffy Lewis to the Yankees in exchange for $15,000 in cash, pitchers Ray Caldwell and Slim Love, catcher Al Walters, and outfielder Frank Gilhooley in 1918.

Dave Kingman was born in 1948 in Pendleton, OR. "King Kong" hit 442 career major league home runs and played with the Yankees briefly in 1977, when he played in each major league division. He hit four of his career home runs in a New York uniform.

After considering an attractive offer from the Orioles, David Cone re-signed with the Yankees as a free-agent, agreeing to a three-year deal worth $18 million in 1995.

22

Matty Alou was born in 1938 in Haina, Dominican Republic. A member of a famous trio of ballplaying brothers, and uncle of Moises, Alou played for the Yankees in 1973. Alou led the National League with a .342 average in 1966 with the Pittsburgh Pirates.

Catcher Elrod Hendricks was born in 1940 in Charlotte Amalie, Virgin Islands. He enjoyed 12 major league seasons, including 1976-77 with the Yankees. Hendricks hit a home run in Game 1 of the 1970 World Series with the Baltimore Orioles.

Tom Underwood was a veteran of 11 major league seasons, including 1980-81 with the Yankees. Underwood was 13–9 with New York in 1980. He was born in Kokomo, IN, in 1957.

Lee Mazzilli was traded for the third time in 1982 as the Yankees dealt him to the Pittsburgh Pirates for four minor leaguers including Tim Burke.

23

Catonsville, MD, native Frederick "Fritz" Maisel was born in 1889. He played for the Yankees 1913–17, hitting .281 in 135 games in 1915.

The Yankees sold submarine pitcher Carl Mays, who recorded 53 victories in 1920-21 and killed Ray Chapman with a pitch, to the Cincinnati Reds for $85,000 in 1923.

Mickey Mantle married Merlyn Johnson, a woman he had met at a high school football game, in 1951.

Major League Baseball in 1994, at an impasse in labor negotiations with the players' union, implemented a revenue-sharing plan and salary cap proposal that provided players with 50 percent of baseball revenue.

24

Suffering from alcoholism and epilepsy, Hall of Fame hurler Grover Cleveland Alexander was found missing an ear and unconscious in Hollywood, CA in 1949. Alexander defeated the Yankees in the deciding game of the 1926 World Series.

Free-agent outfielder Gary Ward signed with the Yankees in 1986. He was generally disappointing in two-plus seasons in New York after hitting .316 with the 1986 Texas Rangers.

Yankee lawyers filed a "cyber squatting" lawsuit in Brooklyn Federal District Court in 1999 against a Queens man who had registered the domain name newyorkyankees.com.

25

Third baseman Eugene Robertson was born in 1899 in St. Louis, MO.

Robertson played for the Yankees 1928-29. He hit .319 for the 1924 St. Louis Browns.

All-time stolen base leader Rickey Henderson played for the Yankees 1985–89 and joined the Mets in 1999. He led the American League in stolen bases eleven different seasons. He was born in 1957 in Chicago, IL.

Yankee player and manager Billy Martin died at the age of 61 as a passenger in a Christmas automobile accident near his home in Binghamton, NY, in 1989.

26

Edward "Doc" Farrell was born in Johnson City, NY, in 1901. Farrell played for the Yankees 1932-33 after starting his career with the New York Giants. He hit .316 playing regularly for the 1927 Giants and Boston Braves.

Although not official until January 1920, the Yankees finalized the deal to buy Babe Ruth from the Red Sox in 1919, paying owner Harry Frazee $100,00 and guaranteeing a loan to finance the Broadway play *No No Nannette*.

First baseman Chris Chambliss was born in 1948 in Dayton, OH. Chambliss played for the Yankees 1974–78 and 1988 (one at-bat). He hit .524 in the 1976 American League Championship Series including a walk-off home run in the bottom of the 9th in Game 5.

27

The *Sporting News* 1939 annual selection of "Baseball Men of the Year" honored baseball executive Larry MacPhail and outfielder Joe DiMaggio of the Yankees.

Yankee infielder Roy White was born in Los Angeles, CA, in 1943. He played 15 years and compiled a lifetime .271 average for New York.

Hero of the 1996 World Series, Jim Leyritz, was born in 1963 in Lakewood, OH. He started his career with the Yankees in 1990.

Free-agent Ed Whitson, 14–8 with the San Diego Padres, signed a 5 year $4.4 million contract with the Yankees in 1984. Whitson pitched inconsistently and was subsequently traded back to the Padres in 1986 after New York fans turned on him.

28

Third baseman Aurelio Rodriguez was born in 1947 in Cananea, Mexico. He played for the Yankees 1980-81. Rodriguez halted Baltimore Oriole Brooks Robinson's 16 consecutive gold glove awards in 1976, won the following two years by Yankee Graig Nettles.

With a history of baseball tradition, the "greatest football game ever played" was held at Yankee Stadium in 1958. The Baltimore Colts defeated the New York Giants in the first sudden death overtime in NFL Championship history, 23–17.

Sal "The Barber" Maglie died in 1992 at the age of 75 in Niagara Falls,

NY. Barber pitched for the Yankees 1957-58 and was known for his "close shaves" to hitters. He was 23–6 with the 1951 New York Giants.

The Yankees acquired outfielder Tim Raines from the Chicago White Sox in 1995.

29

Frank "Pudgie" Delahanty was born in 1885 in Cleveland, OH. Delahanty played six professional seasons, including 1905-06 with the Highlanders.

Infielder William Knickerbocker was born in 1911 in Los Angeles, CA. He played for the Yankees 1938-39. He hit .317 in 1934 as the everyday shortstop for the Cleveland Indians.

Babe Ruth lost an opportunity to manage the Cincinnati Reds in 1933 when Yankee owner Jacob Ruppert refused to release him.

Babe Ruth returned to baseball in 1937 when he was announced as the manager of the De Land Reds of the Florida State League.

Yankee pitcher Red Ruffing was drafted into the U.S. Army Air Corps, placing his career in doubt. Ruffing was 38 with 19 years of major league experience at the time.

Melissa Ludtke, female *Sports Illustrated* writer, sued Major League Baseball, the Yankees and New York City officials for denying access to the locker room for player interviews during the 1977 World Series.

Former Yankee catcher Walt Alexander died in 1979 in Fort Worth, TX. The Atlanta, GA, native played in five major league seasons, ending his career in New York in 1917.

30

Yankee manager Joe Torre was born in 1931 in Brooklyn, NY. Torre led the Yankees to World Series titles in 1996, 1998, 1999 and 2000.

Yankees manager Joe Torre completed radiation therapy for prostate cancer in 1999.

31

Ban Johnson arranged the purchase of the Yankees by Colonel Jacob Ruppert and Cap Huston for $460,000 in 1914. The new owners named long-time Detroit Tiger pitcher Bill Donovan as manager.

Born in Baltimore, MD, in 1919, Thomas Byrne pitched two stints with the Yankees (1943–51 and 54–57). He was 16–5 with the Yankees in 1955.

Jim "Catfish" Hunter became one of the first big free agents to sign when he agreed with the Yankees on a $2.5 million contract in 1974.

Daniel R. McCarthy became general partner of the Yankees in 1991.

Pitcher Orlando "El Duque" Hernandez, half-brother of the 1997 World Series MVP Livan Hernandez, officially defected from Cuba in 1997 and subsequently signed with the Yankees.

BIBLIOGRAPHY

Allen, Maury. *Where Have You Gone, Joe DiMaggio?* New York: E.P. Dutton, 1975.

Bouton, Jim. *Ball Four.* Cleveland: The World Publishing, 1970.

Carroll, Bob. *This Year in Baseball 1990.* New York: Simon and Schuster, 1990.

Gallagher, Mark, and Neil Gallagher. *Mickey Mantle Baseball Legends.* New York: Chelsea House, 1991.

Gutman, Dan. *Baseball's Biggest Bloopers: The Games that Got Away.* New York: Penguin Books, 1993.

Halberstam, David. *Summer of '49.* New York: William Morrow, 1969.

Honig, Donald. *The New York Yankees.* New York: Crown, 1987.

James, Bill. *The Bill James Guide to Baseball Managers from 1870 to Today.* New York: Scribner, 1997.

Kahn, Roger. *The Boys of Summer.* New York: Harper & Row, 1971.

Lyle, Sparky, and Peter Golenbeck. *The Bronx Zoo.* New York: Crown, 1979.

Macht, Norman L. *Babe Ruth Baseball Legends.* New York: Chelsea House, 1991.

Mantle, Mickey, and Phil Pepe. *Mickey Mantle: My Favorite Summer 1956.* New York: Doubleday, 1991.

Martin, Billy, and Phil Pepe. *Billyball.* New York: Doubleday, 1987.

McWhirter, Norris, and Ross McWhirter. *The Guinness Book of World Records.* New York: Sterling, 1979.

_____ and _____. *The Guinness Sports Record Book.* New York: Sterling, 1982.

Meserole, Mike (editor). *The 1990 Information Please Sports Almanac.* Boston: Houghton Mifflin, 1989.

_____. *The 1994 Information Please Sports Almanac.* Boston: Houghton Mifflin, 1994.

Pepe, Phil, and Zander Hollander. *The Book of Sports Lists.* Los Angeles: Pinnacle, 1979.

Pepitone, Lena, and William Stadiem. *Marilyn Monroe Confidential.* New York: Simon and Schuster, 1979.

Reichler, Joseph L. *The Great All-Time Baseball Record Book.* New York: Macmillan, 1981.

_____. *The Baseball Encyclopedia.* New York: Macmillan, 1988.

Schiffer, Don. *World Series Encyclopedia.* New York: Thomas Nelson & Sons, 1961.

Thorn, John, Pete Palmer, Michael Gershman, and David Pietrusza. *Total Baseball 6th Edition*. New York: Total Sports, 1999.
Weldon, Martin. *Babe Ruth*. New York: Thomas Y. Crowell, 1948.
The World Almanac and Book of Facts, 1989–1992. New York: Scripps Howard, 1988–1991.

Chronological information and box score data
from 1990–2000 sports sections of editions of:

The Corning (NY) Leader
The Elmira Star-Gazette
The New York Times
USA Today
Williamsport (PA) Tribune-Review

Miscellaneous 20th century box score information
on microfilm from The New York Times.

Statistics, feats, trivia, and biographical information
gleaned from baseball cards from 1950–1999.

Historical information from on-line resources including:

www.CBS.Sportsline.com
www.Excite.com/sports
www.ESPN.com
www.thenationalpasttime.com
www.baseballhalloffame.com

INDEX

193